PLAIN
REVELATION

PLAIN REVELATION

Ranko Stefanovic

Andrews
University Press

Berrien Springs, Michigan

Andrews University Press
Sutherland House
8360 W. Campus Circle Dr.
Berrien Springs, MI 49104–1700
Telephone: 269-471-6134
Fax: 269-471-6224
Email: aupo@andrews.edu
Website: http://universitypress.andrews.edu

ISBN 978-1-883925-86-4

Printed in the United States of America
17 16 15 14 13   1 2 3 4 5

Quotations from the book of Revelation are the author's own translation. Unless otherwise stated, scripture quotations from other books are taken from the New Ameri-
can Standard Bible®, Copyright © 1960, 1962, 1963, 1968, 1971, 1972, 1973, 1975,
1977, 1995 by The Lockman Foundation. Used by permission (www.Lockman.org).
Scripture quotations marked RSV are from the Revised Standard Version of the Bible,
copyright © 1946, 1952, and 1971 National Council of the Churches of Christ in the
United States of America. Used by permission. All rights reserved.

Library of Congress Cataloging-in-Publication Data

Stefanovic, Ranko.
 Plain Revelation / Ranko Stefanovic.
    pages cm
 Includes bibliographical references and index.
 ISBN 978-1-883925-86-4 (hardcover : alk. paper) 1. Bible. Revelation--Commentaries.
    I. Title.
 BS2825.53.S738 2013
 228'.077--dc23
                          2013041520

Project Director	Ronald Alan Knott
Project Editor	Deborah L. Everhart
Line Editor	Kenneth Wade
Copy Editor	Elsbeth Krumholz
Editorial Assistant	Nathan Berglund
Cover Designer	Robert N. Mason
Text Designer	Robert N. Mason
Typesetter	Arielle Pickett
Proofreader	Rachel Cabose

Typeset: 11/13 Sabon MT

This book is dedicated to

G. David Jang, MD

whose vision and support
led to the realization of this project

We're putting you on notice!

The book you are reading, Ranko Stefanovic's *Plain Revelation*, is a concise introduction to a journey of great discovery in the Apocalypse.

When you finish this book, you will be ready for Dr. Stefanovic to take you further on that amazing journey.

For that, you will need his landmark, verse-by-verse, commentary on this epic book of the Bible.

It's titled *Revelation of Jesus Christ: Commentary on the Book of Revelation*.

Read more about it on page 279.

Contents

Preface

The idea for writing this book was born sometime in the year 2011. Niels-Erik Andreasen, president of Andrews University, invited me to his office one day and explained that he had met with G. David Jang, MD, from Loma Linda University, who had enthusiastically asked him if I might be willing to write a concise, user-friendly book on Revelation that would be accessible to all informed readers. Dr. Andreasen then urged me to seriously consider that suggestion.

The idea was not entirely a surprise for me because, since the publication of my commentary *Revelation of Jesus Christ* in 2002, there have been constant requests from many readers and my listening audiences across the globe for a non-commentary-type book, written in a concise style and plain language, which would be financially affordable to many readers and could be easily translated into different languages. After talking personally to Dr. Jang and consulting Ronald Knott, director of Andrews University Press, I felt compelled to embark on the task.

This book is intended to be an introduction to my commentary and can serve as a personal study guide, a study tool for small groups, and a textbook. I hope that it will be of help to many who are interested in understanding the last book of the Bible, but are afraid to delve into its contents because of a common misperception that the Apocalypse is almost impossible to comprehend. It is my desire that readers will discover that the Apocalypse is actually not as hard to understand as many people think it is. As they read it, may they also realize that the book of Revelation provides guidance for a contented life today and a hope, not fear, for tomorrow. When the book is studied properly, an understanding of its central theme inevitably results in changed lives for God's glory.

I want to express my deep gratitude to Dr. G. David Jang, whose vision and support initiated the realization of this book. I am dedicating this book to him. Many thanks also go to Dr. Niels-Erik Andreasen, who took a personal interest in this project; to my wonderful daughter Zeljka, for spending with love many hours patiently proofreading the text and correcting details; to Evelyn Kissinger, who volunteered to read the manuscript and offer feedback on the content of the book; and to Laura Morrow, my graduate student reader, for proofreading and correcting the text. I also wish to express my thanks to Andrews

University Press personnel—Ronald Knott and Deborah Everhart in particular—for the editing and design of the book.

This book would certainly not have been written without the love and unselfish support of my life partner and dear wife Estera. She did all she could to provide me with the necessary time for writing. She deserves much more than a simple thanks.

The writing of this book has been done with a lot of prayer. I want to give all honor to my God for providing me with good health and wisdom in dealing with the text of Revelation. This book is written to His glory.

Introduction

Of all the books in the Bible, the book of Revelation has provoked the most interest and curiosity. Yet, for many Christians, it is the most obscure book of the Bible. It comes as a surprise that the book entitled "Apocalypse" ("revelation" or "unveiling") has become, for many, a symbol of confusion and obscurity. Strange images and frightening scenes described in the book have caused many to turn away from reading it.

However, Revelation clearly shows that it was written to be understood (see Rev. 22:10). The beginning of the book states: "Blessed is the one who reads and the ones listening" (1:3). The text describes a public reading of Revelation where one person reads the book and others listen. This shows that Revelation is intended to be read in the church. The text in Greek, however, shows that this reading is more than merely reading. The person who reads makes the message of Revelation understandable to the congregation assembled for worship.

This is not to say, however, that the book was given to only a few individuals to study; rather, it was given to all God's people. Great blessings are promised to all who read Revelation, heed its messages, and treasure them in their minds and hearts (Rev. 22:7).

The purpose of this book is to explain Revelation and to explicate this difficult Biblical book in plain language. I hope that readers will discover that Revelation is not as difficult to understand as it appears to be. True, there are and will always be obscure prophecies and symbols that we will probably never be able to understand until they are fulfilled. However, if we understand the messages of Revelation as a whole, we will discover its central theme: Jesus Christ—who is the focal point of Revelation—and His promise to be with His people as the future unfolds.

1

Before moving through the pages of Revelation and attempting to unlock the meaning of what is written in it, it is important to acquaint ourselves with some basic information about the book, including how and when it was written, how the book is organized, and how to interpret its contents.

Authorship and Date

Revelation was written by a person named John (Rev. 1:1–4, 9; 22:8). The fact that the book does not explain who John was shows that he was well known to the original readers. The earliest Christian authors who lived close to the time when Revelation was written agree that John was one of the twelve apostles, the son of Zebedee (cf. Matt. 10:2), and the author of the fourth Gospel and three epistles. Many verbal parallels between Revelation and the Gospel of John confirm such identification.

John wrote Revelation while he was on Patmos (Rev. 1:9). Patmos is a small, rocky island in the Aegean Sea, southwest of Ephesus. The early Christian authors unanimously state that the apostle was banished to the island by the Roman authorities because of his faithful preaching of the gospel. Although the book does not indicate the date, strong evidence suggests that Revelation was written around AD 95 near the end of Emperor Domitian's reign. This date was affirmed by many early Christian authors.

The book was originally sent to the seven Christian congregations located in the large cities of Asia Minor—the southwestern part of modern Turkey (Rev. 1:4, 11). There is sufficient evidence that, at the time, Christians suffered increasing persecution from the Romans. The worst persecution was yet to come, however. Thus, the book was written to encourage Christians facing a difficult future.

Although originally written *to* them, Revelation was not written only *for* them but also for all Christians throughout history until the time of the end. The book points to God, who is in control of the situation in the world; it also concludes with God's triumph over the forces of evil and the establishment of God's everlasting kingdom.

Interpretative Approaches to Revelation

No book of the Bible has been the object of so many interpretative approaches as this one. The question of how to interpret the prophecies of Revelation and apply them historically has generated much debate in the last several centuries. Today, there are four distinctive interpretative approaches to the book.

Preterist. Preterism (from Latin *preter*, meaning "past") is a method of interpretation that places the whole significance of Revelation in the past. The book, from this perspective, deals exclusively with the Christian church in Asia Minor and its struggle with Rome at the time it was written. In this view, Revelation does not predict the future. John the Revelator only wrote about events that took place in his time or in the immediate future. The purpose of the book was to encourage the Christians of John's day to persevere in their faithfulness to God.

Futurist. In contrast to preterism, the futurist method interprets the prophecies of Revelation exclusively from the end-time perspective. Futurist interpreters hold that chapters 4–22 will be fulfilled shortly before the Second Coming. In other words, the prophecies of Revelation will be fulfilled during the last generation of Christians. Futurism interprets the symbols of Revelation as literally as possible. Today, this is the preferred method of most Protestant Evangelicals.

Idealist. The idealist approach is based on preterist ideas. It recognizes that Revelation describes what was happening to the Christians in the first century. However, idealist interpreters contend that the book describes, in vivid symbolism, the ongoing struggle between good and evil that will result in God's ultimate triumph over evil. The book does not speak about literal events fulfilled in the past or to be fulfilled in the future, from our temporal perspective. The messages of Revelation generally provide guidance to every generation of Christians. Idealism is the successor of the allegorical interpretation of the Bible, which characterized the medieval interpretation of the Bible.

Historicist. The historicist approach of prophetic interpretation holds that Revelation portrays, in symbolic presentations, the course of history unfolding from the first century until the end time. Some prophecies of the book were fulfilled in the past, some are yet to be fulfilled, and some refer to the present time. Historicism recognizes that the events predicted in the book are pictured in symbolic language. The events themselves are real; however, they are portrayed in symbolic language. Historicism was the method of prophetic interpretation by Protestants until the nineteenth century, when many Protestants turned to other interpretative approaches.

In evaluating these approaches, one notices that preterism limits the relevance of Revelation's messages to the first-century Christians. Similarly, futurism limits the prophecies of Revelation exclusively to the last generation of Christians. These two methods seem deficient, because they imply that Revelation has nothing to offer to the generations between John's time and the time of the end. Revelation plainly shows that the first three chapters concern John's time (see Rev. 1:11). However, Revelation 4:1 states that chapters 4–22 deal with events that will take place beyond John's time and continue until the time of the end. Careful analysis shows that the focus of chapters 4–11 is on the movements and events in Christian history from the first century until the time of the end, while the second half of the book deals primarily with the events to take place at the end time.

A major problem with preterism and idealism is their denial of the book's predictive prophecies. Revelation claims to be a book of prophecy (Rev. 1:3; 22:7, 10). John clearly states, both in the introduction and conclusion of the book, that its purpose is to show God's people the events to take place in the future (1:1; 22:6). Any interpretative method that denies the predictive nature of Revelation does not do justice to the obvious claims of the book. Both preterism and idealism fail on this ground.

One thus can see the inadequacies of preterism, futurism, and idealism for interpreting the prophecies of Revelation. This sets historicism as the only adequate approach for prophetic interpretation. Historicism sees the events predicted in Revelation as taking place both in the past and the future as well as in the centuries that lie between. This method also recognizes the spiritual applications of the book's messages. It, thus, becomes evident that the historicist interpretation does the best job of discovering the relevance of Revelation's messages for all generations, even until the end of the age.

Organization and Structure of Revelation

Understanding the basic structure of a book may help us fit smaller sections into the overall theme of the book. As such, this understanding serves as a safeguard against interpreting passages in isolation from the rest of the book. The same applies to the last book of the Bible. An understanding of the literary arrangement of Revelation will help us unpack the broad meaning of the text in regard to the entire book's context, which would otherwise not be possible.

We can observe at least three organizational structures in Revelation: the chiastic structure, the sanctuary structure, and the threefold structure. These structures are not mutually exclusive. Considered together, they unpack a wide spectrum of theological themes and motifs in Revelation.

Chiastic Structure

The word "chiasm" is derived from the Greek cross-shaped letter X (read as chi) and refers to a literary feature widely used in the Old Testament. While literary structures today are based on an ABC outline, the chiastic structure is based on an ABA' outline. The climax of the text is set in the center, with the corresponding sections moving up to and away from it: section A parallels section A' at the end, section B to section B', section C to section C' until we come to the center. An understanding of how a chiasm works helps us discern the theological emphasis of the book's content as intended by the inspired author. This book suggests that Revelation follows this chiastic structure:

A. Prologue (1:1–8)
  B. Promises to the overcomers (1:9–3:22)
    C. God's work for humanity's salvation (4:1–8:1)
      D. God's wrath mixed with mercy (8:2–9:21)
        E. Commissioning John to prophesy (10:1–11:18)
          F. Great conflict between Christ and Satan (11:19–13:18)
        E'. Church proclaims the end-time gospel (14:1–20)
      D'. God's final wrath without mercy (15:1–18:24)
    C'. God's work for humanity's salvation completed (19:1–21:4)
  B'. Fulfillment of the promises to the overcomer (21:5–22:5)
A'. Epilogue (22:6–21)

One might observe that the first half of this structure (segment A–E) focuses on the entire history of the Christian age, while its chiastic counterpart (segment E'–A') focuses exclusively on the time of the end. At the center, segment F points to the central theological theme of the book: the Great Controversy between Christ and the counterfeit trinity (Satan and his two associates—the sea and earth beasts). This shows that the entire book is written from the perspective of the Great Controversy, with a special emphasis on the final conflict at the conclusion of this world's history, which includes the coming of Christ and the establishment of God's eternal kingdom.

Sanctuary Structure

The structure of Revelation is also designed according to the sanctuary services in the Old Testament. The book is replete with references to the temple and its articles of furniture. The heavenly temple in Revelation is seen as the center of all divine activity on earth. The entire book appears to be modeled on the Old Testament sanctuary services.

In this structure, Revelation falls into seven major parts. Each of these parts is introduced with a sanctuary scene. The book pictures all the divine actions on earth as resulting from the activities in the heavenly temple:

Prologue (1:1–8)

    1. Introductory sanctuary scene (1:9–20)
    The messages to the seven churches (2–3)
    2. Introductory sanctuary scene (4–5)
    The opening of the seven seals (6:1–8:1)
    3. Introductory sanctuary scene (8:2–5)
    The blowing of the seven trumpets (8:6–11:18)
    4. Introductory sanctuary scene (11:19)
    The wrath of the nations (12:1–15:4)
    5. Introductory sanctuary scene (15:5–8)
    The seven last plagues (16–18)
    6. Introductory sanctuary scene (19:1–10)
    The eschatological consummation (19:11–21:1)
    7. Introductory sanctuary scene (21:2–5)
    The New Jerusalem (21:9–22:5)

Epilogue (22:6–21)

This sevenfold structure of Revelation reflects the daily and annual services of the earthly sanctuary. The sanctuary structure provides an insight into what is going on in the book. Here is a summary of these seven sanctuary scenes. More detailed descriptions will be given later in the book, in the expositions of the respective passages.

1. Revelation 1:9–20—This first vision of Revelation pictures Christ in the midst of the seven lampstands, wearing the garments of the High Priest. The lampstands represent the seven churches in Asia Minor in John's day. Jesus is portrayed as ministering to the churches in their needs, similar to the priests of the earthly temple, who trimmed the lamps to keep them burning. This scene does not describe the heavenly sanctuary, because the whole vision is set on earth, not in heaven. The sanctuary imagery is used only to illustrate Jesus's activities on behalf of the churches.

2. **Revelation 4–5.** With this vision, the scene shifts from earth to heaven (see Rev. 4:1). In these two chapters, there are more allusions to the sanctuary and its furnishings than anywhere else in the book. The scene takes place in the throne room of the heavenly temple, where the Holy Place and the Holy of Holies are merged into one room. Here, John witnessed the inauguration of Christ into His royal and priestly ministry, which took place after His death on Calvary and His subsequent ascension to heaven. With His inauguration, Christ began His mediatory ministry in the heavenly sanctuary on behalf of humans.

3. **Revelation 8:2–5.** This is another sanctuary setting with sanctuary imagery. The scene pictures an angel receiving incense at the altar of sacrifice, representing the prayers of God's people. The angel takes the prayers to the Holy Place of the heavenly temple and offers them on the golden altar of incense before God. In response to these prayers, fiery judgments are hurled upon rebellious humanity. This scene clearly shows that intercession is taking place in the heavenly sanctuary.

4. **Revelation 11:19.** In this vision, the heavenly temple is opened, and the Ark of the Covenant is seen in its innermost part. This is followed by "lightning, sounds, peals of thunder, an earthquake, and great hail," representing the divine presence. The Ark of the Covenant points to the Most Holy Place. While the sanctuary imagery in the first half of the book shows that the events in Revelation chapters 1–11 occur in the context of Christ's mediatory ministry in the Holy Place, Revelation 11:19 points to the beginning of a new phase of Christ's ministry in the heavenly sanctuary. The book shows that before the Second Coming, judgment will take place in heaven (Rev. 14:7). This judgment is introduced in Revelation 11:1–2. Its purpose is to separate the faithful from those who have spurned God's mercy. At the conclusion of the pre-Advent judgment, Christ will come to reward every person according to his or her deeds (22:12).

5. **Revelation 15:5–8.** At the conclusion of the end-time gospel proclamation (Rev. 14:6–20), the temple in heaven is filled with the smoke of God's glory, so nobody is able to enter the temple to receive forgiveness. There is an absence of priestly activities in the heavenly temple. This scene uses language derived from the Old Testament (see 1 Kings 8:10–11). Here, we see the conclusion of Christ's mediatory

ministry in the heavenly sanctuary. There is no further need for intercession, because the destiny of every person has been decided.

6. Revelation 19:1–10. Here, a scene of jubilant rejoicing over the destruction of end-time Babylon is described; the suffering of God's people is over. Although the scene takes place in the heavenly temple (see Rev. 4–5), no reference to the heavenly sanctuary and its furnishings is mentioned. This is because the heavenly temple no longer functions as the place of intercession. Christ's mediatory ministry on behalf of humans is no longer taking place there.

7. Revelation 21:2–22:5. The last vision brings us back to earth. In the New Jerusalem, there is no temple, because the city itself functions as the temple (Rev. 21:22). The Old Testament sanctuary was the place where God symbolically dwelt among His people. On the new earth, there is no longer a need for a temple as a symbol of God's presence, because the New Jerusalem will be the place of God's actual presence with His people throughout eternity (see 21:3).

The sequence of these introductory sanctuary scenes reveals the line of progression of the heavenly sanctuary that starts with the inauguration. The inauguration is then followed by the phases of intercession, judgment, the close of intercession, and the absence of priestly activities. The sequence concludes with the New Jerusalem, where God's presence with His people is actualized.

The structure of Revelation based on the sanctuary's daily and yearly pattern helps us locate the key visions of the book within the context of history. First, it points to Revelation 11:19 as a dividing line between the historical and end-time sections of the book. While the first half of Revelation focuses primarily on the Christian age, the second half focuses exclusively on the end time. This affirms that the scene of Revelation chapters 4–5 is the inauguration of Christ at Pentecost in AD 31. It also shows that the visions of the seven seals and the seven trumpets run throughout Christian history, while the seven last plagues take place exclusively at the time of the end.

Threefold Structure

Apart from the prologue (Rev. 1:1–8) and the epilogue (22:6–21), the main body of Revelation falls into three distinctive parts: (a) the messages to the seven churches, which primarily focus on the historical situation within these churches in Asia Minor during John's time (1:9–3:22); (b) the historical part, which primarily focuses on history's unfolding from the first century until the end of time (chaps. 4–11); and (c) the eschatological part, which primarily focuses on the time of the end and the events leading up to the coming of Christ and the establishment of God's kingdom (12:1–22:5). These divisions are related to the three periods of history within the book's perspective: the time of John, the Christian age, and the end time.

It is especially significant that each of these three divisions begins with a special vision of Jesus Christ. In each of these introductory visions, Jesus is presented in a unique role. His portrayal in these visions defines the theological perspective of the subsequent scenes. This affirms the view that the last book of the Bible is truly a revelation of Jesus Christ in the full meaning of this statement.

While recognizing the importance of the chiastic structure and the structure based on the daily and annual sanctuary services, the exposition of Revelation in this book is based primarily on this threefold structure. I invite you to join me in exploring Revelation chapter by chapter. I urge you to put aside any preconceived ideas and allow the book to speak to you. A proper understanding of Revelation's messages will move us to search our souls, making us ready for the future, so we will not be surprised. "Blessed is the one who heeds the words of the prophecy of this book" (Rev. 22:7).

What Revelation Is All About

 Revelation 1:1–8

The prologue of Revelation (Rev. 1:1–8) identifies God as the author of Revelation and as the One who speaks through His Son to show His people the things that will take place. It further introduces the book's author and its original recipients; then, it describes the central theme and purpose of the book and how it was written. Finally, it introduces the keynote of the book. The first eight verses of Revelation are as follows:

> ¹The revelation of Jesus Christ, which God gave Him to show to His servants the things which must soon take place, and He signified it by sending it through His angel to His servant John, ²who testified to all that he saw, that is, the word of God and the testimony of Jesus Christ. ³Blessed is the one who reads and the ones listening to the words of the prophecy and keeping the things that are written in it, for the time is near.
>
> ⁴John to the seven churches that are in Asia: Grace to you and peace from the One who is, and who was, and who is coming, and from the seven Spirits who are before His throne, ⁵and from Jesus Christ, the faithful witness, the firstborn from the dead, and the ruler of the kings of the earth. To the One who loves us and released us from our sins by His blood ⁶and made us a kingdom, priests to His God and Father, to Him be glory and might forever and ever. Amen.
>
> ⁷Behold, He is coming with the clouds, and every eye will see Him, even those who pierced Him, and every tribe of the earth will mourn over Him. Yes, amen! ⁸"I am the

Alpha and the Omega," says the Lord God, "the One who is, and who was, and who is coming, the Almighty."

The Central Theme of Revelation (1:1a)

The opening statement generates the title of the book, naming it "the revelation of Jesus Christ." The Greek word *apokalupsis* (apocalypse) means "unveiling," "uncovering," or "revealing." The Apocalypse is, thus, an unveiling of Jesus Christ.

In the original language, the phrase "a revelation of Jesus Christ" may mean either that the revelation is *from* Jesus or that it is *about* Jesus as the One revealed. In a sense, both meanings are implied here. While the revelation came from God through Jesus Christ, who communicated it to John through an angel (Rev. 1:1; cf. 22:16), the rest of the book testifies that Jesus is the main subject of its contents. He is "the Alpha and Omega" (that is, the A to Z) of the book's content, "the beginning and the end" (21:6; 22:13), and "the first and the last" (1:17; 22:13). The book begins and concludes with Jesus.

The title indicates what one should find in the book. The statement "[this is a] revelation of Jesus Christ" shows that the primary focus of the Apocalypse is Jesus Christ. He is the key that unlocks the true meaning of the book. Revelation is not a kind of "Hollywood apocalypse" littered with bizarre and horrible events that come upon the world, causing fear. By naming his book "the revelation of Jesus Christ," John, the inspired author, wanted to tell the reader that the book he wrote offers a unique portrayal of Christ that is not found elsewhere in the Scriptures.

The book of Revelation is a gospel as much as the four Gospels are. The four Gospels and Revelation talk about the same Jesus; however, they focus on different aspects of His roles and existence. The four Gospels portray Jesus as the preexistent Son of God who entered into human experience to save fallen human beings, and who, after His death on the cross and subsequent resurrection, ascended to heaven. What is He doing in heaven now? Revelation unveils the answer to this question. The book reveals that after His ascension to heaven, Jesus was seated on the heavenly throne, and He now rules over the entire universe.

The Gospels also tell us that before His ascension, Jesus made two promises about His future interactions with His people: first, that He will always be with them, until the time of the end (Matt. 28:20); and second, that He will come again to take them to Himself (John 14:1–3). Revelation picks up on these two promises. The book describes, first, how Jesus fulfills the promise to be with His people throughout history, even to the end (Rev. 1–18); and it describes, second, how He will come at the conclusion of this world's history and be united with them (chaps. 19–22).

Without Revelation, our knowledge of Christ's ministry in heaven on behalf of His people would be vague. Revelation is the gospel in the full sense of the word. It conveys the substance of the gospel as "the good news." It emphatically points to the glorified Christ as the One who, by virtue of His own death, conquered death and the grave (Rev. 1:17–18). He will never forsake His people; He will always be with them until He comes the second time to take them to Himself.

Purpose of the Book (1:1b)

The prologue further states that the purpose of Revelation is to show God's people "the things which must soon take place" (Rev. 1:1). It is obvious that the portrayal of future events occupies much of the book. While the first half of Revelation (chaps. 1–11) delineates worldwide events that take place between the first century and the time of the end, its second half (chaps. 12–22) deals primarily with the time of the end and the events leading to the Second Coming. This division suggests the question: How can the book be both the unveiling of Jesus Christ and the unveiling of events that will take place?

For one, the prophecies of Revelation explain, from God's perspective, why the predicted events will happen. They provide assurance that, no matter what the future brings, God is in control. Whatever happens accomplishes His plans and purpose for this world.

However, the future events predicted in Revelation—whether those already fulfilled or those yet to take place—are evidently not the primary theme. They are not recorded to make the Apocalypse a divine fortune-telling book, nor are these prophecies given to satisfy our obsessive curiosity about the future. Their primary purpose is to assure us of Jesus's presence with His people throughout history and its final events.

Christ knew, however, that the full impact of His promise to be with His people would not be effective without unpacking future events through His prophetic word. The graphic portrayal of these events in His message is designed to impress on us the seriousness of the final crisis and our need to depend on God during this time. This time of crisis will remind God's people of Christ's promise to be with them in order to sustain them during these difficult times. "These things I have spoken to you," Jesus said, "so that when their hour comes, you may remember that I told you of them" (John 16:4).

We must keep in mind that the fulfillment of end-time prophecies must not be a subject of speculations and sensationalism. Revelation informs us about *what* will happen in the world at the time of the end. What the book does not show us, however, is exactly *when* and *how* the end-time events will take place. Books have been written and web pages have been created predicting exactly how these prophecies will be fulfilled. However, most of the ideas expressed are misleading, for they are drawn not from the Bible but rather from imaginings based on allegorical interpretations or headline news. The timing and manner of the unfolding of the final events are secrets God has reserved only for Himself (Matt. 24:36; Acts 1:7). They will be clear to us only when they are fulfilled, not before (John 14:29; 16:4).

When understood properly, the prophecies of Revelation have practical purposes: to teach us how to live today and to prepare us for the future. Studying them should make us better people, motivate us to take seriously our eternal destiny, and inspire us to try to reach people around us with the gospel message.

Symbolic Language of the Book (1:1c)

The prologue further explains that the contents of Revelation were "signified" to John in a vision. The Greek word *semaino* (signify) carries the primary meaning: "To show by signs or symbols." This word is used in the Greek translation of the Old Testament (the Septuagint) where Daniel explained to King Nebuchadnezzar that, by means of a symbol—the statue made of gold, silver, bronze, and iron—God had shown to the king "what will take place in the future (Dan. 2:45). Similarly, by employing this word in the prologue of Revelation, the revelator, John, informs the reader that the things recorded in the book were shown to him on Patmos in visions using symbols.

The book of Revelation does not provide photographic descriptions of heavenly realities or future events that should be interpreted literally. Although the scenes and events predicted per se are real, they were shown to John in symbolic presentations. Under the inspiration of the Holy Spirit, John faithfully recorded these symbolic presentations exactly as they were shown to him (Rev. 1:2). However, due to the inadequacy of human language, John added symbols of his own. His attempts at putting heavenly realities in human words are delineated by marker words such as "like" and "as."

Keeping the symbolic character of Revelation in mind will safeguard us against the literal application of symbols, which would distort the prophetic message. While reading the Bible in general presupposes a literal understanding of the text (unless it clearly points to intended symbolism), studying Revelation calls for a symbolic understanding of the scenes and events recorded, unless the text clearly indicates that a literal meaning is intended.

It is not, however, easy to determine what should be understood symbolically and what should be understood literally in Revelation. While some symbols are defined in the book (cf. Rev. 1:20; 12:9; 17:9–11, 15), most are not. In trying to determine their meaning, we must be careful not to impose a meaning on the text that comes out of allegorical imagination or from current meanings of those symbols. Their meaning must be controlled by the divine intention and the meaning the symbols conveyed to those the book was originally addressed to.

In dealing with the symbols in Revelation, we must keep in mind that Revelation was written almost two millennia ago to the Christians of John's time (Rev. 1:4, 11). The symbolic language of Revelation is that of the first century. As we study Revelation today, we must determine the meaning those symbols had for the original recipients. This will safeguard us against our natural tendency to impose on the symbols of Revelation meanings that coincide with our time and situation rather than the time and place within which God originally communicated them to His people.

The symbolic language of Revelation was not born in a vacuum but was drawn from historical reality. Most of the symbolism of the book was taken from the Old Testament—some three-fourths of the book's text has direct or indirect allusions to the Old Testament. In portraying future events, inspiration often uses the language of the past. God wants to impress upon our minds that His acts of salvation in the future will be much like His acts of salvation in the past. What He did for His people in the past, He will do for them in the future. There is no doubt that first-century readers of Revelation would have understood most of the symbols in Revelation in light of their Old Testament background.

Thus, in unlocking the meaning of the symbols and images in Revelation, we must first pay attention to the Old Testament. However, many symbols in the book—such as beasts, heads, horns, stars, the four winds of the earth, women, a seven-headed dragon, and so on—were also widely used in the Jewish apocalyptic writings of the time. As such, they were very much a part of people's vocabulary in the first century. In addition, Revelation's images would have also evoked contemporary Greco-Roman scenes in the minds of first-century Christians.

Ellen White notes that "in the Revelation all the books of the Bible meet and end."[1] Many passages in Revelation have direct parallels in other New Testament texts. Paying careful attention to New Testament parallels helps us achieve deeper insights into the book's message.

Blessing to the Reader (1:3)

The book promises a special blessing to readers. The word "blessed" (*makarios*) in the original Greek means "happy." This is the same word that Jesus used in the Sermon on the Mount (Matt. 5:3–12) with reference to the deep inner joy that nobody and nothing in life can take away (John 16:22), which buoys the faithful through the hardships of life. The readers of Revelation are promised this special happiness when they observe the instructions specified in the prophetic word.

One might notice the change in the text from "the one who reads" (singular) to "the ones listening" (plural), which suggests a public reading of Revelation in a church setting. The listeners were the congregation assembled to hear the expository reading of the book's prophecies. Revelation, thus, envisions individuals in the church who are appointed by God to make the prophecies of Revelation understandable to the congregation. However, this does not suggest that the book is intended to be studied by only a few individuals; rather, it should be studied by the whole body of believers. When believers understand the prophecies of Revelation and respond by taking these prophecies to heart, a great blessing comes upon them.

The Trinitarian Greetings (1:4–6)

Revelation was originally written in the form of an epistle. As such, it starts with the threefold opening of letters that was customary at that time. First, it introduces the sender and the recipients of the letter: "John to the seven churches that are in Asia" (Rev. 1:4). John was one

of the twelve disciples. He was writing to seven Christian congregations in the Roman province of Asia (now the southwestern part of
Turkey), which were in dire spiritual circumstances that threatened to
destroy their existence as God's people.

In Revelation, those seven churches represent the church throughout
the Christian age. The number seven also has symbolic meaning: it is
the number of fullness and completeness. Thus, although originally
written *to* those churches, Revelation was also written *for* all God's
people throughout the Christian age.

The second part of the letter's opening gives the common epistolary
greeting among the early Christians: "Grace and peace to you" (cf. Rom.
1:7; 1 Pet. 1:2). The phrase consists of the customary Greek greeting
word *charis* (grace) and the Hebrew greeting word *shalom* (peace). In
the New Testament, "grace and peace" is more than just a casual
greeting. The order of these two words is always "grace and peace,"
never "peace and grace."[2] Bruce M. Metzger points out that this is
because grace is the divine favor bestowed upon human beings and
"peace is the state of spiritual well-being, which follows as the result."[3]

The givers of grace and peace are the three persons of the Godhead.
The first mentioned is God the Father, referred to as "the One who is,
and who was, and who is coming" (Rev. 1:8; cf. 4:8). This tripartite
title echoes the divine name "I am who I am," which interpreted the
Old Testament covenant name Yahweh and pointed to God's eternal
existence (Exod. 3:14).

The second person in the Trinity of the Godhead is called "the
seven Spirits" (cf. Rev. 4:5; 5:6). This name refers to the Holy Spirit,
with seven being a number of fullness. The Old Testament background
of this identification is the sevenfold designation of the Spirit, found
in the Septuagint version of Isaiah 11:2 (the spirit of wisdom and
understanding, the spirit of counsel and strength, the spirit of
knowledge and godliness, and the spirit of the fear of God).[4] Also, in
Zechariah 4, the seven lamps symbolize the universal activity of the
Holy Spirit in the world (Zech. 4:2). In Revelation, "the seven Spirits"
parallel the seven churches in which the Spirit operates. The phrase,
thus, denotes the fullness and universality of the Holy Spirit's work in
the church, enabling the church to fulfill her calling.

The list concludes with Jesus Christ, who is identified with a threefold
title: "The faithful witness, the firstborn from the dead, and the ruler of
the kings of the earth" (Rev. 1:5a). This threefold title echoes Psalm 89,
in which the Davidic king is the firstborn of Yahweh, the exalted king

on earth, and the faithful witness for Yahweh (89:27, 37). These three titles of Jesus in Revelation 1:5a correspond to His titles of Prophet, Priest, and King. By virtue of His faithful witness during His earthly sojourn, Jesus has received the honor of the firstborn and has been exalted to the highest rank, above all powers and authority in heaven and on earth (Eph. 1:20–22; 1 Pet. 3:22).

Having stated who Jesus truly is, John then describes what Jesus does: He "loves us and released us from our sins by His blood, and made us a kingdom, priests to His God and Father" (Rev. 1:5b–6). This threefold activity of Jesus corresponds to His three titles. In the original text, "[He] loves us" is an ongoing activity: He loves us continually. This love embraces equally the past, the present, and the future. The One who loves us has loosed us from our sins by His blood. In the original text, the verb "loosed" refers to the completed act in the past. On the cross Jesus died and released us from our sins forever.

Revelation tells us not only what Christ has done for us but also what we become in Him. He has made us "a kingdom, priests to His God and Father" (cf. Rev. 5:9–10). This is the status that the redeemed enjoy because of what Christ did on the cross of Calvary. This status was originally promised to ancient Israel. Because God loved Israel, He redeemed them from the slavery of Egypt and promised that they would be His kingdom of priests (Exod. 19:5–6). This privileged title is now offered to the Christian church as the true Israel of God (1 Pet. 2:9–10).

What Israel was offered as a future promise is now offered to Christians on the basis of what Christ did in the past. Because of Christ's ongoing love, the redeemed are already elevated to the glorious status of "a kingdom and priests" (Rev. 5:9–10). Paul explains that the redeemed are already raised and made to sit with Christ in the heavenly places (Eph. 2:6). While we are elevated to that status, we must keep in mind that we are still in this world. Although in the world, we do not belong to this world. "For our citizenship is in heaven, from which also we eagerly wait for a Savior, the Lord Jesus Christ" (Phil. 3:20).

The Keynote of the Book (1:7–8)

In concluding the prologue, John directs attention to the keynote of the letter: the return of Jesus in majesty and glory. He employs the wording from Daniel 7:13 ("coming with the clouds") and Zechariah 12:10 ("whom they have pierced" and "they will mourn for Him") as well as the words of Jesus from His discourse on the Mount of Olives: "Coming on the clouds of the sky" and "all the tribes of the earth will mourn" (Matt. 24:30). John wants us to understand that Christ's coming is rooted in biblical prophecy as well as in Christ's promise to come again. The language used here points to a special resurrection of certain people immediately before the return of Christ.

The promise to come again is restated by Jesus three times in the conclusion of the book (Rev. 22:7, 12, 20). The Second Coming is the keynote of the book; it opens and closes the book. It is the climax of prophecy and the point that history moves toward. Christ's coming in glory will mark the conclusion of this world's history and the beginning of God's eternal kingdom.

In the New Testament, Christ always refers to His coming with the words "I am coming" rather than "I will come." The futuristic present tense refers to the future event as already occurring, thus demonstrating the certainty of Christ's promise to come again. This certainty is affirmed with the statement: "Yes, amen." In Greek, it reads as "*Nai*, amen." *Nai* is a Greek word that means *amen,* a Hebrew affirmative. When combined, the two words express an emphatic affirmation. This affirmation also concludes the book: "'Yes, I am coming soon.' Amen. Come, Lord Jesus" (Rev. 22:20).

This text refers to the literal and personal coming of Christ in majesty and glory. In this way, Revelation is in line with the teaching of the rest of the Bible. The Bible nowhere teaches an invisible and secret coming of Christ. On the contrary, every human will witness Him coming, and this includes "those who pierced Him" (Rev. 1:7). Nobody will be exempt. While His coming brings deliverance to the ones waiting for Him, it will bring judgment to those who have spurned His mercy and love.

The certainty of the Second Coming is rooted in the fact that it has been promised by God Himself, the great "I am," who is "the Alpha and the Omega, . . . the One who is, and who was, and who is coming, the Almighty" (Rev. 1:8). A promise is as strong as the person giving the promise; it is as certain as the integrity and ability of the person to do what he or she says. In the Bible, the promise to come again is given by God, who, in the past, has kept all His promises. He has provided us with an assurance that His promise to come back will be fulfilled, just as all His promises have been fulfilled in the past.

Vision of the Risen Christ

 Revelation 1:9–20

his section describes the circumstances in which John received the visions of Revelation and his visionary encounter with the glorified Christ, who commissioned him to write the things he was about to see in vision and pass them on to the seven churches in Asia Minor:

> ⁹I, John, your brother and fellow partaker in the affliction and kingdom and endurance in Jesus, was on the island called Patmos because of the word of God and the testimony of Jesus Christ. ¹⁰I was in the Spirit on the Lord's day, and I heard behind me a loud voice as of a trumpet, ¹¹saying: "Write down what you see in a scroll and send it to the seven churches, to Ephesus and to Smyrna and to Pergamum and to Thyatira and to Sardis and to Philadelphia and to Laodicea."
>
> ¹²And I turned to see the voice that was speaking with me, and having turned, I saw seven golden lampstands, ¹³and in the midst of the lampstands, I saw one like a son of man clothed in a robe reaching down to the feet and girded with a golden girdle. ¹⁴His head and hair were white as white wool, as snow, and His eyes as a flame of fire, ¹⁵and His feet were like burnished bronze as refined in a furnace, and His voice was like the sound of many waters, ¹⁶and He had in His right hand seven stars, and out of His mouth proceeded a sharp two-edged sword, and His countenance was as the sun shining in its power.
>
> ¹⁷And when I saw Him, I fell at His feet as a dead person, and He placed His right hand on me, saying: "Stop being afraid! I am the first and the last, ¹⁸and the living

One, and I was dead, and behold, I am alive forever and ever, and I have the keys of Death and Hades. [19]Write, therefore, the things which you saw, namely, the things which are and the things which are about to take place after these things. [20]With regard to the mystery of the seven stars that you saw in My right hand, and the seven golden lampstands, the seven stars are the angels of the seven churches, and the seven lampstands are the seven churches."

John on Patmos (1:9)

John begins his story by telling the readers that he was on Patmos because of his faithful witness to the gospel (Rev. 1:9). Patmos was a barren, rocky island in the Aegean Sea about fifty miles from Ephesus; the island is ten miles long and six miles across its widest part. It has been commonly held that the island was used by the Romans as a penal colony for political offenders, as were some other Sporades islands.[1] Early Christian authors who lived close to the time when Revelation was written are unanimous that John was banished to Patmos by Roman authorities to prevent him from spreading the gospel.

As a prisoner, the aged apostle endured all hardships in his exile on Patmos. For one thing, the Roman authorities treated him as a criminal. Early Christian tradition testifies that he was forced to perform hard labor in quarries.[2] The hardship John suffered was marked by "perpetual fetters, scanty clothing, insufficient food, sleep on the bare ground in a dark prison, and work under the lash of military overseers."[3]

John's experience on Patmos left marks on the language and imagery of Revelation. For instance, the tribulation that he endured because of his faithful witness to the gospel became a precursor of the faithful people's experience in a hostile world throughout history but especially of the great tribulation that God's people will have to go through at the time of the end (cf. Rev. 7:14). Also, when he mentioned the islands and mountains disappearing at the eschatological denouement (6:14; 16:20), he probably had the mountainous island of Patmos, together with its sister islands, in mind.

Especially noticeable is the prominence of sea and water imagery in the book (it occurs twenty-six times). Expressions such as "like the sound of many waters" (1:15; 14:2) evoke the melodic sound of the restless sea around Patmos; the area before the throne of God in the visions appeared to the apostle "like a sea of glass, like crystal" (4:6), while the reflection of the rising and setting sun in the sea at Patmos became the source for the metaphor "like a sea of glass mixed with fire" (15:2).

The metaphoric meaning of the sea in the book eventually shifts from positive to negative. Since John was confined on Patmos, the sea came to mean separation and suffering to him. The stormy waters around Patmos became the symbol of the disturbing social and political conditions in the world. The sea is obviously related to the abyss (bottomless pit), the abode of Satan and his demons (cf. Rev. 13:1 with 17:8). It is out of that metaphoric sea that the apostle saw the beast coming to oppress God's people (13:1). The prostitute Babylon was seen as dwelling "on many waters" (17:1; cf. v. 15). It is also from the symbolic sea that the figurative merchants of Babylon, selling her corrupt doctrines and policies, get all their wealth and luxuries (18:17–24).

With this in mind, it is no wonder that in his last vision of the new heaven and the new earth, John first observed that "the sea is no longer there" (Rev. 21:1). The text does not refer to just any sea but to *the* sea that surrounded Patmos, filling the aged apostle with a deep longing for the time when the sea will be no longer. The absence of the "sea" on the new earth means the absence of all evil that the "Patmos" suffering and pain brings in this life.

The real pain, however, that the Revelator felt on Patmos was greater than his physical suffering. He was overwhelmingly concerned with the situation in the churches, located in seven cities in the province of Asia (cf. Rev. 1:11), that had been deprived of his leadership. The exiled apostle knew about potential threats to those churches. The situation in the churches gradually became destabilized by the increasing hostility of Roman authorities in Asia toward Christians. There were also some disturbing reports that those churches were in dire straits. Most of them were divided, while in some churches, the majority of the believers were involved in spreading apostasy. John's authority also was coming under attack.

Many Christians in Asia were struggling with regard to their identity. The dire circumstances and distress might have led many of them to question whether God was still in control and what the future would bring to the church. They were in urgent need of guidance and encouragement. However, the aged apostle could not be with them.

His concern for their spiritual welfare was, at times, overwhelming. John was, himself, in great distress, and he needed a word of assurance and encouragement.

Christians should never forget that whenever they find themselves on a "Patmos" surrounded by an endless raging "sea"—whatever that sea may mean to them—they are not alone. The Patmos experience always results in a revelation of Jesus Christ. It is because Daniel experienced the Babylonian captivity that there is the book of Daniel in the Bible. In the same way, John had to go to Patmos so today we may have the book of Revelation. Jesus, who visited John in a vision on that barren island, is the same Jesus who is present with His people to sustain and support them today. He will be with them always, until the very end of the age (Matt. 28:20).

John's Encounter with Christ (1:10–20)

On the Lord's Day (1:10a)

We do not know how long John was actually on Patmos before Christ appeared to him in the vision. John states only briefly that while he was in the midst of his distress, he was taken into a vision on "the Lord's day" (Rev. 1:10). It appears that, for him, "the Lord's day" was a special day. However, nowhere does he state what day that was, although the first-century Christians evidently understood it.

In the Bible, there are two days that are specified as the Lord's. The first one is the seventh-day Sabbath. The Sabbath is called "my [God's] Sabbath" (Exod. 31:13; Ezek. 20:12, 20) and the Lord's holy day (Isa. 58:13). Jesus called himself "Lord of the Sabbath" (Matt. 12:8; Mark 2:28). This clearly shows that John could have received the vision on the seventh-day Sabbath as the Lord's Day.

Another day referred to as the Lord's in the Bible is the eschatological "day of the Lord," mentioned often in both the Old Testament (Isa. 13:6–13; Joel 2:11, 31; Amos 5:18–20; Zeph. 1:14; Mal. 4:5) and the New Testament (1 Thess. 5:2; 2 Pet. 3:10). It refers to the time when God will bring the history of this world to its end and establish a new order. In the New Testament, the day of the Lord refers exclusively to the Second Coming.

It is particularly significant that the Sabbath in the Bible has eschatological significance (Isa. 58:13–14; 66:23) and is a sign of deliverance (Deut. 5:15; Ezek. 20:10–12). It is, thus, quite possible that

John coined the phrase "the Lord's day" to combine the two biblical concepts into one: to tell his readers that he was taken in vision to the eschatological day of the Lord to witness the events during the conclusion of this earth's history (cf. Rev. 1:7) and to tell them this vision actually took place on the seventh-day Sabbath. This would fit the portrayal of the final events in Revelation, within which the Sabbath, as I will show later, plays a central role in the end-time drama.

Christ as a Priest (1:10–12)

While John was in vision, he heard behind him a loud voice speaking to him (Rev. 1:10). The voice sounded like a trumpet. A trumpet-like sound in the Bible represents the voice of God. That was the voice that proclaimed the Ten Commandments from Mount Sinai (Exod. 19:16), and it will be heard again announcing the coming of Christ on the clouds (Matt. 24:31; 1 Cor. 15:52; 1 Thess. 4:16). That voice now commissions John to write on a scroll the things he is about to see and to send it to the seven churches (Rev. 1:11).

The voice that John heard sounded familiar to him, for it was the voice of Jesus, whom he had listened to for about three and a half years. When he turned to see the One speaking to him, he saw seven golden lampstands and, in their midst, "one like a son of man" (Rev. 1:12–13). These were separate lampstands with lamps on the top. John later explains that the lampstands represented the seven churches in Asia to whom the book of Revelation was originally sent (1:20; cf. 1:11).

The vision is reminiscent of the ancient Jewish temple. In the Jewish temple in Jerusalem, the lampstands provided light (1 Kings 7:49). They also signified God's plan for Israel to be His light-bearing witness to the surrounding nations (Isa. 42:6–7; 49:6; 60:1–3). Jesus defined the role of the church in terms of a lamp giving light to a world enshrouded in darkness (Matt. 5:14–16; cf. Phil. 2:15). The lamp needs to be on a lampstand to disperse its light (cf. Mark 4:21; Luke 8:16). If the church failed in its role of shining the light on the world, it would lose its reason for existence (Rev. 2:5).

The focus of the scene, however, is not on the churches but on Christ in their midst. John sees Him dressed in a long robe with a girdle around His waist. Jewish historian Josephus describes the high priest serving in the Jerusalem temple as dressed in a long robe that reaches to his feet, with a girdle around his waist.[4] Isaiah prophesied of the Messiah, saying that "righteousness will be the belt about His loins, and faithfulness the belt about His waist" (Isa. 11:5). A daily task of the priests in the Jerusalem temple was to keep the lamps in the holy place burning brightly. They would trim and refill the lamps that were waning, replace the wick on the lamps that had gone out, refill them with fresh oil, and relight them (Exod. 30:7–8).[5]

The picture of Jesus dressed in a priestly robe and walking among the lampstands (Rev. 2:1) portrays Him as a priest ministering to the churches and helping them in their needs and circumstances. The scene brings to mind the covenant promise given to ancient Israel on their way toward the Promised Land: "I will also walk among you and be your God, and you shall be My people" (Lev. 26:12). Now, in the symbolic walk among the lampstands, Jesus fulfilled this covenant promise. All of this was intended to assure both John and the churches of Christ's presence and His promise to be continually with His people until the end of the age.

Portrayal of Christ (1:13–16)

Jesus comes to John as the exalted Lord, yet He appears as "one like a son of man" (Rev. 1:13)—that is, like a human. This was the favorite self-designation of Jesus (Matt. 26:46; Mark 13:26; Luke 19:10). John had an earlier glimpse of Jesus's glory on the Mount of Transfiguration (Mark 9:2–3; cf. 2 Pet. 1:16–17). However, the exalted Christ that John sees in his vision has a totally different appearance from the Jesus he knew while in the flesh. The apostle finds human language inadequate to describe Jesus's appearance. In endeavoring to portray Jesus, John uses some ancient images and some Old Testament descriptions of God.

John's portrayal of Jesus is similar to the manlike divine figure in Daniel 10:5–12. But Jesus is much more than that. He also bears the characteristics of God in the Old Testament. The phrase "one like a son of man" echoes the same from Daniel 7:13–14. Jesus has the white hair of "the Ancient of Days" in Daniel 7:9. His eyes are like flaming fire, His feet are like burnished bronze, and His face is shining like the divine figure from Daniel's vision (Dan. 10:6; cf. Matt. 17:2). His voice, like the sound of many waters, was the voice of God in Ezekiel 43:2 (cf. Dan. 10:6). In the images of this manlike figure, John quickly recognized the glorified Lord with all His divine characteristics and prerogatives.

In applying these Old Testament images to Christ, John uses the words "like" or "as," which suggest a metaphoric rather than literal meaning. In the ancient world, white or gray hair signified wisdom and experience (Job 15:10; Prov. 20:29). Christ's eyes, like the flame of fire, denoted His ability to penetrate the innermost secrets of the human heart (Rev. 2:18, 23); His feet, like burnished bronze, symbolized stability and strength (Ezek. 1:7); His voice, like a trumpet and the sound of many waters, was the voice of God speaking (Ezek. 43:2); His shining face was referred to in Jesus's exaltation (Matt. 17:2–3). Furthermore, equipped with the two-edged sword coming out of His mouth (Heb. 4:12), Christ appears and acts as the full authority of God.

In terms of the Old Testament descriptions of God, this portrayal of Jesus appealed in particular to the Jews. However, for Gentiles, the same description could evoke the image of the Hellenistic goddess Hekate, popularly worshiped in western Asia Minor during John's time. Pagans ascribed to her universal authority; they considered her the source and ruler of heaven, earth, and Hades (the underworld), and the agent by which they would come to their end. She manifested herself in three forms, corresponding to each part of the universe: her heavenly form was Selene or Luna (the moon), her earthly form was Artemis or Diana, and her underworld form was Persephone. She was called the "keybearer," because she was thought to possess keys to the gates of heaven and Hades. She was referred to as follows: the "beginning and end are you, and you alone rule all. For all things are from you, and in you do all things. Eternal one, come to their end."[6]

We see how Jesus presents Himself to Gentiles as their only hope. Everything they hoped for in the pagan religion they could find in Christ. His authority surpassed the authority of Hekate and any other authority in heaven, on earth, or under the earth (cf. Phil. 2:10). By virtue of His own death on the cross, Jesus broke the power of death, and this empowered Him to possess "the keys of Death and Hades" (Rev. 1:18). Because of His death and resurrection, Jesus lives forevermore, being with His people and sustaining them.

Words of Encouragement to John (1:17–20)

Jesus came to Patmos to provide encouragement for John. John was the pastor of the churches in Asia, and as a leader, he also needed encouragement. Overwhelmed by the glory of the Lord, the aged apostle collapsed at Jesus's feet in awe, just as he had done earlier on the Mount of Transfiguration (Matt. 17:6–7). In turning, John once again experienced the calming hand of Christ with His reassuring words: "Stop being afraid!" (from the original Greek; Rev. 1:17). John had often heard these words from Jesus (Matt. 14:27; 17:7; 28:10; Luke 5:10; John 6:20). Yet on Patmos these words had a special meaning for him.

By referring to Himself as "the first and the last" (Rev. 1:17), Jesus reveals Himself to John as the God of the Old Testament (Isa. 44:6; 48:12). The Greek word for "last" is *eschatos,* which the word "eschatology" comes from. This shows that the focus of eschatology in Revelation is not about the end-time events but about Jesus Christ and His presence with His people. He has the last word with regard to the final events. As the eternal God, He is "the same yesterday and today and forever" (Heb. 13:8). He is "the living One" and is in possession of "the keys of death and Hades" (Rev. 1:18). Keys are a symbol of power and authority. Christ has conquered death. His followers do not need to fear death any longer, because death and the abode of the dead are under His control. The day is coming when death as "the last enemy . . . will be abolished" (1 Cor. 15:26).

Encouragement for the Churches

What Jesus did for John, He also did for the churches. Jesus's second reason for coming to Patmos was to give John seven distinctive messages, commissioning him to pass them on to the churches. In those messages, Jesus had full knowledge of the spiritual condition of each church. He knew that the Ephesians were backsliding in love, and that the Smyrnians were suffering and in constant fear of what the future would bring. He knew the circumstances in which the Christians in Pergamum lived and that the church in Thyatira was divided. He knew about the spiritual complacency of the Christians in Sardis and the spiritual weakness of the Philadelphians. And He knew about the self-sufficiency and blindness of the Laodiceans.

Since Jesus knew the particular situations and needs of the churches, He was able to relate to their circumstances and needs. In addressing the churches, He introduced Himself to each by mentioning some of the characteristics from the composite picture of Himself within the first chapter of Revelation:

- To the church in Ephesus, He comes as "the One who holds the seven stars in His right hand, who walks in the midst of the seven golden lampstands" (Rev. 2:1; cf. 1:13, 16).
- To the church in Smyrna, He comes as "the first and the last, One who was dead and came to life" (2:8; cf. 1:17–18).
- To the church in Pergamum, He comes as "the One who has the sharp two-edged sword" (2:12; cf. 1:16).

- To the church in Thyatira, He comes as "the Son of God, the One whose eyes are as a flame of fire, and His feet like burnished bronze" (2:18; cf. 1:14–15).
- To the church in Sardis, He comes as "the One who has the seven Spirits of God and seven stars" (3:1; cf. 1:4, 16).
- To the church in Philadelphia, He comes as "the holy One, the true One, the One who has the key of David, who opens and no one shuts, and shuts and no one opens" (3:7; cf. 1:18).
- To the church in Laodicea, He comes as "the Amen, the faithful and true Witness, the beginning of God's creation" (3:14; cf. 1:5a).

In each case, the characteristics of Jesus are related to the particular situations and needs of the churches. For instance, to the church in Ephesus, which is losing its first love and is threatened by false teachers, Jesus comes as the One who holds their situation in His hand and who walks in their midst (Rev. 2:1). Also, to the church in Smyrna going through dire persecution, Jesus suitably presents Himself as the One who has also experienced what they are going through (2:8). He also gives them a promise of resurrection (2:10–11). He makes similar promises and presentations of Himself to the rest of the churches.

Several observations may be made here. First, Jesus presents Himself to each church in a distinctive manner. However, no individual church has the full picture of Jesus. Each receives only some of Him. However, all the churches together have the full picture of Jesus. It is important to keep in mind that the full revelation of Jesus comes through the whole church of Christ—not through individuals or factions separated from the larger body of believers. Furthermore, no two churches share the same aspect of Christ. The obvious reason is that since each church is in a unique situation and has unique needs, Jesus is able to adapt to each situation.

The same concept may be observed in the four Gospels. The four Gospels tell the same story of Jesus, but from different angles. As such, each gives a distinctive picture of Jesus's ability to meet the different and particular needs of the people to whom the Gospels were originally sent.

The situation here applies to the lives of Christians in many ways. Many Christians today know much *about* Jesus, but what they lack is knowing Him *personally*. Their spiritual lives hinge on someone else's knowledge of Jesus: parents, spouses, or their pastors. The strong appeal of Revelation is to discover Jesus personally, as the One who meets us where we are. As the church proclaims the gospel message to the world, it must follow Christ's way in presenting the gospel message to the world. The focus should be on Jesus Christ—the world's greatest need—and to proclaim Him in words and actions. What Christ wants is to reveal Himself to the world through the church as the only One who can meet people in their distinctive circumstances and satisfy their spiritual needs. This is the kind of light Jesus wants to shine through the church. If the church fails in this calling, it loses its very reason for existence.

As Sin Increases, Grace Abounds

As all seven messages begin alike, they also conclude alike. Each concludes with a personal appeal: "The one who has an ear, let him hear what the Spirit says to the churches" (see Rev. 2:7). Every Christian living in a particular church was urged to heed these messages. Every appeal to the churches also contains a promise to the overcomers.

The messages indicate a spiritual decline in the seven churches. The first church in Ephesus is still faithful to God, even though it is not quite what Jesus wants it to be. The second and third churches—Smyrna and Pergamum—are generally faithful; only a small number of wayward members are unfaithful. Thyatira is a divided church, with two phases of its faithfulness to Christ. The fifth and sixth churches—Sardis and Philadelphia—are in very serious conditions. The majority of followers in these churches are out of harmony with the gospel, while the remnant represents the faithful few. When it comes to Laodicea, there is nothing good to be said about that church. It is self-sufficient and indifferent. It receives a threat: "I am about to vomit you out of My mouth" (Rev. 3:16).

However, along with the evident spiritual decline in the churches, there is a proportionate increase in the promises Jesus gives.[7] Although each church is in greater decline compared with the preceding one, each receives more promises than the previous one:

- Ephesus is given one promise: to obtain the tree of life (Rev. 2:7).
- Smyrna is given two promises: to have the crown of life and to escape from the second death (2:10–11).
- Pergamum is given three promises: to have the hidden manna, to have a white stone, and to be called by a new name (2:17).
- Thyatira is given four promises: to have the authority over the nations, to rule over the nations with an iron scepter, to dash the nations into pieces, and to be given the morning star (2:26–28).

- Sardis is given five promises: to walk with Jesus, to be dressed in white robes, to have their names not blotted out of the book of life, to be acknowledged before the Father, and to be acknowledged before the angels (3:4–5).
- Philadelphia is given six promises: to be kept from the hour of trial; to be pillars in the temple; to never leave the temple; and to have the name of God, the name of the city of God, and God's new name written on them (3:10–12).
- Laodicea is given only one promise: to sit with Jesus on His throne (3:21). However, this promise incorporates all other promises that were made to the churches. To sit with Jesus on His throne means to have all these promises.

This increase in promises in proportion to the spiritual decline in the churches brings to mind Paul's statement that where sin increases, grace abounds all the more (Rom. 5:20).

It is important to keep in mind that, in the words of Ellen White, "the church, enfeebled and defective though it be, is the only object on earth on which Christ bestows his supreme regard. He is constantly watching it with solicitude, and is strengthening it by his Holy Spirit."[8] The church's only hope is in Christ. He knows His people, because He walks among them, and He cares for them. As the church is facing the eschatological trial, she has the promise of the exalted Christ: "Stop being afraid! I am the first and last" (Rev. 1:17). "Behold, I am with you always, even to the end of the age" (Matt. 28:20).

Messages to the Churches (Part 1)

 Revelation 2:1–17

The seven messages were sent to the Christian congregations located in seven cities of the Roman province of Asia at the end of the first century. There were, however, more than seven churches in Asia Minor—including those in Colossae, Troas, and Hierapolis. That only seven churches were chosen suggests their symbolic significance—seven is a number of fullness. This indicates that they represented the entire Christian church. Their contents may be applied on three levels:

Historical application. It is primarily important to keep in mind that the seven messages were originally sent to their respective churches in Asia Minor. These were actual churches with real challenges. These churches were located in important, prosperous city centers located on the main postal road that connected them. Under the Roman government, they generally enjoyed peace and prosperity. As a token of their gratitude and loyalty to Rome, a number of cities set up emperor worship in their temples. Emperor worship was compulsory as the duty of all citizens. The citizens were also expected to be involved in the city's public events and participate in pagan religious ceremonies. Serious consequences awaited those who did not participate.

Commissioned by Christ, John wrote to the churches as their pastor to help them with the challenges of their pagan environment. It is, thus, primarily important to discover how these messages applied to the Christians in Asia to whom they were originally sent.

Universal application. Although originally sent *to* the churches in Asia Minor, these messages were not written *only* for them. Just as Paul wrote his epistles primarily to the churches of his day, yet they still contain timeless messages for subsequent generations of Christians. Similarly, the messages to the seven churches contain valuable lessons that apply to Christians in all time periods.

These messages were not sent separately but together as one letter (cf. Rev. 1:11). The entire letter was to be read by all the churches. Since each message concludes with an exhortation to heed what the Spirit says to the churches, each message applies equally to all the churches, although each was written to an individual church. These messages, thus, speak to all Christians and can generally represent different types of Christians in certain periods of history or in different locations. For instance, while the general characteristic of today's Christianity is essentially Laodicean, some churches or individual Christians might, instead, have the characteristics of the church in Ephesus or Smyrna.

Prophetic application. The book of Revelation does not specify that the seven messages are written as predictive history. However, since there were more than seven churches in Asia in the first century and only these seven were selected, a symbolic function is implied. Also, Revelation claims to be a book of prophecy, and this points to the prophetic significance of these messages (Rev. 1:1–3). Therefore, the spiritual conditions of the seven churches correspond remarkably to the spiritual conditions of Christianity in different periods of history.[1] All this shows that the seven messages are intended to provide, from heaven's perspective, a panoramic survey of Christianity from the first century until the time of the end.

As we look at these messages one by one, we will first explore the cities in which the seven churches were located to see how pagan practices affected the Christians there. Then we will take a closer look at each message to discover the valuable lessons they provided for the Christians in John's day as well as for us today. Finally, we will see how each message applies to a particular period of Christian history.

Each message follows the same format, consisting of: (1) an address, (2) an introduction of Jesus, (3) Jesus's appraisal of the church, (4) Jesus's counsel and warning to the church, (5) an appeal to hear the Spirit, and (6) promises to the overcomers. By comparing the parallel parts of the messages, we can gain deeper insight into the meaning of these messages.

The Message to Ephesus (2:1–7)

The first church addressed by Jesus was located in Ephesus (modern Selçuk, Turkey), the nearest of the seven cities to Patmos:

¹To the angel of the church in Ephesus write: "Thus says the One who holds the seven stars in His right hand, who walks in the midst of the seven golden lampstands: ²I know your works, namely, your labor and endurance, and that you cannot bear evil ones, and that you have tested those who call themselves apostles—and they are not—and you have found them to be liars; ³and you have perseverance and you have borne up because of My name, and you have not grown weary. ⁴But I have against you that you have left your first love. ⁵Keep remembering, therefore, from where you have fallen, and repent and do the first works; but if not, I am coming to you, and I will remove your lampstand from its place, unless you repent. ⁶But this you have, that you hate the works of the Nicolaitans, which I, Myself, also hate.

⁷"The one who has an ear, let him hear what the Spirit says to the churches. To the one who overcomes, I will give the right to eat from the tree of life, which is in the paradise of God."

The City of Ephesus

Ephesus was the capital city of the province of Asia. It was the fourth-largest city in the Roman Empire, with a population of about a quarter million. Located on the Aegean Sea, at the mouth of the Cayster River, and at the crossroads of two major trade roads, this cosmopolitan city was known as the gateway to Asia. The city was a famous political, commercial, and religious center. It was filled with public and commercial buildings, including temples, theaters, gymnasiums, bathhouses, and brothels. The city was the home of the Panionian Games: these annual athletic events drew the whole population of Asia to Ephesus.

In the city, there were two temples devoted to the worship of the emperor. In addition, about fifteen temples of different deities have been identified in this first-century city. Ephesus was also famous for magical practices and arts (cf. Acts 19:19). The city's pride was the grandeur of the temple of Artemis (or Diana to the Romans), considered to be one of the seven wonders of the ancient world; it attracted multitudes of pilgrims each year for the annual Artemisia festivals. A great silversmith business was associated with the temple, contributing to the city's wealth. The temple was, at the same time, a treasury house and a refuge for fleeing criminals; it also played a vital role in community life.

The city was, however, notorious for immorality and superstition; it was viewed as full of criminals. It was in this city that the most influential Christian church in the province was located. Established by Paul during his three years of ministry there, the church grew rapidly, soon becoming an important center of early Christianity (Acts 19). At the time Revelation was written, the church was still strong in faith and had preserved the purity of the gospel. The city was most likely the residence of John prior to and after his exile.

The Christians living in Ephesus experienced all kinds of pressure from pagans. This included opposition from pagans and accusations for their refusal to participate in pagan religious activities. They were accused of atheism for not participating in emperor worship and the worship of pagan gods. They were also charged with cannibalism in connection with the Lord's Supper. Stories that accused Christians of sacrificing children at their services, eating their flesh, and drinking their blood were circulated. Because of this, Christians faced losing their legal status in the city and suffering social isolation and possible persecution.

Jesus's Message to the Church

Jesus presents Himself to the church in Ephesus as "the One who holds the seven stars in His right hand, who walks in the midst of the seven golden lampstands" (Rev. 2:1), which denotes His presence in the church and His knowledge of its situation and needs. Jesus commends the church for a number of great qualities. In spite of living in a pagan environment and being surrounded by a pagan lifestyle and immoral practices, the members worked hard and demonstrated patient endurance for the sake of the gospel. They also stood firm in the face of persecution. Despite the pressure from outside, they had not grown weary. The church was doctrinally sound, exercised discernment in testing false apostles, and did not tolerate their false teachings in its midst (2:2–3).

The members, in particular, resisted the practices of the Nicolaitans (Rev. 2:6). It is not clear who exactly these people were. Some early Christian authors describe them as heretical followers of Nicolas of Antioch, one of the seven deacons of the Jerusalem church, who ultimately fell into heresy (Acts 6:5).[2] They advocated compromise and conformity with pagan practices to avoid the discomfort and hardships of social isolation and impending persecution. The Nicolaitans are mentioned also in the message to the church in Pergamum, in which they are linked with another heretical group: the followers of the teaching of Balaam (Rev. 2:14–15).

Several decades earlier, Paul had warned the Ephesians that "men will arise, speaking perverse things, to draw away the disciples after them" (Acts 20:30). This prediction was now fulfilled. The church, however, was not enticed by the perverse doctrines of the false teachers. It made every effort to preserve the purity of the gospel and prevent the falsehood from corrupting the members. Not long after Revelation was written, Ignatius, the bishop of Antioch, wrote a letter to the Ephesians, in which he similarly praised their brave stand for the truth.

In spite of these great qualities, this hard-working and faithful church had a serious flaw: it was backsliding in love. In their early days, the Christians in Ephesus were known for their "faith in the Lord Jesus" and their "love for all the saints" (Eph. 1:15). Now, several decades later, that love was fading. In putting all the emphasis on right actions and sound doctrine, the members were declining in love for Christ, and as a result, their love for each other faded. Their religion became legalistic and loveless. They were doing what was right, but their works became cold, lacking love for Christ and their fellow humans.

The situation of the church in Ephesus reflects the situation of Israel before the Exile, which, in the words of Jeremiah, lost the ardent love and devotion it had for God during the early days (Jer. 2:2). The people of Israel were appointed to be God's light-bearing witnesses to the world. However, in their later history, they renounced their love for God, mistreating and oppressing their fellow humans. As a result, God took the privilege of being His light-bearing people from them. A similar punishment could happen to the church in Ephesus. If the church does not reflect the love of God, it loses the very reason for its existence. It is in danger of having its lampstand removed from its place (Rev. 2:5), similar to how ancient Israel also lost this privilege.

Jesus appeals to the church with three imperatives: "Keep remembering," "repent," and "do the first works" (Rev. 2:5). First, the Ephesians must keep remembering. As the Greek text indicates, they had not forgotten the relationship they once had with Christ but failed to continue in it. By recalling the ardent love for Christ and each other that flowed from their hearts when they accepted the gospel, the members would realize their present spiritual condition. Then they should repent. Repentance in the Bible denotes a radical turnaround in one's life. Jesus calls the Ephesians to turn away from their present condition and turn back to God.

Finally, the Ephesians must start doing their first works. Jesus does not urge them to love to the detriment of doing right. The revitalization of their first love, which is for Christ, will result in doing right. If the Christians in Ephesus return to their first devotion to Christ, love for their fellow humans will overflow in their midst.

Throughout history, Christians have always found themselves strained between strict religious observances and practices and expressing Christ's love and compassion. The message to the church in Ephesus is a perennial warning to all Christians, whose primary concern is doing the right thing, to always keep in mind the central theme of the gospel: the love of God.

The overcomers—the ones who heed Christ's counsel—in Ephesus are given the promise "to eat from the tree of life, which is in the paradise of God" (Rev. 2:7). After Adam and Eve sinned, they were forbidden to eat from the tree of life. Now, those in Ephesus who stay faithful and do not participate in pagan practices will be allowed to eat from the tree in the restored Eden (22:2).

The situation of the church in Ephesus corresponds aptly to the situation and spiritual condition of the church in general in the first century. The first century was a period characterized by love and faithfulness to the gospel. But by the time John wrote the book of Revelation, the church had begun losing the fire of its first love, thus departing from the simplicity and purity of the gospel.

The Message to Smyrna (2:8–11)

The second message was addressed to the church in Smyrna (modern Izmir, Turkey), a city about thirty-five miles north of Ephesus. Christ's message to this church is the shortest of the seven:

> *8To the angel of the church in Smyrna write: "Thus says the first and the last, the One who was dead and came to life: 9I know your affliction and poverty—but you are rich—and the slander of those who say that they are Jews, and they are not but are the synagogue of Satan. 10Stop fearing the things which you are about to suffer! Behold, the devil is about to cast some of you into prison that you may be tested, and you will have*

tribulation for ten days. Remain faithful to the point of death, and I will give you the crown of life.

[11]"The one who has an ear, let him hear what the Spirit says to the churches. The one who overcomes shall not be harmed by the second death."

The City of Smyrna

Smyrna was another important city located next to Ephesus. Its geographical location earned it the reputation of having the most convenient and safest harbor of any trade city in Asia. The city also stood on the major crossroad to Phrygia and Lydia that made it an important trade route connecting Greece and Asia. Its location, the trade, and the fertile area made Smyrna a very wealthy city with a population of some two hundred thousand residents.

The city was also a political, religious, and cultural center. It was proud of its famous stadium, library, and the largest public theater in the province, which seated twenty thousand people. Because of its wealth and exceptional beauty, the city claimed to be "the glory of Asia." It was also noted for the science and medicine industries that flourished there. The city proudly claimed to be the birthplace of the famous epic poet Homer.

Smyrna had the status of a free city. Its special relationship with Rome earned many privileges for the city. The Roman Senate granted the city the privilege to build a temple in honor of Tiberius. This made Smyrna a center of emperor worship. Late in the first century and after, emperor worship became compulsory for all citizens. As an act of loyalty, it was a civic duty of all citizens to go to the temple once a year and burn incense before the statue of the emperor and proclaim: "Caesar is Lord!" Those who did this would then receive a certificate, allowing them to hold a job or conduct business. Those who refused to comply faced persecution and death.[3]

This may explain the situation of the Christians in Smyrna. Because they didn't participate in emperor worship and pagan religious rituals, they faced losing their legal status, persecution, and even martyrdom.

Jesus's Message to the Church

Jesus introduces himself to the church in Smyrna as "the first and the last, the One who was dead and came to life" (Rev. 2:8). These characteristics of Jesus correspond aptly with their situation. The members were going through the hardships of persecution, anticipating an even more severe persecution. Jesus comes to them as the One who understands their situation, because He was also persecuted to the point of death. He will be with them in their trials to sustain them.

First, Jesus knows their affliction. The Greek word for affliction here denotes the pressure of a burden that crushes.[4] Second, they are in extreme poverty and destitute; they possess nothing. Their poverty is related to the persecution they are experiencing. Because of their loyalty to Christ, many church members were ostracized and lost their jobs, while some suffered imprisonment and even death. However, in spite of their poverty in material goods, the Smyrnians were rich in grace and faith.

Jesus also mentions malignant slander from the Jews that contributed significantly to their plight. Jews in the Roman Empire were usually exempted from worshiping the emperor and pagan gods. However, toward the end of the first century, the Jews in Smyrna found themselves in a difficult situation with the local officials. Since Romans often identified early Christians with Jews, Jews wanted to disassociate themselves from Christians. They slandered Christians before the local officials by making malicious accusations and inciting the authorities to persecute them. Although they considered themselves to be the synagogue of God, these Jews actually constituted "the synagogue of Satan" by being used by Satan to harm God's people (Rev. 2:9).

The Christians in Smyrna were in constant fear for their future. Jesus gently admonishes them to "stop fearing" (Rev. 2:10). "There is no fear in love; but perfect love casts out fear" (1 John 4:18). They are about to experience even more serious trials and imprisonment in a period of ten days—like the ten days of testing assigned for Daniel and his friends in Babylon (Dan. 1:12–15). However, Jesus urges them to remain faithful, even to the point of death, and He will give them "the crown of life" (Rev. 2:10). The crown referred to here is the garland given to the winner at the ancient Olympic Games. The crown that Jesus promises the faithful in Smyrna is eternal life, to be given at His Second Coming (2 Tim. 4:8). As James stated: "Blessed is a man who perseveres under trial; for once he has been approved, he will receive the crown of life which the Lord has promised to those who love Him" (James 1:12).

The overcomers in Smyrna are given the promise that they will not be hurt by the second death (Rev. 2:11). Physical death is a temporary sleep and, as such, is not a tragedy because of the hope of the resurrection. It is the second death that should be feared: eternal death, from which there will be no resurrection. Jesus warned His followers: "Do not fear those who kill the body but are unable to kill the soul; but rather fear Him who is able to destroy both soul and body in hell" (Matt. 10:28).

The experience of the church in Smyrna coincided with the severe persecution of Christians throughout the Roman Empire during the second and third centuries. The "ten days" (Rev. 2:10) mentioned in the message could be applied prophetically to the notorious imperial persecution initiated by the emperor Diocletian and continued under his successor Galerius (AD 303–313). In this way, the church in Smyrna could represent the period in church history from the beginning of the second century until approximately AD 313, when Constantine the Great issued the famous Edict of Milan, granting Christians religious freedom.

The Message to Pergamum (2:12–17)

The third message was addressed to the church located in Pergamum (modern Bergama, Turkey), a city about forty miles northeast of Smyrna:

> *12To the angel of the church in Pergamum write: "Thus says the One who has the sharp two-edged sword: 13I know where you dwell, where the throne of Satan is, and you are holding fast My name, and you did not deny My faith, even in the days of Antipas, My faithful witness, who was killed among you, where Satan dwells. 14But I have a few things against you, that you have there some who hold the teaching of Balaam, who taught Balak to cast a stumbling block before the sons of Israel to eat the things sacrificed to idols and to commit fornication. 15Thus, you also have those who hold the teaching of the Nicolaitans. 16Repent, therefore; but if not, I am coming to you quickly, and I will make war against them with the sword of My mouth.*
> *17"The one who has an ear, let him hear what the Spirit says to the churches. To the one who overcomes, I will give of the hidden manna, and I will give him a white*

stone, and on the stone a new name written, which nobody knows except the one who receives it."

The City of Pergamum

Pergamum served as the capital city of the province of Asia for more than two and a half centuries (although this honor was also claimed by Ephesus). In addition to its political importance, Pergamum was the reputed center of intellectual life in the Hellenistic world. Its famous library of nearly two hundred thousand volumes was the second largest library, after the one in Alexandria. The city was the home of Galen, the famous physician of the ancient world, who studied there at the medical school of Asclepius.

Pergamum was also a reputed religious center. It was the first city in Asia to embrace emperor worship and to build a large temple to the emperor Augustus. As in Smyrna, emperor worship was compulsory in Pergamum; to secure the certificate allowing them to work or to run a business, the citizens were obliged to offer incense before the statue of the emperor and proclaim: "Caesar is Lord." A refusal to do so would result in losing one's legal status and facing persecution.

The city was also famed for its magnificent temples to Zeus, Athena, Dionysus, and Asclepius. On the acropolis of the city stood the remarkable altar of Zeus (the central portion of which is now exhibited in the Pergamon Museum in Berlin). Near the city stood the immense shrine of Asclepius, the Greek god of healing. Asclepius was called "the Savior" and was represented by a serpent (an emblem retained by the modern medical profession). In John's time, the shrine of Asclepius experienced great popularity; people came from around the world to be healed by this savior-god. This made Pergamum the "Lourdes of the province of Asia."[5]

All these things created a difficult situation for the Christians in Pergamum. They were surrounded by paganism and its splendid temples. They lived in a climate hostile to their faith. They constantly witnessed the smoke arising from the altar of Zeus, located above the city and dominating the whole area. They could hear stories of the miraculous healings at the asclepeion (the healing center named after Asclepius) circulating at the time when miracles were fading in their midst. These things made the city the place "where Satan dwells" and where his throne was located (Rev. 2:13).

Jesus's Message to the Church

Jesus identifies Himself to the Christians in Pergamum as "the One who has the sharp two-edged sword" (Rev. 2:12). The Roman governor in Pergamum had *ius gladii* (the right of the sword)—that is, the power to put a person to death.[6] No doubt he used that power against Christians. However, Jesus assures the church that the power over life and death belongs only to Him (cf. Rev. 1:17–18). Humans might claim that power, but the last word belongs to Jesus: "In the world you have tribulation, but take courage; I have overcome the world" (John 16:33).

Jesus said to the Christians in Pergamum that He knew they lived in a place that was antagonistic toward them. They lived in the city where Satan dwelt and where his throne was situated, namely, at the very headquarters of Satan's activities. Yet, most of them remained unwavering in their faithfulness to Christ. They were ostracized in society for not condoning emperor worship and for not respecting pagan gods and practices. Some of them paid for their faithfulness to Christ. Antipas, a prominent Christian, was put to death by the Roman governor because of his loyalty to Christ.

Not all Christians in Pergamum remained faithful, though. There were some who compromised their Christianity with pagan practices. They belonged to two camps: the Nicolaitans and the ones "who hold the teaching of Balaam" (Rev. 2:14–15). The fact that Jesus mentions the two groups together suggests that they were related. Actually, *Balaam* and *Nicolaos* are the names in Hebrew and Greek respectively, both meaning "the one who conquers nations." Just as Balaam seduced the Israelites on the way to the Promised Land to engage in illicit relationships with Moabite women and practice idolatry (Num. 31:16), these people encouraged their fellow Christians to avoid persecution by compromising with regard to emperor worship and participation in pagan socio-religious activities (Rev. 2:14). While the church in Ephesus strongly resisted the teaching of these false teachers (cf. Rev. 2:6), these teachers clearly won some adherents among the members in Pergamum.

Jesus encourages the church not to compromise with pagan religious practices. He exhorts them to repent. If they do not repent and turn from the course of their action, judgment is imminent. Christ is coming to wage war against them with the sword of His mouth (Rev. 2:16). Just as Balaam, along with those whom he had seduced into sin, was killed by the sword (Num. 31:8; cf. 25:1–9), a similar judgment will visit the Balaamites and Nicolaitans. The only way to avoid the impending judgment is to repent and make a decisive turnaround in their relationship with Christ.

The overcomers in Pergamum, who refused to participate in pagan practices, were promised the privilege of eating the hidden manna— "the bread of angels" (Ps. 78:25). Because of their refusal to participate in emperor worship, they were deprived of the certificate with their names on it, issued by the Roman governor. However, Jesus promises them a white stone with a new name engraved, entitling them to special privileges that surpass any pleasure of the pagan life.

The situation in the church of Pergamum represents the situation of the Christian church at large during the period following the conversion of Constantine the Great to Christianity in AD 313. As the church finally won its struggle with paganism, the Christians no longer had to fear persecution or pressure from outside. However, many in the church chose to compromise Christianity with paganism. Pagan philosophical ideas and customs made their way into the church, gradually replacing the Bible as the source of teaching and belief. Although many Christians remained unwavering and faithful to the gospel during this period, the fourth and fifth centuries witnessed spiritual decline and apostasy, during which the church wrestled with the temptation of compromise.

Messages to the Churches (Part 2)

 Revelation 2:18–3:22

The messages to the seven churches reveal Jesus's keen interest and care for the spiritual well-being of His people. In these messages, He also urges them to faithfulness, no matter what the consequences.

The Message to Thyatira (2:18–29)

The fourth message was sent to the church in Thyatira (modern Akhisar, Turkey) located some forty miles southeast of Pergamum. The message to this church is the longest of the seven:

> *18To the angel of the church in Thyatira write: "Thus says the Son of God, the One whose eyes are as a flame of fire, and His feet like burnished bronze: 19I know your works, namely, your love and faith, that is, your service and perseverance, and that your last works are greater than the former. 20But I have against you that you tolerate the woman Jezebel who calls herself a prophetess and teaches and leads astray My servants to commit fornication and eat things sacrificed to idols. 21And I gave her time that she might repent, and she does not want to repent of her fornication. 22Behold, I am casting her into a bed and those who commit adultery with her into great affliction, unless they repent of her works, and 23I will kill her children, and all the churches will know that I am the One who searches kidneys and hearts, and I will give to each of you according to your works.*
> *24"Now, I say to you, those the remaining ones in Thyatira, all those who do not have this teaching, who*

have not known the deep things of Satan, as they say: I do not lay on you another burden, ²⁵except, hold what you have until I come.

²⁶*"To the one who overcomes and who keeps My works until the end, I shall give to him authority over the nations, ²⁷and he will shepherd them with a rod of iron, as the vessels of a potter are smashed together, as I also have received it from My Father, ²⁸and I will give him the morning star. ²⁹The one who has an ear, let him hear what the Spirit says to the churches."*

The City of Thyatira

Thyatira was the smallest and least important of the seven cities addressed in Revelation. It had no political importance or cultural significance. The city was known for many trades, such as garment making, bronze smithing, tanning, leather working, pottery, baking, dyeing, and the manufacture of royal purple and woolen goods.[1] Lydia, the purple dealer in Philippi—the first Christian convert in Europe—was from Thyatira (Acts 16:14). The citizens of Thyatira were mainly poor laborers and tradesmen, in contrast to the well-situated residents of the previous three cities.

The city had many trade guilds. In order to run a business or have a job, a person had to belong to a trade guild. Each guild had a patron god. Guild members were expected to attend the guild festivals in honor of the patron god and to share a common meal in the temple that included drunkenness and eating meat sacrificed to the patron god. The festivals usually ended with immoral activities with temple prostitutes. Those who refused to participate in the festivals could suffer serious consequences: expulsion from the trade guilds, ridicule, as well as the hardships of social isolation and economic sanctions.

This created serious problems for the Christians in Thyatira, because they could not join the trade guilds without participating in the guild festivals.

Jesus's Message to the Church

Christ introduces Himself to this church as "the Son of God, the One whose eyes are as a flame of fire, and His feet like burnished bronze" (cf. Rev. 2:18). While to John, Jesus appeared as a son of man (1:13), to the church in Thyatira He comes as the Son of God. His flaming eyes denote His penetrating ability to see what is in the innermost parts of humans (2:23). He is the One who searches kidneys (the seat of emotions) and hearts (the seat of intelligence). The ability to search kidneys and hearts belongs only to God (Jer. 17:10). Christ's feet, which look like burnished bronze, symbolize His uncompromising stance against the seductive influences in the church.

Thyatira is described by Jesus as a loving, faithful, service-oriented, and persevering church. Unlike the church in Ephesus, whose love was fading, this church is noted for an increase in faith and love: their last works are greater than the first. In the New Testament, love and faith go together (Gal. 5:6; Eph. 1:15; 1 Thess. 3:6); furthermore, service is an outcome of love (1:3), and perseverance is a product of faith (Col. 1:23; 2 Thess. 1:3–4).

The big problem for this church was that they tolerated the teaching of an influential woman in their midst. Jesus names her Jezebel after the notorious wife of King Ahab in the time of Elijah, who led all Israel into apostasy (1 Kings 16:31–33). This woman claimed to be a prophetess with a direct message from God, stating that it was all right for Christians to go along with the requirements set by the guild (Rev. 2:20). Her teaching was similar to the teaching of the Nicolaitans and the teaching of Balaam, because she seduced the members "to eat the things sacrificed to idols and to commit fornication" (cf. 2:14–15). Her seductive influences made a great impact on the church, leading many astray into compromise with paganism and apostasy.

Jezebel is referred to as a spiritual harlot and her seductive activities as immorality (Rev. 2:21)—a symbolic reference to her activities of advocating compromise with paganism. She functions as a forerunner to the great harlot Babylon, who will at the time of the end seduce the leaders of the world into the service of Satan (17:1–7). All those who condone her teaching are committing spiritual adultery with her (2:22). Since harlots' activities take place in bed, the bed is the place where Jezebel and those who are in adulterous relationships with her will be judged. If they do not repent, Jesus will throw them together into great affliction. A similar fate will come upon Jezebel's offspring, who will follow in her footsteps. By using this severe language, Jesus wants to impress upon their minds the seriousness of their action. Everyone will be judged according to their works (2:23).

Not all members of the church have sided with Jezebel. There is a remnant who has not "known the deep things of Satan" (Rev. 2:24). Jezebel offers the members arcane teachings; however, her teachings are diabolically deep. In the Old Testament, the word "to know" denotes an experiential knowledge, and as such, it is used for sexual relations (Gen. 4:1; 19:5). This remnant is not involved in spiritual adultery with Jezebel to experience the depth of Satan's deceptive teachings. Jesus promises not to place upon them additional burdens and instead tells them to hold fast to what they have received thus far.

To the ones who remain faithful in Thyatira, Jesus promises a share in His victory. He will give them authority over the nations, just as He has received authority from the Father (Rev. 2:27). He will also give them the morning star, which is a symbol of Jesus Christ (22:16). To those who remain faithful, Jesus promises the greatest gift, the gift *of* Himself.

The situation in the church in Thyatira aptly applies to the condition of the church at large during the Middle Ages. The danger to the church did not come from outside but from those who claimed authority from God. During that period, tradition completely replaced the Bible as the basis for teaching and belief. A human priesthood and sacred relics replaced Christ's priesthood, and works were regarded as the means of salvation. Those who did not condone the corrupting influences of the institutional church experienced severe persecution and even death.

The Message to Sardis (3:1–6)

The fifth message was sent to the church in Sardis (modern Izmir in Smyrna), a city located about thirty miles south of Thyatira:

> *¹To the angel of the church in Sardis write: "Thus says the One who has the seven Spirits of God and seven stars: I know your works, that you have a name that you live, and you are dead. ²Keep watching and strengthen the remaining ones who are about to die, for I have not found your works fulfilled before My God. ³Keep remembering, therefore, how you have received and heard, and keep it and repent. If therefore you do not watch, I will come as a thief; you will in no way know at what hour I will come upon you. ⁴But you have a few names in Sardis who have not defiled their garments, and they will walk with me in white, because they are worthy.*
>
> *⁵"The one who overcomes thus will be clothed in white garments, and I will not erase his name from the*

book of life, and I will confess his name before My Father and before His angels. ⁶The one who has an ear, let him hear what the Spirit says to the churches."

The City of Sardis

Sardis was built on top of a steep hill overlooking the fertile Hermus Valley. Because the platform of the hill upon which the city stood eventually became too small for the growing city, the city gradually spread down into the valley.

The city had a splendid history. Some six centuries prior to the writing of the book of Revelation, Sardis had been one of the greatest cities in the ancient world. It was the capital of the kingdom of Lydia, ruled by the wealthy King Croesus until he was defeated by Cyrus the Great of Persia in the sixth century BC. By the Roman period, the city had lost its prestige. While continuing to enjoy prosperity and wealth, the city's glory and pride was rooted in its past rather than its present reality.[2]

The city was known as a trading center for the wool, dyeing, and garment-making industries, providing its citizens with a luxurious lifestyle. The largest building in the city was the temple of Artemis. The city's patron deity was Cybele, the Great Mother of the gods, whose temple hosted eunuch priests. The goddess was believed to possess the special power of restoring the dead to life.[3]

Due to its location on a particularly steep hill, the city was a natural citadel, inaccessible except by one route, and, as such, was easy to defend. Because of this, the citizens were so arrogant and overconfident that the city walls were carelessly guarded or not guarded at all. The city was captured by surprise on two occasions, first by Cyrus the Great of Persia (549 BC) and later by Antiochus III (218 BC). On both occasions, enemy soldiers climbed the precipice by night and found that the Sardians had not posted a guard on the walls. The city was taken and destroyed because of the overconfidence of its citizens and the failure of the guards to keep watch.

Jesus's Message to the Church

Jesus introduces himself to the church in Sardis as "the One who has the seven Spirits of God and seven stars" (Rev. 3:1). The church is about to receive a strong rebuke from Christ; however, Jesus comes to it with the fullness of the Holy Spirit to awake this lifeless church and bring it back to life (cf. Rom. 8:11).

The tone Jesus uses to address the church is alarming from the start. The church is not commended for any qualities; it receives only a rebuke. Jesus knows their works and their real spiritual condition. The church has a name to be alive, but in reality, it has reached the point of spiritual death. This situation in the church reflects the characteristics of the city itself: based on their history, they had a great reputation to be alive, but in the present, they are lifeless. Their works do not measure up to God's standard: "I have not found your works fulfilled before My God" (Rev. 3:2). Their deeds lack the transforming power of the gospel.

The Sardians were not blamed for specific sins or heresy but for being lifeless. Their real problem was spiritual complacency and lethargy. Their compromise with the pagan environment had killed their spiritual life and their witness for the gospel. Jesus exhorts them to keep watch and strengthen those who still have some life in themselves but are ready to die (Rev. 3:2a).

As with the church in Ephesus, Jesus exhorts the Sardians to remember how they heard and received the gospel in the beginning of their Christian experience (Rev. 3:3a). The only way to reclaim a whole-hearted devotion to Christ is to recall and keep past experience fresh in mind and apply it to the present. This will result in repentance and turning away from their present lethargic condition to a new beginning in their relationship with Christ. In such a way, their love and devotion to Christ will be rekindled by the life-giving Spirit of God.

However, if they do not wake up and repent, Jesus will come to them in judgment unexpectedly, like a thief in the night. Watchfulness is a characteristic of faithful Christians (Rev. 16:15). If the church fails to watch, its destiny will mirror the history of the city. Just as Sardis was unexpectedly conquered two times due to its citizens' lack of vigilance, so Christ will visit them in judgment unexpectedly, like a thief, in their spiritual lethargy (3:3b). It will be too late to repent.

However, there are still some Christians in Sardis who are unwavering in their faithfulness to Christ. These members have not defiled their clothes by compromise with paganism (Rev. 3:4). They are a minority in the church, though, and even they are in danger of dying (3:2). Jesus promises that they will walk with Him in white robes, for they are worthy. The white robes that they will receive correspond to their faithfulness to Christ.

Jesus promises the overcomers in the church that they will be clothed in white garments (Rev. 3:5). This reaffirms the promise made in the previous verse. (Those who keep their garments undefiled—either from the pagan environment or the lethargic situation in the church—will walk with Jesus in white robes.) The fulfillment of this promise is described in Revelation 7:9–17. Jesus also promises not to erase their names from the book of life but to confess their names before the Father and His angels. This echoes the words Jesus spoke to His disciples: "Everyone who confesses Me before men, I will also confess him before My Father who is in heaven" (Matt. 10:32).

The message to the church in Sardis fits appropriately with the condition of the church in the post-Reformation period, known as the period of Protestant Scholasticism. The vibrant generation of Reformers rediscovered the gospel, forgotten during the medieval period, and put the Bible into the hands of the people. New churches were established and Christianity became rejuvenated. Sadly, once the Reformers passed away, lifeless formalism began invading the church. Their successors became more and more involved in doctrinal polemics and controversies, gradually degenerating into a state of spiritual lethargy. Toward the end of this period, under the impact of the rising tide of philosophical rationalism and secularism, the saving grace of the gospel and commitment to Christ waned, giving place to rationalism and theological arguments. The church during this period, although appearing to be alive, was in reality spiritually dead.

The Message to Philadelphia (3:7–13)

The sixth message was addressed to the church in Philadelphia (modern Alaşehir, Turkey), located some twenty-five miles southeast of Sardis:

750-1844

> [7]To the angel of the church in Philadelphia write: "Thus says the holy One, the true One, the One who has the key of David, who opens and no one shuts, and shuts and no one opens: [8]I know your works; behold, I have given before you an open door, which no one is able to shut, because you have little strength, and you kept My word and did not deny My name. [9]Behold, I am giving some of the synagogue of Satan who say that they are Jews, and they are not, but they lie—behold, I will make them come and bow before your feet and to know that I have loved you. [10]Because you have kept the word of My endurance, I will also keep you from the hour of trial that is about to

48

come on those who dwell on the earth. ¹¹I am coming
soon; hold what you have, that no one takes your crown.
¹²"The one who overcomes I will make a pillar in the
temple of My God, and he will never go out of it, and I will
write upon him the name of My God and the name of the
city of My God, the new Jerusalem, which descends out of
heaven from My God, and My new name. ¹³The one who has
an ear, let him hear what the Spirit says to the churches."

The City of Philadelphia

Philadelphia was the youngest of the seven cities in Revelation 2–3.
It was situated on a high volcanic plateau in a mountainous region,
making it a strong fortress city. The city was founded by Attalus II
Philadelphus (159–138 BC), the king of Pergamum, who named the
city Philadelphia (brotherly love) for the love he had for his brother
Eumenes II. When Eumenes ascended to the throne, Attalus served
him faithfully as an army general, in spite of his power and many
opportunities to overthrow him. Only after the death of his brother
did Attalus occupy the throne.

Philadelphia was a prosperous city that stood on the imperial trade
road, connecting all parts east with all parts west of the province. It
also stood on the major postal road running from Pergamum to
Laodicea. From its inception, Philadelphia was intended to serve as a
missionary city for promoting the Greek language and culture in the
areas of Lydia and Phrygia. Its geographical location, however, made
it subject to occasional earthquakes. The most severe one took place
in AD 17 and devastated Philadelphia, Sardis, and other surrounding
cities. It was rebuilt by Romans under the emperor Tiberius.

Jesus's Message to the Church

To the church in Philadelphia, Jesus presents himself as the holy and
true One who holds the key of David. "The Holy One" is a reference to
God in the Old Testament (Isa. 43:15; 57:15; Hab. 3:3). In the New
Testament, it also designates Jesus (Mark 1:24; John 6:69). Jesus is also
the true One (Rev. 3:14; 19:11); the church, thus, may fully rely on Him.
He has the key of David: when He opens, no one can shut, and when
He shuts, no one is able to open. This picture of Jesus alludes to Isaiah
22:22, which concerns Eliakim, King Hezekiah's chief steward, who
was given the key to the royal palace, therefore exercising the full
authority of the king. Jesus, thus, presents Himself to the church as the

One with full authority and access to the heavenly storehouse. This is why He is able to make those great promises to His church.

In contrast to Sardis, which does not receive any praise from Jesus, the church in Philadelphia does not receive any rebuke. Jesus knows their works: they have kept His word and did not deny His name (Rev. 3:8b). Like the Smyrnians, they also suffer from Jewish opposition. Even though these Jews say that they serve God, they do not; they are actually "the synagogue of Satan" (2:9). They have put themselves in the service of Satan to menace God's people (3:9). However, Jesus assures the church that He is already dealing with their opponents. The day is coming when those who harm them will be forced to admit that God is with them.

Although faithful, the church in Philadelphia has little strength. This church is not spiritually strong. Jesus does not point to any specific sin or heresy. Their situation seems to be like that in Sardis: the appealing influence of the pagan environment has greatly impacted their spiritual life and their witness for the gospel. Yet, as weak as the church may be, Christ promises to set before them an open door of opportunities. He assures them that when He opens the door for this weak church, all the power of the enemy will not be able to shut that door.

Because they have kept the word of Jesus's endurance constantly before their eyes, Jesus promises to preserve them during the time of severe trial that is to "come on those who dwell on the earth" (Rev. 3:10). "Those who dwell on the earth" in Revelation is a regular reference to the wicked. This time of trial to come upon the wicked involves the seven last plagues, which God will pour upon those who receive the mark of the beast (15–16). Jesus promises to be with His faithful people and to protect them during this time of trial.

Jesus is coming soon, and He exhorts the Philadelphians to hold fast to what they have, so no one can take their crown of victory (Rev. 3:11). Although weak, they must hold fast to what they have—the spark of their faithfulness that is still burning. If they do, neither Satan nor humans will be able to take the crown that is reserved for them.

Those who overcome are promised to be permanent pillars in the temple in the New Jerusalem, with the names of God, the New Jerusalem, and Christ written on them. Pillars in the earthly temple provided stability and permanence. They are a symbol of the church in the New Testament (1 Tim. 3:15). The faithful are promised that they will always be in God's presence. They will serve God in His temple (Rev. 7:15).

The situation of the church in Philadelphia coincided with the situation in Christianity during the eighteenth and nineteenth centuries. This period was characterized by a great revival of Protestantism. Various movements revitalized genuine faith in the saving grace of Christ, and that resulted in a restoration of the spirit of Christian fellowship and self-sacrifice. The church during this period was driven by a genuine desire to carry the gospel to the whole world. As a result, there was a great propagation of the gospel that had never before been experienced.

The Message to Laodicea (3:14–22)

The last of the seven messages was addressed to the church in Laodicea (modern Eskihisar, Turkey), located some forty-five miles southeast of Philadelphia and one hundred miles east of Smyrna.

14To the angel of the church in Laodicea write: "Thus says the Amen, the faithful and true Witness, the beginning of God's creation: 15I know your works, that you are neither cold nor hot. I would that you were cold or hot. 16Thus, because you are lukewarm and neither cold nor hot, I am about to vomit you out of My mouth. 17Because you say, "I am rich and have become wealthy and have need of nothing," and you do not know that you are wretched and miserable and poor and blind and naked, 18I counsel you to buy from Me gold refined in fire that you may be rich and white garments that you may clothe yourself, so that the shame of your nakedness may not be exposed, and eye salve to anoint your eyes, so that you may see. 19As many as I love, I discipline and reprove; therefore, be zealous and repent.

20"Behold, I am standing at the door and knocking; if anyone hears My voice and opens the door, I will come in to him and eat supper with him and he with Me.

21"To the one who overcomes, I will grant him to sit with Me on My throne, as I also overcame and sat with My Father on His throne. 22The one who has an ear, let him hear what the Spirit says to the churches."

The City of Laodicea

Laodicea was situated in the Lycus Valley on the major trade road between Ephesus and Syria and near the cities of Hierapolis and Colossae. Because of its favorable location, the city became one of the greatest commercial and financial centers of the ancient world. Laodicea was enormously wealthy. Most of the wealth came from the clothing manufacturing industry and banking transactions. Laodicea was widely known for the fine quality of a soft and glossy black wool used for making different kinds of garments and carpets that were exported all over the world. This commercial prosperity made the city a great banking center, where a large quantity of gold was stored. In addition, Laodicea was famous for its medical school, which had a reputation throughout the ancient world for its treatment of eye diseases by means of an ointment made from Phrygian powder mixed with oil.

The commercial, financial, and industrial prosperity and success filled the wealthy citizens of Laodicea with a spirit of pride. When it was devastated by an earthquake around AD 60, its citizens were so rich and filled with pride that, according to the Roman historian Tacitus, they proudly refused imperial help and rebuilt the city using their own resources.[4] The proud spirit of the city evidently pervaded the church: "I am rich and have become wealthy and have need of nothing" (Rev. 3:17a).

For all its prosperity, the city had a great problem with water. A six-mile-long aqueduct supplied the city with water from the vicinity of Hierapolis, and they also received water from Colossae, known for its cold mountain water. Whether water came from the hot springs of Hierapolis or the cool water of Colossae, it became lukewarm in the aqueduct by the time it reached the city. This situation could have provided a background for the metaphoric lukewarmness of the Laodicean church.

Jesus's Message to the Church

To the church in Laodicea, Jesus presents Himself with the threefold designation: "The Amen, the faithful and true Witness, the beginning of God's creation" (Rev. 3:14). The word *amen* comes from Hebrew and basically means "in truth." In the Old Testament, God is called "the God of truth [*amen*]" (Isa. 65:16). Christ's discerning testimony exposes the true condition of this church. His creative power to bring something out of nothing is the only hope for this halfhearted and lukewarm yet loved-by-Christ church.

This church is in such a bad condition that Jesus has nothing positive to say to it. Surprisingly, the members are not charged with sin, apostasy, or heresy. Yet, no other church receives such a stern rebuke. Jesus likens it to the city's water supply. The members are neither refreshingly cold nor hot but lukewarm, and as such, Jesus is about to vomit them out of His mouth (Rev. 3:16).

The church reflects the complacency of the very city that prided itself on its accomplishments and wealth. The members claim to be rich and have need of nothing. They regard their wealth as divine favor, just as Ephraim did in the Old Testament: "Surely I have become rich, I have found wealth for myself; in all my labors they will find in me no iniquity, which would be sin" (Hos. 12:8). In contrast to the Christians in Smyrna, who are poor but are spiritually rich, the Laodiceans are rich and wealthy, yet in reality, they are miserable and spiritually poor, blind, and naked (Rev. 3:17). The Greek word *ptōchos* denotes their extreme poverty. They are blind to their condition. The irony is that they live in a city famous for eye treatment, yet they are spiritually blind. Their self-deluded pride prevents them from seeing themselves as they truly are.

Jesus counsels the church to buy from Him three things. The first is gold refined in fire. According to Peter, gold refined in fire symbolizes a tested, proven faith that can last until the end (1 Pet. 1:7). This will make the Laodiceans truly rich. Jesus also offers them white garments to cover their wretched condition. The garments are a symbol of salvation (Rev. 3:4–5; 7:9, 13–14). Isaiah exclaimed: "He has clothed me with garments of salvation, He has wrapped me with a robe of righteousness" (Isa. 61:10). To be dressed in white and clean garments means to be in a right relationship with God (Rev. 3:4). When the prodigal son returned to his father, the father covered his nakedness with a special robe (Luke 15:22). These garments are also offered to the last-day Christians living during the intensive preparation for the battle of Armageddon (Rev. 16:15).

Lastly, Jesus offers to the Laodiceans eye salve to anoint their eyes, so they may see their true spiritual condition. The psalmist prayed: "Open my eyes that I may behold" (Ps. 119:18). Paul prayed to God on behalf of the Ephesians to give them "a spirit of wisdom and of revelation in the knowledge of Him," so "the eyes of your heart may be enlightened" that they may know "what are the riches of the glory of His inheritance in the saints" (Eph. 1:17–18). The Christians in Laodicea need the discerning influence of the Holy Spirit to open their spiritual eyes, so they may see their true condition on one hand

and the true riches of the inheritance Christ makes available to them on the other hand.

Jesus counsels them to buy gold, garments, and eye salve from Him. The fact that items are not offered for free indicates that the Laodiceans must give something in exchange for what they need. They must give up their pride, complacency, and self-sufficiency to receive riches from Christ.

Of the seven churches, only the Laodiceans and Philadelphians are explicitly told that they are loved by Jesus (Rev. 3:19). But, to Laodicea, this love is expressed through rebuke and discipline: "As many as I love, I discipline and reprove" (3:19). These words echo Proverbs 3:12: "For whom the LORD loves He reproves." God disciplines us "so that we may not be condemned along with the world" (1 Cor. 11:32; cf. Heb. 12:5–11). Christ has not given up on the church. He makes every effort to make His church realize its own condition and to break the chains of self-sufficiency, which hold it down.

The only remedy for the church is genuine repentance. Jesus urges its members to turn away from their complacency and make a fresh start. Jesus concludes His appeal to them with one of the most impressive pictures: He portrays Himself as standing at the door and knocking (Rev. 3:20). This picture evokes that of the lover in the Song of Songs who is knocking at the door of his beloved and pleading with her to let him in (Song of Sol. 5:2–6). Up to this point, the whole church is admonished, but now, Jesus addresses individuals in the church. All those who open the door and welcome Him in will have an intimate, loving dinner with Him. Eating a meal together refers to an intimate relationship with a person—in this case with Christ.

Jesus promises to share His throne with the overcomers in the church, just as He overcame and sat with His Father on His Father's throne. The fulfillment of this promise will be realized after His return to earth (Rev. 20:4–6). It is significant that while the number of promises to other churches increases in proportion with the decline of their spiritual condition, Laodicea, as bad as it is, is given only one promise. However, this promise incorporates all other promises given to the churches. To sit with Jesus on His throne means to have everything.

The spiritual condition of the church in Laodicea represents the spiritual condition of the church today. The strong verbal links with the warning given in the context of preparing for the battle of Armageddon (Rev. 16:15) show that the message to the church in

Laodicea was to be the model for the church at the time of the end. This last church exists in peculiar times: it goes through the motions of great political, religious, and secular upheavals, and it faces challenges that were not faced by any previous generation. Yet, this church is self-sufficient and lukewarm, struggling with its authenticity. Christ's warning to this church has a far-reaching implication for all who are part of that church at the closing period of this earth's history.

The Throne-Room Scene

 Revelation 4:1–11

Chapter 4 begins a new section of Revelation. At this point, the scene shifts from earth to heaven and from John's time to the future (Rev. 4:1). There is also a shift in language. While the seven messages are written in straightforward language—the meaning of the infrequent symbols used may generally be easily understood—from this point on, the book employs complex symbolic language that is not easy to interpret. John's description of the future is reminiscent of Jewish apocalyptic literature, which is known for its use of peculiar symbolic language:

>¹After these things I looked, and behold, a door opened in heaven, and the first voice which I heard was as a trumpet speaking to me, saying: "Come up here, and I will show you the things that must take place after these things." ²Immediately, I was in the Spirit; and behold, a throne stood in heaven, and upon the throne was One sitting; ³and the One sitting was in appearance like a jasper and a sardius stone, and a rainbow around the throne was in appearance like an emerald. ⁴And around the throne were twenty-four thrones, and upon the thrones were sitting twenty-four elders clothed in white garments, and upon their heads were golden crowns. ⁵And from the throne were proceeding flashes of lightning and sounds and peals of thunder; and seven torches of fire were burning before the throne, which are the seven Spirits of God, ⁶and before the throne was something like a sea of glass, like crystal.
>   And in the midst of the throne and around the throne were four living beings full of eyes in front and back; ⁷the

first living being was like a lion, the second living being like a calf, the third living being having a face like that of a man, and the fourth living being like a flying eagle. ⁸And the four living beings, each one of them having six wings, are full of eyes around and inside; and they do not have rest day and night, saying: "Holy, holy, holy Lord God, the Almighty, who was and who is and who is coming!" ⁹And whenever the living beings give glory and honor and thanks to the One sitting on the throne, the One who lives forever and ever, ¹⁰the twenty-four elders fall before the One sitting on the throne and worship the One who lives forever and ever, and they cast their crowns before the throne and say: ¹¹"You are worthy, our Lord and God, to receive glory and honor and power, because You created all things, and because of Your will, they existed and were created."

In Revelation 4, John is transported in vision from earth to heaven, and there he sees an open door. The trumpet-like voice of Jesus, which spoke to him earlier in chapter 1, now invites him to come to heaven, where he will be shown "the things that must take place after these things" (Rev. 4:1). The expression "after these things" points to Revelation 1:19, where Jesus instructed John to write down what was to be revealed to him, which consisted of "the things which are"—the messages to the seven churches—and "the things which are about to take place after these things." Having heard the messages to the churches (2–3), the Revelator will now be shown the things that must take place in the future, after his time through to the time of the end.

It is important to realize that "the things that must take place after" the seven churches in Revelation 4:1 does not refer to the content of chapters 4–5 but to chapters 6–22, which provide a panoramic survey of history from John's time until Christ's return. The scene in chapters 4–5 is introductory to the rest of the book and, as such, does not fit chronologically into the sequence of the vision. Before the future is revealed to John, he is taken into the heavenly throne room, where he is given a glimpse of Christ's exaltation on the throne at the right hand of the Father. In this manner, the Revelator is given heaven's perspective on what the future events about to be revealed to him mean. As history unfolds, Jesus Christ, who rules as sovereign over the universe, will bring the history of this world to its conclusion and decisively deal with the problem of sin.

The Throne Room (4:2–3, 5–6)

Through the open door in heaven, John is able to look into the heavenly temple. What first catches his attention is the majestic throne with God the Father sitting upon it. The throne is central to everything that takes place in the scene—it is featured seventeen times in chapters 4–5. Everything in the throne room is portrayed in relation to the throne: "Around the throne" (Rev. 4:3–4, 6; 5:11), "from the throne" (4:5), "before the throne" (4:5–6, 10), or "in the midst of the throne" (4:6; 5:6). The centrality of the throne in the vision is fundamental to the theology of the scene.

John was not the first to observe the splendor of the heavenly throne room. Micaiah in 1 Kings (22:19), Isaiah (6:1–3), and Daniel (7:9–10) each provide a unique description of the grandeur of God's throne and the heavenly hosts in service to God. However, Ezekiel 1 most closely resembles Revelation 4. About one-third of the words in Revelation 4 also occur in the throne vision of Ezekiel 1.

In all the Old Testament throne visions, God was regularly seen as sitting upon a throne. In the ancient world, a throne denoted power and authority. The person who sat on the throne ruled over a territory. The throne of God, thus, stands for His ruling authority over the universe. His ruling authority is, however, challenged by a usurping enemy power. The book of Revelation refers to the throne of Satan and his earthly cohorts, who are set in opposition to God's sovereignty and power (Rev. 2:13; 13:2; 16:10). The central issue in the ongoing great conflict between God and Satan is who has the right to rule. Revelation 4–5 portrays a decisive event in that conflict: the exaltation of Christ to the heavenly throne because of His sacrificial death on the cross of Calvary.

John does not attempt to describe God by using the anthropomorphic language used by the Old Testament prophets. He focuses instead on God's radiant glory, which takes a characteristic form. The Apostle Paul reminds us that God "dwells in unapproachable light, whom no man has seen or can see" (1 Tim. 6:16). The Old Testament often speaks of the splendid glory surrounding God (Ps. 104:2; Ezek. 1:26–28), which can hardly be expressed in human language. John describes it in terms of the dazzling glow of precious stones: jasper, sardius (carnelian), and emerald (Rev. 4:3). These three stones were regarded in the ancient world as representatives of precious stones.[1] Ezekiel mentions them, along with other precious stones that adorned Lucifer, portraying him as a paradigm for the king of Tyre (Ezek. 28:13).

The selection of these three precious stones accents their theological significance in the scene. Sardius and jasper were the first and last stones on the breastplate of the high priest in the Old Testament, representing Reuben as the eldest and Benjamin as the youngest of Jacob's sons. The emerald, as the fourth stone on the breastplate, represented Judah (Exod. 28:17–21).[2] These three stones are also found among the foundation stones in the New Jerusalem, which are inscribed with the names of the twelve apostles (Rev. 21:14, 19–20).

The flashing brilliance of the precious stones produces a rainbow that surrounds the throne (Rev. 4:3b). Centuries earlier, Ezekiel witnessed in a vision a rainbow around God's throne, signifying "the likeness of the glory of the LORD" (Ezek. 1:28). The rainbow functions as the sign of God's covenant. The precious stones and the rainbow, thus, are intended to provide confidence in God's covenant promise to His people and in His faithfulness to that promise (Gen. 9:12–17).

Before the throne, there is a flat expanse that appeared to John like "a sea of glass, like crystal" (Rev. 4:6)—resembling the sea at Patmos. The crystal-like expanse again echoes Ezekiel's vision (Ezek. 1:22). Also, centuries earlier, God was seen by Moses and the elders as standing on something that "appeared to be a pavement of sapphire, as clear as the sky itself" (Exod. 24:10).

Finally, John observes flashes of lightning, sounds, and peals of thunder issuing from the throne (Rev. 4:5) that accentuate the splendor of the occasion. The scene evokes the giving of the law to Moses at Mount Sinai (Exod. 19:16; 20:18) when Israel, having been redeemed from Egypt, was inaugurated as the people of God and "a kingdom of priests" (Exod. 19:4–6). In a similar fashion, John now observes as Christ, having redeemed humanity by His blood, receives the sealed scroll from God and inaugurates the redeemed as "a kingdom and priests" to God (Rev. 5:7–10).[3]

The Throne-Room Assembly (4:4–11)

The throne room of the heavenly temple is a grand, majestic place, accommodating countless heavenly beings. John specifies four distinct groups of participants in the scene.

The Members of the Godhead

The first person John observes in the throne room is God the Father sitting on the throne (Rev. 4:2). He is the object of worship for the entire heavenly assembly. The next one mentioned is the Holy Spirit, the second member of the Godhead (cf. 1:4). He is referred to as "the seven Spirits of God" and is symbolized by the seven torches of fire before the throne (4:5). The phrase "the seven Spirits of God" denotes the fullness and universality of the work of the Holy Spirit in the church. The one whose absence is felt is the third member of the Godhead. Jesus does not appear in the scene until chapter 5, when He is greeted and worshiped by the whole heavenly assembly.

The Twenty-Four Elders (4:4)

In a circle around the throne, there are twenty-four other thrones, with twenty-four elders sitting on them. They are dressed in white and wear gold crowns. The elders are mentioned throughout the book.[4] They are always seen as sitting upon thrones surrounding God's throne, worshiping God, and offering praises to Him.[5] Also, one of them twice helped John understand his visions (5:5; 7:13–14).

Some view these elders as a group of angels. However, nowhere in the Bible or Jewish tradition are angels ever called elders; this title is reserved for humans. In Revelation 7:11, they are clearly distinguished from the angels. Furthermore, the elders share God's throne, in contrast to angels, who always stand in God's presence. They represent the overcomers, who receive the promise to sit with Jesus Christ on His throne (Rev. 3:21). Also, the elders wear white robes, which, in Revelation, are the attire of God's faithful people (3:4–5, 18; 6:11; 7:9, 13–14). Finally, they have golden victory crowns (Gr. *stephanoi*) on their heads. The victory crowns are reserved exclusively for the victorious saints (2:10; 3:11; cf. 2 Tim. 4:8; James 1:12). The fact that they wear victory crowns, not royal crowns, shows that the twenty-four elders are not rulers from the other worlds in the universe but are humans.

All these things point to the twenty-four elders being a symbolic group, representative of redeemed humanity. Their number is symbolic, incorporating two sets of twelve—referring to the twelve tribes of Israel as the symbol of God's people in the Old Testament and the twelve apostles as the symbol of God's people in the New Testament. In the New Jerusalem, the twelve gates are named after the twelve tribes of Israel, and the twelve foundations are named after the twelve apostles (Rev. 21:12–14). The twenty-four elders, thus, represent the entire body of God's people from both the Old and New Testament—the church in its totality.

In the Old Testament temple, there were twenty-four divisions of priests, who took turns in the temple services (1 Chron. 24:4–19). Each division was led by a chief priest, with twenty-four chief priests in total (24:5). In Jewish tradition, these chief priests were called "elders."[6] Similarly, the singers in the temple were organized into twenty-four groups (25:1–3). Notice that the activities of the twenty-four elders in Revelation consist of continuous worship and adoration to God (Rev. 5:9–10; 19:4) and the presentation of the saints' prayers to God (5:8)—activities similar to the work of the priests and singers in the earthly temple. Therefore, seated on the thrones, the twenty-four elders function in their twofold role as priests and kings (cf. 5:8–10).

The twenty-four elders appear in Revelation 4 for the first time in the Bible. They are never mentioned in any record of the Old Testament visions of God's throne. While cherubim and seraphim are regularly mentioned, no elders are ever observed by the prophets. This indicates that the twenty-four elders, when John sees them, are a new group not previously present in the heavenly throne room. They must have appeared there shortly before the scene was set up, sometime after Jesus's resurrection. They could have been the ones who were raised from the dead when Jesus died (see Matt. 27:51–53). Paul tells us that, when Jesus ascended to heaven, He took "a host of captives" with Him (Eph. 4:8). These resurrected saints ascended with Jesus into heaven as the representatives of humanity, to witness God's fairness in His actions and to participate in the heavenly judgment.

These representatives of humanity were ushered into the heavenly throne room at some point while the ceremony was set up. They were brought there, with envoys from the whole universe, to welcome Jesus back to heaven after His victorious death on the cross and to witness His enthronement at the right hand of the Father.

The Four Living Beings (4:6b–8)

On each side of the throne there are four heavenly beings facing the four directions of the universe. According to John, they are unlike any heavenly being he had seen before. Their description, however, resembles the heavenly beings in Ezekiel's vision of God's throne (Ezek. 1:5–14; 10:12–15). The similarities are obvious. Both Ezekiel and John saw the same number of beings, and both refer to them as "the four living beings." Both compare their appearance to a lion, a calf or ox, a man, and a flying eagle, and in both cases, they are covered with eyes. Finally, in both visions, they are closely associated with the throne. Ezekiel further explains that these four living beings are cherubim, the exalted order of angels who stand in service to God (10:20–22).

However, while the living beings in Ezekiel's vision have four faces and four wings (Ezek. 1:6), the four living beings in Revelation have six wings like the seraphim in Isaiah's vision (Isa. 6:2). Also, like the seraphim in Isaiah's vision, the four living beings in Revelation 4 unceasingly praise God with these words of acclamation: "Holy, holy, holy Lord God, the Almighty" (Rev. 4:8; cf. Isa. 6:3).

All this indicates that the four living beings are the exalted angels close to God, who serve Him as His agents and as the guardians of His throne. They are always seen in proximity to the throne (Rev. 4:6; 5:6; 14:3). Their association with the throne is reminiscent of the cherubim on the Ark of the Covenant, which faced each other with their wings stretched over the mercy seat (Exod. 25:18–21; 1 Kings 6:23–28). God is often referred to in the Bible as the one sitting on the throne between the cherubim (2 Kings 19:15; Pss. 80:1; 99:1; Isa. 37:16).

The portrayal of the living beings is symbolic. The wings point to their swiftness in carrying out God's orders. The eyes represent their intelligence and discernment. Their appearances in terms of a lion, a calf or ox, a man, and a flying eagle represent the entire order of creation, as one scholar said: everything that is noblest, strongest, wisest, and swiftest in nature.[7] As the representatives of the entire creation, they are constantly engaged in leading the heavenly hosts in worship and praise to God (Rev. 4:8–9; 5:8–9, 14; 7:11–12; 19:4). On the negative side, they are the divine agents involved in the execution of God's wrath upon the earth (6:1, 3, 5, 7; 15:7).

The Heavenly Hosts

The largest group in the throne room assembly consists of the multitude of the angelic hosts, the number of which is "myriads of myriads and thousands of thousands" (Rev. 5:11). Ellen G. White suggests that, since this group is joined in their praises by "every creature," they are envoys from the rest of the universe, representing the unfallen worlds (Rev. 5:13).[8] These envoys, together with the twenty-four elders and the four living beings, are assembled in the heavenly throne room to celebrate Christ's triumph over Satan and to express their approval and endorsement of His enthronement.

The Throne-Room Scene (4:9-11)

After describing the heavenly throne room, John tells us about what he witnessed: the unceasing worship of the heavenly assembly. The worship starts with the acclamation of praise by the four exalted angels: "Holy, holy, holy Lord God, the Almighty, who was and who is and who is coming!" (Rev. 4:8). This echoes the praise of the seraphim in Isaiah's vision (Isa. 6:1–3). The threefold repetition of "holy" emphasizes God's holiness and omnipotence, which are manifested in the past, present, and future.

The praise of the exalted angels is, on every occasion, immediately followed by the response of the twenty-four elders, who, as the representatives of redeemed humanity, fall down and lay their crowns before the throne, acclaiming: "You are worthy, our Lord and God, to receive glory and honor and power, because You created all things, and because of Your will, they existed and were created" (Rev. 4:10–11). With their praise, the elders recognize God as the creator of everything—every created thing owes its life to Him. However, in chapter 5, their praise stresses Christ's act of redemption (5:8–10).

The worship scene in Revelation 4–5 emphatically points to two things: creation (chap. 4) and redemption (chap. 5). It shows that the essence of true worship is to recount and celebrate God's mighty acts of creation and redemption. The scene shows that the God who created the world also has the power and ability to restore it and, therefore, to provide eternal salvation for lost and suffering humanity.

The portrayal of the elders as falling down and presenting their crowns before God, who is seated on the throne, reflects the Roman court ceremony where kings presented their crowns before the emperor as tokens of subordination and obeisance. "You are worthy" was the acclamation the emperors were greeted with in triumphal entry. Also, "our Lord and God" was the title claimed by Domitian—the emperor at the time Revelation was written. Because they refused to acknowledge the emperor as lord and god, the Christians of John's day suffered persecution and the threat of death. This foreshadows the final crisis in this world's history. The scene of Revelation 4 is intended to assure God's faithful people that the God whom they serve is the only one worthy to be worshiped as the Lord and God of the universe.

It appears that the scene in chapter 4 does not refer to a specific event. Rather, it provides a general description of the heavenly throne room and what takes place in it.[9] The picture of God sitting on the throne in His glory, surrounded by countless heavenly beings, is not a new scene witnessed for the first time by John. Instead, this scene was commonly witnessed by the Old Testament prophets in their visions of God.[10] The text does not indicate that God's throne was set up in the throne room while John was watching, as in Daniel's vision (Dan. 7:9). This was because Daniel's vision involved a specific event. However, in John's vision, the worship in the throne room is not a one-time event; rather, it is an event that regularly takes place in heaven.[11] The text states that "whenever the living beings give glory and honor and thanks to the One sitting on the throne," the twenty-four elders fall before God and worship Him (Rev. 4:9). This clearly shows that the worship in chapter 4 is an ongoing activity that repeatedly occurs in the heavenly throne room.

Although it is not a specific event, the scene in chapter 4 is preparatory for what is about to occur in chapter 5. During the preparation for the inaugural ceremony, envoys from the whole universe—including the representatives of humanity (the twenty-four elders) and the unfallen worlds in the universe—were ushered into the throne room. They were brought there to welcome Jesus at His return to heaven and to witness and celebrate His installation on the heavenly throne at the right hand of the Father. This splendid occasion is the subject of chapter 5.

The Enthronement of Christ

 Revelation 5:1–14

In trying to understand the scene in chapter 5, we must keep in mind a significant literary feature in the book of Revelation. The concluding passage of a scene at times summarizes the preceding section and prefigures what occurs in the next scene (cf. Rev. 1:20; 6:17; 12:17; 11:19). Revelation 3:21 is such a passage: it promises the overcomers in Laodicea that they will eventually sit with Jesus on His throne, just as Jesus overcame and sat with His Father on His throne. While concluding the messages to the seven churches, this passage also specifies the content of chapters 4–7.

Before revealing how Jesus's promise to the overcomers to join Him on the throne will be realized, John shows how Jesus overcame and sat with His Father on His throne. Chapters 4–5 encompass the throne-room scene. While the focus of chapter 4 is the heavenly throne with God the Father upon it, chapter 5 focuses upon Jesus who overcame and joined the Father on the throne after His ascension to heaven (Rev. 5:5). It is not until chapter 7 that the redeemed are seen before the throne of God, participating in heavenly worship. Between these chapters is chapter 6, which describes the opening of the seven seals. The seals, thus, symbolically describe the overcomers' experience of overcoming, which demonstrates that they may share the throne of Jesus.

Revelation 4–5	Christ overcoming and joining the Father on His throne
Revelation 6	The seven seals describing God's people in the process of overcoming, so they may share the throne with Jesus
Revelation 7	God's people sharing the throne with Jesus

As we move through the scene in chapters 4–5, we must keep in mind Revelation 3:21, which provides the key for unlocking the meaning of the scene in Revelation 4–5:

¹And I saw at the right hand of the One sitting on the throne a scroll written inside and on the back, sealed with seven seals. ²And I saw a strong angel proclaiming with a loud voice: "Who is worthy to open the scroll and to break its seals?" ³And nobody in heaven or on the earth or under the earth was able to open the scroll or to look into it. ⁴And I began to weep much, because nobody was found worthy to open the scroll or to look at it. ⁵And one of the elders said to me: "Stop crying! Behold, the Lion from the tribe of Judah, who is the Sprout of David, has overcome, so that He is able to open the scroll and its seven seals."

⁶And I saw in the midst of the throne and the four living beings and in the midst of the twenty-four elders a Lamb, standing as having been slain, having seven horns and seven eyes, which are the seven Spirits of God sent into all the earth. ⁷And He came and took the scroll from the right hand of the One sitting on the throne. ⁸And when He had taken the scroll, the four living beings and the twenty-four elders fell down before the Lamb, each having a harp and golden bowls full of incense, which are the prayers of the saints. ⁹And they sang a new song and said: "You are worthy to take the scroll and open its seals, for You were slain and purchased for God with Your blood from every tribe and tongue and people and nation, ¹⁰and You have made them a kingdom and priests to our God, and they will reign on the earth."

¹¹And I looked, and I heard the voice of many angels around the throne and the living beings and the elders, the number of which was myriads of myriads and thousands of thousands, ¹²saying with a loud voice: "Worthy is the slain Lamb to receive power and riches and wisdom and strength and honor and glory and blessing!"

¹³And every creature which was in heaven and on the earth and under the earth and on the sea, and all things which are in them, I heard saying: "To the One sitting on

the throne and to the Lamb be blessing and honor and glory and might forever and ever!"
    ¹⁴And the four living beings kept saying: "Amen!" And the elders fell down and worshiped.

Revelation 5 continues the throne-room scene that started in the previous chapter. While chapter 4 provides a general view of the heavenly throne room and what occurs there on a regular basis, chapter 5 describes an event that took place at a specific point in time. While the glorious throne is at the very center of the vision in chapter 4, attention now focuses on a seven-sealed scroll lying on the throne at the right hand of God.

The Seven-Sealed Scroll (5:1)

The magnificent liturgy in the throne room is interrupted for a moment as everyone's eyes focus on the throne. As John watches, he sees a scroll on the throne at the right hand of God. Scrolls were a common medium of writing in John's day (Rev. 6:13).

The Greek text clearly shows that the scroll lay on the throne at the right side of God—not "in the right hand" of God as various Bible translations suggest (Rev. 5:1). In ancient Israel, thrones were large enough for more than one person to sit on. To sit at the right side of the king was the highest place of honor (cf. 1 Kings 2:19). The Israelites understood that the king in Israel sat at God's right side as co-ruler with God (Pss. 80:17; 110:1). The scroll lying on the throne implies that the person who takes the scroll is to take its place on the throne. Thus, when Jesus a few moments later picked up the scroll (Rev. 5:8), He took His seat on the throne at the right hand of the Father, thereby assuming His role as the new ruler of the Davidic royal line (5:5).

The scroll is described as an opisthograph, a document written on both sides, "inside and on the back" (Rev. 5:1). While this implies a great amount of written material, it also brings to mind the two tablets of the testimony that Moses brought down from Mount Sinai, "which were written on both sides; they were written on one side and the other" (Exod. 32:15). Likewise, Ezekiel saw in his vision a scroll spread before him that had writing "on the front and back," containing the impending judgments against Israel (Ezek. 2:9–10). This suggests that the scroll of Revelation 5 concerns God's covenant with His people and the prophetic revelation of the future.

The scroll is "sealed with seven seals" (Rev. 5:1). In ancient times, to ratify the contents of a legal document, an impression was made with a ring at the end of the content. However, to protect the document from tampering, it was rolled up and tied with threads, and the seal was impressed in blobs of clay or wax at the knots. Because of this, the document could not be opened nor its contents disclosed until the seal was broken. Only an authorized person could break the seals and open the document.

That the scroll was sealed with seven seals shows that it was totally and securely sealed, for nobody in the entire universe could open it and read its contents (Rev. 5:3). In John's day, the practice of sealing documents with more than one seal was not uncommon. Roman law dictated that to prove its contents were valid, a will or testament had to be sealed with a minimum of seven seals belonging to the document's witnesses. The symbolic scroll John saw in the vision was like a legal document rolled up, tied with a cord, and sealed along the outside edge with seals of wax affixed to the knots. As such, it could not be opened nor could its contents be disclosed until all seven seals were broken. Breaking the seven seals is preparatory to opening the scroll and disclosing its contents (Rev. 6).[1]

Daniel and Revelation show that the idea of sealing denotes a concealment of God's revelation until the appointed time because of people's inability to understand it (Dan. 12:4, 9; Rev. 10:4). The scroll in Revelation 5 is sealed for the obvious purpose of concealing its contents and keeping them hidden. Because it is sealed, nobody is "able to open the scroll or to look into it" (5:3). It is not possible to open it and disclose its contents, unless an authorized person breaks all the seals.

There are many views regarding what exactly the sealed scroll stands for. However, Revelation 10:7 shows that its contents are related to "the mystery of God" with regard to God's purpose to solve the problem of sin, to save fallen humanity, and to establish His eternal kingdom (Rev. 10:7). This mystery has been hidden for ages, but it has been revealed, in part, with the coming of Christ and the preaching of the gospel (Rom. 16:25–26; 1 Cor. 6:10; Eph. 3:1–12). However, it is at the sound of the seventh trumpet that this mystery will ultimately be realized (Rev. 10:7).

Ellen G. White comments that the sealed scroll contains the record of the Great Controversy, which includes

> the history of God's providences, the prophetic history of nations and the church. Herein was contained the divine utterances,

His authority, His commandments, His laws, the whole symbolic counsel of the Eternal, and the history of all ruling powers in the nations. In symbolic language was contained in that roll the influence of every nation, tongue, and people from the beginning of earth's history to its close.[2]

The sealed scroll, thus, functions as a symbolic reference to the divine plan of salvation. If the scroll is sealed, the plan of salvation remains unrealized. When it is unsealed upon breaking the seals at the sound of the seventh trumpet—the Second Coming—then the plan of salvation will be ultimately realized (Rev. 10:7).

The Crisis in the Throne Room (5:2–6)

As John continues to watch, a crisis develops in the throne room. All the worship stops at the shout of a mighty angel who challenges the assembly: "Who is worthy to open the scroll and to break its seals?" (Rev. 5:2). To take the scroll from the throne, open it, and read its contents, the person must be deemed worthy. In John's day, worthiness denoted a distinctive qualification that made a person fit or eligible for a highly honored office. Such a qualification was based on outstanding achievements, such as prowess and bravery displayed on the battlefield. In Revelation 4:11, only God is worthy to receive glory, honor, and power on the basis of His creative power. He is worthy to reign on the throne over the universe. Thus, taking and opening the scroll requires a unique qualification, possessed only by someone who is divine: the blood of the Lamb (5:9).

It is therefore understandable why no created being in the universe fulfills this qualification (Rev. 5:3). This causes sorrow for John, and he starts weeping (5:4). One of the elders approaches him, telling him not to weep, because "the Lion from the tribe of Judah, who is the Sprout of David, has overcome" and is able to break the seals and open the scroll, because He has conquered (5:5).

The figure of the Lion refers to *what* Jesus did: He overcame. Jesus is fully qualified to take the scroll and sit on the throne and reign because of *who* He is. First, He is from the lineage of David and from the tribe of Judah, as was prophesied concerning the Messiah. Second, He alone, out of the entire universe, is equal to God. Thus, He is worthy to sit on the throne of the universe at the right hand of the Father and, as the eschatological sovereign, bring the history of this world to its end.

When John turns to see the Lion, however, he actually sees a Lamb "as having been slain" (Rev. 5:6). While the figure of the Lion refers to *what* Jesus did, the figure of the Lamb shows *how* He did it—by His sacrificial death on the cross by which He has been able to redeem humanity and win the victory over death (5:5–6). It is the cross that makes Jesus unique. It is His victory on the cross that makes Him eligible to take the scroll, break its seals, and retake the heavenly throne, which He has shared with the Father throughout eternity and which He voluntarily left to come to earth and die on the cross (3:21).

Christ the Lamb is described as having seven horns and seven eyes (Rev. 5:6). Horns symbolize authority, and eyes symbolize discernment and intelligence. Seven is the number of fullness. Jesus has full authority to rule over the universe. The seven eyes signify the fullness of His discernment and intelligence. The number seven is particularly significant because the scroll is sealed with seven seals. The seven horns illustrate His omnipotence, which empowers Him to take the sealed scroll and open it. The seven eyes symbolize His omniscience, which enables Him to read the scroll and instruct His people in its contents.

The Old Testament Background of Revelation 5

The key to unlocking the scene portrayed in chapter 5 is found in the history of Israelite kingship in Old Testament times.

Enthronement of Israelite Kings

During the early period of their history, the Israelites' only king was God. Without an earthly ruler to govern the people, the situation in the land was rather chaotic (Judg. 17:6; 21:25). At the request of the people, God eventually allowed them to institute a monarchy, even though God was their King (8:23; 1 Sam. 8:7). However, the Israelite king was required at his installment to secure a copy of the scroll of the law and keep it by the throne throughout his reign (Deut. 17:18–20). His primary duty was to read the scroll regularly, obey it, and instruct people of its contents. His faithfulness to the covenant scroll would result in blessings for the nation.

The scroll which the king of Israel was to govern by was Deuteronomy[3]—the book of God's covenant with the people of Israel. Placed at the royal throne, it functioned, in many respects, as the constitution of the kingdom, containing God's instructions for the life of the nation. It also specified the covenant terms and conditions of God's promises to His people.

At the crowning of the first Israelite king, Samuel provided a scroll of the law for Saul (1 Sam. 10:25). However, Saul did not comply with the covenant scroll and was succeeded by David. The period under the reign of David and his son Solomon marked the golden age of Israel's history. David's reign became the model of ideal kingship in Israel (cf. Ps. 72).[4] God made the covenant promise to David that his descendants would perpetually rule on the throne in Jerusalem (Ps. 132:11–12). This concept of the Davidic throne is the background for the scene in Revelation 5, where Jesus is referred to as "the Lion from the tribe of Judah" and "the Sprout of David" (Rev. 5:5). Elsewhere in the New Testament, Jesus is called the Son of David, who will sit on the throne of David and rule (Luke 1:32–33; Acts 13:22–23). After His ascension into heaven, Jesus sat on the throne at the right hand of the Father (cf. Matt. 26:64; Heb. 8:1).

Later in Israelite history, the covenant scroll became a symbol of installation upon the throne. By taking it, the newly crowned king would sit on the throne and begin his reign. At his enthronement in the temple, King Joash was presented with a copy of the covenant scroll and the crown as the royal emblem. By taking these, he was officially proclaimed king (2 Kings 11:12). The scroll in the young king's hand and the crown on his head entitled him to sit on the throne. The ceremony concluded with joyful acclamation by the people, as they recognized the king's authority and submitted themselves to it.

To the people, the possession of the covenant scroll and the ability to open and read it demonstrated the king's right to rule and judge the nation. The scroll in the king's hand was his royal scepter, so to speak. However, for the king, the obligation to read and obey the scroll was a reminder that he was accountable to an authority higher than himself when exercising his power. The king was not the sole ruler of the nation. He was sitting on the throne of God (1 Chron. 29:23; 28:5). As such, he represented God to the people and his duty was to instruct them in God's law that was specified in the covenant scroll. In such a way, the Israelite king was to be the covenant mediator and guardian of God's law in the land.

Sealing of the Covenant Scroll

The Old Testament shows that the Israelite kings rarely followed the covenant book. Because of the kings' and the people's disobedience, the prophets declared that the covenant scroll of the law would be sealed (cf. Isa. 8:16). Isaiah 29:9–14 shows that the inability to read the scroll directly resulted from sealing the scroll.[5] Sealing symbolically denotes a human inability to discern and understand the will of God, which is revealed in the book of the law and the prophetic oracles.

After the Exile, the Jews no longer had a king from the line of David on the throne in Jerusalem governing people according to the covenant book. The Jewish sources show that the Jews of John's day widely believed, on the basis of Isaiah 8:16, that the scroll of the law (as the covenant book) was sealed at the time of the Babylonian Exile because of the Israelite kings' and the people's disobedience.[6]

It was at the demise of the Davidic kingship that the prophets spoke of the future messianic king of the Davidic lineage, who would be worthy to sit on the throne of David and rule (Jer. 23:5–6; 33:15–22; Ezek. 34:23–25; 37:24–28).[7] The people hoped and longed for the ideal king from the line of David, who would sit on the throne of Israel and rule with justice over the people. He would open the sealed covenant book and instruct the people regarding the will of God.[8]

It was on this concept that Jews of John's day built their understanding of the coming Messiah, who would fulfill the role of the ideal and true king of Israel. The Messiah was expected to be the Son of David and from the tribe of Judah. The New Testament reveals that these hopes and expectations were fulfilled in Jesus Christ (cf. Luke 1:32–33; Acts 2:29–36).

The Enthronement of Christ (5:7–14)

Revelation 5 describes the enthronement of Jesus in the heavenly temple after His ascension into heaven. The language used to portray the scene is connected with the Israelite kings in the Old Testament. The seven-sealed scroll that John saw Jesus take from the throne at the right hand of the Father is comparable to the covenant scroll of the law that was handed to the Israelite kings at their enthronement. To take the scroll symbolized the right to sit on the throne and reign. To unfold the scroll meant to unfold God's plan of salvation for fallen humanity.

Christ's victory on the cross made Him worthy to take and unseal the covenant scroll that, because of human disobedience, was sealed. In the heavenly throne room, when Christ the Lamb approached the throne to take the scroll, an anthem of praise and adoration arose from the heavenly assembly, acknowledging that act (Rev. 5:7–14).

This was the climactic moment of the scene. The covenant book, which had been sealed and stored for ages, was handed to the triumphant Christ—the long-awaited King of the Davidic lineage and the Lion from the tribe of Judah.

Since the scroll signifies the right to reign, the symbolic act of taking the scroll makes Christ the rightful king over the universe. He takes His seat on the throne and shares the ruling prerogatives with the Father (Rev. 3:21). The Father now governs the universe through the Son. All authority and sovereignty is now given to Him (Matt. 28:18). Christ is now "far above all rule and authority and power and dominion, and every name that is named, not only in this age but also in the one to come" (Eph. 1:21).

As such, Christ receives the glory and adoration of the four living beings and the twenty-four elders as they fall down and worship: "You are worthy to take the scroll and open its seals" (5:9). This is joined by the acclamation of countless heavenly hosts: "Worthy is the slain Lamb to receive power and riches and wisdom and strength and honor and glory and blessing!" (5:12). Finally, the Father and Christ together receive honor and worship from all the heavenly beings: "To the One sitting on the throne and to the Lamb be blessing and honor and glory and might forever and ever!" (5:13). These are qualities that apply only to royalty.

The symbolic taking of the scroll by Christ the Lamb signified the transference of authority from Satan to Christ. As the scholar Adela Yarbro Collins notes, "The problem facing the heavenly council is the rebellion of Satan, which is paralleled by rebellion on earth." The tears of John "express the desire of the faithful to have this situation rectified."[9] With the fall of the human race into the bondage of sin, humanity became lost and hopeless. By usurping the lordship and dominion on earth (cf. Luke 4:6), Satan became "the ruler of this world" (John 12:31; 14:30; 16:11).

However, what was lost with Adam has now been regained by Christ. His installment on the heavenly throne demonstrates that His sacrifice has been accepted on behalf of humanity. The death of Jesus purchased people for God from every tribe, language, people, and nation (Rev. 5:9). White describes this in a way that helps explain what is happening in Revelation 5:

> All heaven was waiting to welcome the Savior to the celestial courts. As He ascended, He led the way, and the multitude of captives set free at His resurrection followed. The heavenly host,

with shouts and acclamations of praise and celestial song, attended the joyous train. . . . There is the throne, and around it, the rainbow of promise. There are cherubim and seraphim. The commanders of the angel hosts, the sons of God, the representatives of the unfallen worlds, are assembled. The heavenly council, before which Lucifer had accused God and His Son, the representatives of those sinless realms over which Satan had thought to establish his dominion, all are there to welcome the Redeemer. They are eager to celebrate His triumph and to glorify their King.

But He waves them back. Not yet; He cannot now receive the coronet of glory and the royal robe. He enters into the presence of His Father. He points to His wounded head, the pierced side, the marred feet; He lifts His hands, bearing the print of nails. He points to the tokens of His triumph; He presents to God the wave sheaf, those raised with Him as representatives of that great multitude who shall come forth from the grave at His Second Coming. He approaches the Father, with whom there is joy over one sinner that repents; who rejoices over one with singing. Before the foundations of the earth were laid, the Father and the Son had united in a covenant to redeem man if he should be overcome by Satan. They had clasped their hands in a solemn pledge that Christ should become the surety for the human race. This pledge Christ has fulfilled. . . . The voice of God is heard proclaiming that justice is satisfied. Satan is vanquished. Christ's toiling, struggling ones on earth are accepted in the Beloved. . . . The Father's arms encircle His Son, and the word is given, "Let all the angels of God worship Him" (Heb. 1:6).

With joy unutterable, rulers and principalities and powers acknowledge the supremacy of the Prince of life. The angel host prostrate themselves before Him, while the glad shout fills all the courts of heaven, "Worthy is the Lamb that was slain to receive power, and riches, and wisdom, and strength, and honor, and glory, and blessing" (Rev. 5:12).

Songs of triumph mingle with the music from angel harps, till heaven seems to overflow with joy and praise. Love has conquered. The lost is found. Heaven rings with voices in lofty strains proclaiming, "Blessing, and honor, and glory, and power, be unto Him that sitteth upon the throne, and unto the Lamb forever and ever" (Rev. 5:13).[10]

In Revelation 5, Christ has been inaugurated into His royal and priestly ministry in the heavenly sanctuary. By receiving the scroll, He takes the destiny of all humanity into His hands. His ability to break the seals and open the scroll entitles Him to carry the plan of salvation to its ultimate realization. The scroll contains the terms and conditions of God's promise to His people. It points to the only hope for God's people: that their Lord reigns on the throne of the universe. He will ever be present with them to sustain and protect them until He comes again and takes them home.

The Pentecost Scene

The installment of Christ on the heavenly throne took place at the time of Pentecost (Acts 2:32–36).[11] During His installment at the right hand of the Father, Jesus became the legitimate ruler of earth. The Holy Spirit descended upon the disciples to fulfill the promise Jesus made to them (John 14:16–18). Revelation 5:6 mentions the seven Spirits "sent into all the earth." The seven Spirits denote the fullness of the Holy Spirit's activity in the world (seven is a number of fullness). While earlier in the book, the Holy Spirit is regularly before the throne (cf. Rev. 1:4; 4:5), in chapter 5, He is sent to the earth. Sending the Holy Spirit is related to the inauguration of Christ into His post-Calvary ministry. White comments:

> When Christ passed within the heavenly gates, He was enthroned amidst the adoration of the angels. As soon as this ceremony was completed, the Holy Spirit descended upon the disciples in rich currents. . . . The Pentecostal outpouring was Heaven's communication that the Redeemer's inauguration was accomplished. According to His promise, He had sent the Holy Spirit from heaven to His followers as a token that He had, as priest and king, received all authority in heaven and on earth, and was the Anointed One over His people.[12]

Sending the Holy Spirit in connection with Christ's exaltation to the heavenly throne is significant. According to John 7:39, the Holy Spirit "was not yet given, because Jesus was not yet glorified." However, in His Pentecost sermon, Peter explained that the coming of the Holy Spirit to earth was the result of Christ's exaltation on the heavenly throne at the right hand of God (Acts 2:32–36). The coming of the Holy Spirit at Pentecost was, thus, heaven's message that Jesus had appeared before the Father and that His sacrifice had been accepted on behalf of humanity. After this, He was inaugurated into His post-Calvary ministry as our King and Priest. He is now our mediator in the heavenly sanctuary, and through Him, we fallen humans have access to God.

Since Christ is exalted on the throne of the universe and inaugurated into His post-Calvary ministry, the work of the Holy Spirit is unlimited in applying Christ's victorious death to the lives of humans and announcing God's kingdom throughout the earth. Pentecost marks the beginning of spreading the gospel throughout the world. With the proclamation of the gospel, Christ is expanding His kingdom by winning human hearts. For those who respond to the gospel, divine grace is available. For those who reject the gospel, there are consequences. This sets the ground for the opening of the seven seals scene that is portrayed in Revelation 6.

The Seven Seals

 Revelation 6:1–17; 8:1

In Revelation 4–5, we witnessed the heavenly worship service, celebrating the enthronement of Christ at His ascension into heaven. By taking the sealed scroll, Christ took His place on the Father's throne as the legitimate ruler of earth. All things have now been subjected under His feet (Eph. 1:22). Yet, He is not the undisputed ruler of this world. There are still many rebellious people who do not accept His authority. They have yet to be conquered, so those people who are captive to sin can be set free.

As He sits on the throne, Christ the Lamb begins to open the seals of the scroll. The opening of the seals triggers a series of events on earth. These events do not comprise the contents of the sealed scroll; rather, they are the events that take place on earth as a result of Christ's actions in heaven. The contents of the scroll will only be revealed when all seals have been opened.

We must keep in mind that the opening of the seals began with the enthronement of Christ at Pentecost in AD 31. The opening of the sixth seal brings us to the Second Coming (cf. Rev. 6:12–17). Thus, chapter 6 encompasses the history of the Christian church within the hostile world from the first century to the return of Christ.

The Four Horsemen (6:1–8)

The descriptions that accompany the opening of the first four seals follow the same literary pattern. As Christ the Lamb opens each of the four seals, John hears each of the four living beings in turn say: "Come!" Some manuscripts read: "Come and see!" to denote that the call was addressed to John (Rev. 6:1). However, it is more likely that this is a summons to the horsemen.

At the breaking of the first four seals, four colorful horses with their riders appear. In Revelation, horses are regularly associated with warfare and conquest (Rev. 9:7; 19:11, 14). Prior to John, Zechariah saw in a vision four colorful horses with their riders, resembling those in Revelation 6 (Zech. 1:8–10). The riders were obviously angelic figures executing divine judgments (1:11). In a later vision, the horses are defined as "the four spirits of heaven" in the Lord's service (6:5). Zechariah's vision helps unlock the symbolism of the horse imagery in Revelation 6:

> ¹And I looked when the Lamb opened the first of the seven seals, and I heard one of the four living beings saying as with a voice of thunder: "Come!" ²And I looked, and behold, a white horse, and the one sitting upon it had a bow, and a crown was given to him, and he went forth conquering and that he might conquer.
>
> ³When He opened the second seal, I heard the second living being saying: "Come!" ⁴And another horse, fiery red, came forth, and the one sitting upon it was given to take peace from the earth in order that they might slay one another, and a great sword was given to him.
>
> ⁵When he opened the third seal, I heard the third living being saying: "Come!" And I looked, and behold, a black horse, and the one sitting upon it had a balance in his hand. ⁶And I heard as a voice in the midst of the four living beings saying: "A quart of wheat for a denarius, and three quarts of barley for a denarius, and do not harm the oil and the wine."
>
> ⁷When he opened the fourth seal, I heard the voice of the fourth living being saying: "Come!" ⁸And I looked, and behold, a pale horse, and the one sitting upon it had the name Death, and Hades was following him; and authority over one-fourth of the earth was given to them to kill with the sword and with famine and with pestilence and by wild beasts.

The First Seal (6:1–2)

As Christ the Lamb opens the first seal, a white horse steps onto the scene. The rider on the horse holds a bow and is given a crown. The Greek word used for crown here is *stephanos*, which is the crown of victory (cf. 2 Tim. 4:8), a garland given to winners at the ancient Olympic games. This rider is a conqueror; he goes forward to completely conquer. In John's day, Roman generals would ride white horses to celebrate a great victory.

The scene here is symbolic. In the Old Testament, God is sometimes pictured as riding a horse with a bow in His hand, conquering the enemies of His people (Hab. 3:8–13; Ps. 45:4–5). Revelation 19:11–16 portrays Christ as riding a white horse, leading the heavenly armies into the final battle of this earth's history. Furthermore, in Revelation, white is a symbol of purity and is regularly associated with Christ and His followers.[1] Also, the *stephanos* crown worn by the horseman is regularly associated with Christ and His victorious people. Finally, the concept of conquering clearly echoes Revelation 3:21 and 5:5, which refer to Christ's "overcoming" on Calvary. This concept is a dominant theme in the book.

The rider on the white horse signifies the spreading of the gospel of Jesus Christ, which started at Pentecost (conquering people for Christ). When Christ was exalted on the heavenly throne, at the right hand of the Father, He began the expansion of His kingdom by waging warfare against the forces of evil. There were many territories to conquer and many people to win for the kingdom. In its initial stage, the proclamation of the gospel had a powerful start as a result of the manifestation of the Holy Spirit's power. Thousands were converted in one day (Acts 2:41, 47; 4:4). However, this "conquest of the gospel" will continue throughout history until the ultimate conquest is realized at the time of the end (cf. Matt. 24:14).

The Second Seal (6:3–4)

Christ's opening of the second seal ushers a fiery-red horse onto the scene. Red is the color of blood and corresponds to the mission of this horse. The rider, who has a large sword, does not do the killing himself. Instead, he takes away peace from the earth, and as a result, people slay one another.

The fiery-red horse follows the white horse. The first horseman shows that, through preaching the gospel, Christ is waging spiritual warfare against the forces of evil. However, the forces of evil render strong resistance to spreading the gospel. They rally those who reject the gospel against those who accept it. Inevitably, persecution follows.

The gospel always divides people; some accept it, and others reject it. While its acceptance brings peace, its rejection results in a loss of peace. "Do not think that I came to bring peace on the earth," Jesus said. "I did not come to bring peace, but a sword. For I came to set a man against his father, and a daughter against her mother, and a daughter-in-law against her mother-in-law; and a man's enemies will be the members of his household" (Matt. 10:34–36). As in the Old Testament, the enemies of God's people often turned against each other;[2] so in the second seal scene, those who resist and reject the gospel turn against each other in persecution.

The Third Seal (6:5–6)

As Christ the Lamb opens the third seal, a black horse appears, following the red horse. The rider is seen holding a scale for weighing food. John also hears an announcement by one of the four living beings: "A quart of wheat for a denarius, and three quarts of barley for a denarius, and do not harm the oil and the wine" (Rev. 6:6).

In Palestine, grain, oil, and wine were the three main crops. They are mentioned in the Old Testament as the basic necessities of life.[3] God promised that Israel would have food in abundance. To carefully weigh grain denoted great scarcity or famine (cf. Lev. 26:26; Ezek. 4:16). In John's day, a denarius was a daily wage (cf. Matt. 20:2). In normal circumstances, a daily wage would buy all the necessities for a family. However, a famine would inflate the normal price some twelve times. In the third seal scene, it would take a day's wage to buy enough food for only one person, since a quart of wheat was the daily ration for one person. To feed a small family, a day's wage would buy three quarts of barley—a cheaper, coarser food for the poor.

The imagery of the black horse and its rider points to what will befall those who reject the gospel. The black color corresponds to the mission of the horse and its rider. Black is the opposite of white. If the white horse represents preaching the gospel, then the black horse denotes the absence of the gospel. Grain in the Bible symbolizes the Word of God (Luke 8:11). Bread also stands for the words of Jesus (John 6:35–58). The rejection of the gospel results in a famine of God's word, similar to the spiritual famine prophesied by Amos concerning the Israelites (Amos 8:11–13).

However, the famine of the third seal is not fatal. The same voice that commissioned the horseman also announces that the oil and wine will not be affected by the famine but will continue to be available. Spiritually, oil symbolizes the Holy Spirit, and wine symbolizes salvation in Jesus Christ. Even when the Word of God is scarce, the Holy Spirit is still at work among people, and salvation is still available to all who want it.

The Fourth Seal (6:7–8)

With the opening of the fourth seal, a pale horse appears, following the black horse. The word in Greek for the horse's color is *chloros*, denoting the ashen-gray color of a decomposing corpse. The rider's name is Death, and he is accompanied by Hades, the place of the dead. They are allowed to destroy people by sword, famine, plague, and wild beasts over one-fourth of the earth. Noticeably, the action of the fourth horseman comprises the actions of the previous three horsemen.

The fourth seal calls forth pestilence and death. The graphic portrayal of the fourth horseman provides a further warning to those who reject the gospel. The pale horse following the black one conveys the perennial truth that spiritual famine of the Word of God typically results in spiritual death.

The good news, however, is that the power of Death and Hades is very limited; they are given authority over only one-fourth of the earth. The beginning of the book provides the assurance that, by His own death and resurrection, Jesus has won the victory over Death and Hades—the two enemies of the human race (Rev. 1:18). When the gospel is accepted, life is received as a gift. Death does not have power or authority over those who accept the gospel. Christ has the keys of Death and Hades.

Meaning of the Four Horsemen

The key to unlocking the theological meaning of the four horsemen of the Apocalypse lies in the Old Testament covenant relationship between God and Israel, as well as in Jesus's apocalyptic sermon on the Mount of Olives.

Judgement on God people + also on the ones that are persecuting God people

Curses of the Covenant

When interpreting the seven seals, remember that the symbolism of Revelation is rooted in the Old Testament. In the seven seal scenes, Revelation uses the experience of ancient Israel in Palestine to describe the experience of Christians. The mission of the horsemen is portrayed using the terms sword, famine, plague, and wild beasts (Rev. 6:8). In the Old Testament, these terms were instruments of divine judgment against unfaithful Israel, used to bring them to repentance. These plagues were known as covenant curses and were used as a punishment for breaking the covenant of God.

When God brought Israel out of Egypt, He made a covenant with them at Sinai. He promised that, if they obeyed Him, He would recognize them as His chosen people (Exod. 19:5–6). As long as the Israelites stayed within the covenant relationship, God promised to bless them. The books of Leviticus (26:3–9) and Deuteronomy (28:1–14) contain a long list of blessings for the Israelites if they lived according to God's instruction. God said He would faithfully keep His promise as long as His people were obedient to Him.

On the other hand, if Israel turned away from God to worship other gods, then curses would follow:

> If you act with hostility against Me and are unwilling to obey Me, I will increase the plague on you seven times according to your sins. I will let loose among you *the beasts* of the field, which will bereave you of your children and destroy your cattle and reduce your number, so that your roads lie deserted. And if by these things you are not turned to me but act with hostility against Me, then I will act with hostility against you: and I, even I, will strike you seven times for your sins. I will also bring upon you *a sword*, which will execute vengeance for the covenant; and when you gather together into your cities, I will send *pestilence* among you, so that you shall be delivered into enemy hands. When I *break your staff of bread*, ten women will bake your bread in one oven, and they will bring back your bread by weight, so that you will eat and not be satisfied. (Lev. 26:21–26; emphasis supplied)

This warning includes four plagues—wild beasts, the sword, pestilence, and famine—that would come upon Israel for breaking the covenant. They are repeated again in Deuteronomy 32:23–25.

Sadly, throughout their history, Israel was unfaithful to God and consistently broke the covenant. As they wandered from God and worshiped other gods, the prophets urged them to repent by threatening them with these four curses.[4] Ezekiel referred to them as God's "four severe judgments" (Ezek. 14:21), and Jeremiah called them "four kinds of destroyers" (Jer. 15:3). Because the people continued in their apostasy, God finally exiled them to Babylon.

The covenant curses were the means by which God kept Israel in line with His will. They functioned as disciplinary measures. By them, God chastised His people when they wandered away from Him, in order to win them back. If the people repented and turned back to God, He promised to forgive their sins.

These curses also came upon Israel when God incited enemy nations, such as Assyria and Babylon, against His people.[5] For instance, God referred to Assyria as "the rod of My anger" (Isa. 10:5) and to the king of Babylon as God's servant (Jer. 25:9; 27:6); therefore, God chastised His people through these foreign nations. When these nations destroyed Israel's cities, famine and disease ensued; finally, wild beasts came to prey upon those who were left. These nations tended to treat Israel harshly, often trying to totally destroy them. The Israelites then turned to God for succor in their plight. Then, in response, God judged the enemy nations who mercilessly afflicted His people (Jer. 51:24; Joel 3:2–7).

Seals 1–4	The means God uses to keep His people on track
Seal 5	God's people harmed and martyred by hostile enemies
Seals 6–7	God comes in judgment against those who harmed His people

Revelation uses the imagery of the Old Testament covenant curses to describe, in graphic terms, the experience of the church from Pentecost to the Second Coming. The seven seals, in general, refer to Christians and their response to the gospel. The four horsemen symbolize the experience God's people have in spiritual overcoming, which entitles them to share the throne of Jesus (cf. Rev. 3:21). The rider on the white horse symbolizes the victorious spreading of the gospel. However, the rider on the white horse is followed by the rider on the fiery-red horse. Wherever the gospel is preached, the forces of darkness resist it. Also, as the gospel is preached, Christians often fall into unfaithfulness and disobedience. To keep them on track, God allows the world to chastise them in the same way He chastised Israel in the Old Testament. The rider on the fiery-red horse brings persecution; the rider on the black horse brings spiritual famine; and the rider on the ashen-gray horse brings spiritual plague and death. The graphic picture of the four horsemen gives a solemn warning to Christians throughout history not to take Christ's gospel lightly in their lives.

The Synoptic Apocalypse

By studying the seals, we may observe a close correlation between the seven seals and the Synoptic Apocalypse (Matt. 24; Mark 13; Luke 21). The Synoptic Apocalypse was a discourse Jesus delivered to His disciples on the Mount of Olives shortly before His crucifixion. In that speech, Jesus explained to the disciples what would happen throughout history, up to the end time.

The speech consists of three parts. First, Jesus described the general realities of the Christian era in terms of wars and rumors of wars, famine, pestilence, persecution, earthquakes, deception, and heavenly signs (Matt. 24:4–14). All these events also occur in Revelation 6 and are not the signs of the end; rather, they are the events that will take place throughout history as God's people wait for the end to come. These events are how God keeps the reality of His coming fresh in the minds of His people. Second, Jesus talked about a long interval in history from the destruction of Jerusalem until the great tribulation, during which God's people will experience heightened persecution (24:15–28). Third, Jesus pointed to the heavenly signs that indicate the nearness of the Second Coming. They are followed by specific signs announcing the coming of Christ in power and glory (24:29–31).

The vision of the seven seals parallels the Synoptic Apocalypse in content and sequence:

Matthew 24	Parallels with Synoptic Apocalypse	Revelation 6
4–14	General realities of the Christian age	1–8
15–28	The great tribulation of God's people	9–11
29–31	Specific signs of the Second Coming	12–17

These comparisons show that both Matthew 24:4–14 and the first four seals (Rev. 6:1–8) refer to the general realities of the Christian age. The horsemen of the Apocalypse and the covenant curses in Leviticus 26 have the same function as the general signs foretold by Jesus (Matt. 24:4–14). These signs remind God's people of the reality of Christ's return to keep them awake and on the right track.

Historical Application of the Four Horsemen

The four horsemen of the Apocalypse may also be understood historically. As with the seven churches, there is a correlation between the seven seals and the different epochs in Christian history (Rev. 2–3). Like the church in Ephesus, the first seal coincides with the apostolic period, which was characterized by general faithfulness (2:1–7). During this time, the gospel spread rapidly throughout the world (cf. Col. 1:23). The second seal corresponds remarkably to the period of persecution that took place in the Roman Empire from the end of the first to the beginning of the fourth century (cf. Rev. 2:8–11). The third seal may aptly apply to the fourth and fifth centuries of Christian history, which were characterized by gradual spiritual decline (cf. 2:12–17). In this period, there was a spiritual famine of God's word. The fourth seal applies to the spiritual death that characterized Christianity during the Middle Ages, when the Bible was unavailable to people and tradition overruled teaching the Bible (cf. 2:18–29).

In applying the seals historically, however, it is important not to limit the realities of the four horsemen to one particular period. The first horseman goes forth and conquers until there is nothing left to conquer. The "conquering" preaching of the gospel is not limited to the apostolic period; it continues until Christ returns (Matt. 24:14; Rev. 14:6–12). The same applies to the other horsemen. For neither persecution nor spiritual famine nor death are limited to certain historical periods. They are the general realities that accompany preaching the gospel from Pentecost until Christ's coming in power and glory (19:11–16).

The descriptions of opening the last three seals are very different from the first four. There are no horses or riders. While the horsemen of the first four seals exclusively concern God's people, the remaining three seals refer to judgments that fall on those who oppress God's people.

The Fifth Seal (6:9-11) *Mat 24*

mid ages
inquisition

When ancient Israel was unfaithful to the covenant, God chastised them through their enemies to bring them to repentance. However, those nations viciously afflicted God's people, seeking to destroy them. In turn, God's wrath turned against those enemy nations to deliver His people (cf. Deut. 32:41–43). The same pattern is in the seven seals. The fifth seal describes God's people martyred (as a result of persecution) and praying to God for vindication:

⁹And when He opened the fifth seal, I saw under the altar the souls of those who had been slain because of the word of God and because of the testimony that they had. ¹⁰And they cried with a loud voice: "How long, O Lord, holy and true, will You not judge and avenge our blood upon those who dwell on earth?" ¹¹And to each of them was given a white robe, and it was said to them that they should rest for a little while yet, until their fellow servants, that is, their brothers who are about to be killed, might be made complete as they themselves had been.

The fifth seal scene portrays the souls of those who have been martyred for the sake of the gospel as residing underneath the altar. The term "soul" in the Bible denotes the whole person (Gen. 2:7; Acts 2:41; 27:37). In this scene, the martyrs are "under the altar," alluding to the sacrificial blood poured at the base of the altar of sacrifice in the earthly sanctuary (Exod. 29:12; Lev. 4:7; 8:15). In the Old Testament, life was regarded as being in the blood (17:11). The death of the martyrs is described here as pouring their sacrificial blood before God (2 Tim. 4:6).

John hears the martyrs crying to God for vindication against those who persecuted them: "How long, O Lord, holy and true, will You not judge and avenge our blood upon those who dwell on earth?" The expression "those who dwell on earth" in Revelation consistently refers to those who oppose the gospel and are against God and His people (cf. Rev. 8:13; 11:10; 13:8; 17:2). The martyrs' plea brings to mind how the blood of Abel cried out about Abel's unjust death (Gen. 4:10). The martyrs' plea is not for vengeance against those who took their lives but for vindication concerning the injustice of their death. They placed their trust in God. Now they are asking God to step in and bring justice, so their blood will not have been shed in vain.

"How long, O Lord?" has been the cry of God's oppressed and persecuted people throughout history (cf. Ps. 79:5; Dan. 12:6–7; Hab. 1:2). Thus, the martyrs' plea in the scene of the fifth seal represents the plea of God's suffering people throughout history, from the time of Abel until the time when God will judge and avenge "the blood of His servants" on their enemies (Rev. 19:2).

It often looks as if the prayers of God's people go unanswered and as if injustice prevails. However, God hears the prayers of His people. God responds to the plea of the martyred saints in two ways. First, they are given a white robe. The white robe in Revelation signifies Christ's righteousness with which God covers those who are accepted by Christ (Rev. 3:18). The white robes also represent the future reward for overcomers (3:5). The martyred saints have received the assurance of salvation and eternal life, not because of their martyrdom but because of what God has done for them.

Second, the martyrs are told that they will have to wait for a little while until their brothers in experience—those who must go through a similar martyrdom—are made complete. God promised that He will "avenge the blood of His servants" (Deut. 32:43; Ps. 79:10). In Revelation 8, God's judgments have already been poured out on "those who dwell on the earth" throughout Christian history (8:13). The day is coming, however, when Christ will come in judgment to "those who do not obey the gospel of our Lord Jesus. These will pay the penalty of eternal destruction, away from the presence of the Lord and from the glory of His power, when He comes to be glorified in His saints on that day, and to be marveled at among all who have believed" (2 Thess. 1:8–10). The fulfillment of this prophecy is the subject of the sixth seal scene.

Most Bible translations insert the word "number," postulating that the martyrs had to wait until the number of martyred saints is completed. However, "number" is not in the original Greek text. Revelation does not refer to a number of martyred saints that must be reached but to the completeness of their character. Those who have yet to go through martyrdom are to be made complete, just as the slain martyrs under the altar were. The text clearly indicates that those martyrs were perfected by receiving the robe of Christ's righteousness rather than by their own merits.

While the fifth seal scene represents the experience of God's oppressed people throughout the Christian era, it may also apply to a specific period in history following the Middle Ages. During this period, more than fifty million Christians were martyred because of their faithfulness to the Bible. The prophecies of Daniel speak of the enemy power, described as a little horn "waging war with the saints and overpowering them" (Dan. 7:21, 25). The question was raised: How long would such a situation last? The answer came: it would last for the prophetic period of 1,260 days, meaning years (12:6–7). Opening the sixth seal brings us to that point in time.

The Sixth Seal (6:12–17)

The fifth seal is essential for understanding what goes on in the sixth seal scene. The time has come for God to intervene in answer to the prayers of His people who are suffering injustice in a hostile world.

The sixth seal, thus, portrays the judgments against those who have harmed God's people:

> *¹²And I looked when He opened the sixth seal, and a great earthquake occurred, and the sun became black as a sackcloth made of hair, and the moon became like blood, ¹³and the stars of heaven fell down to the earth as a fig tree casts its figs when shaken by a strong wind, ¹⁴and the sky was parted as a scroll being rolled up, and every mountain and island were moved from their places. ¹⁵And the kings of the earth and the magistrates and the military commanders and the rich and the powerful and every slave and free person hid themselves in the caves and among the rocks of the mountains. ¹⁶And they said to the mountains and the rocks: "Fall on us and hide us from the face of the One sitting on the throne and from the wrath of the Lamb, ¹⁷for the great day of His wrath has come, and who is able to stand?"*

The breaking of the sixth seal by Christ the Lamb results in cosmic and cataclysmic signs, such as a darkening of the sun and moon, a falling of meteors, a disastrous earthquake, and a convulsion of the sky. These cosmic signs are reminders that bring to mind the same events foretold by Jesus in Matthew 24:29–30, which occur at the conclusion of the tribulation of the Middle Ages. In the Old Testament, these events regularly accompany a theophany of judgment.[6]

The sun, moon, stars, and sky are clearly literal here. The text says that the sun and moon become darkened *as* sackcloth and blood respectively, that the stars fall down to earth *as* figs from a fig tree, and that the sky rolls up *as* a scroll. The words "as" or "like" point to a symbolic analogy rather than to an actual thing or event.[7] Christians in the Western world recognized the fulfillment of the prophecy of Christ's coming in the Lisbon earthquake in 1755; the dark day of May 19, 1780, in eastern New York and southern New England; and the spectacular meteor shower over the Atlantic Ocean on November 13, 1833. This awareness led to a series of revivals in North America known as the Second Great Awakening.

However, these supernatural events will be witnessed again at Christ's return to earth. Isaiah prophesied that the day of the Lord would come as "destruction from the Almighty" (Isa. 13:6). Here, John observes people from all walks of life filled with fear and trying to hide themselves from the terrifying upheaval at Christ's coming. They ask the rocks and mountains to protect them from the wrath of God and the Lamb.

This scene is similar to Isaiah's prophecy regarding the day of the Lord: "Men will go into caves in the rocks and into holes in the ground before the terror of the LORD and the splendor of His majesty, when He arises to make the earth tremble" (Isa. 2:19). This verse also echoes Jesus's warning when He quotes Hosea, saying that the time will come when humanity will "say to the mountains, 'Fall on us,' and to the hills, 'Cover us'" (Luke 23:30; cf. Hos. 10:8).

The day of divine wrath has finally come. It is with Christ's coming in power and glory that the prayers of the martyred saints underneath the altar in the fifth seal scene are ultimately answered (Rev. 6:9–11). The time has come for justice to be dispensed, when Christ "comes to be glorified in His saints on that day, and to be marveled at among all who have believed" (2 Thess. 1:10).

The scene concludes with the rhetorical question of the terror-stricken wicked: "The great day of His wrath has come, and who is able to stand?" (Rev. 6:17). Their question echoes that of the people in Nahum: "Who can stand before His indignation? Who can endure the burning of His anger?" (Nah. 1:6). It also echoes Malachi: "Who can endure the day of His coming? And who can stand when He appears?" (Mal. 3:2). Revelation 7 answers that question: those who will be able to stand in that day are the sealed people of God, who are washed in the blood of the Lamb (Rev. 7:14). Before moving into chapter 7, we will briefly explore the seventh seal.

The Seventh Seal (8:1)

After describing those who will be able to stand at the upheaval of Christ's coming, John describes the opening of the seventh seal by the Lamb:

> *¹And when He opened the seventh seal, there was silence in heaven for about half an hour.*

John does not explain the reason for this silence in heaven. In the Bible, silence is regularly associated with the coming of God in judgment (Zeph. 1:7; Zech. 2:13). The Jews of John's day believed that silence occurs in heaven so the prayers of the saints can be heard and answered in judgment on the wicked.[8] The silence in heaven when the seventh seal is broken occurs because heaven is focused on the final judgment and the conclusion of the Great Controversy between good and evil. "Half an hour" refers to a relatively short time, and the day-year principle does not apply here.

The Sealed Saints

 Revelation 7:1-17

hapter 7 is inserted parenthetically between the sixth and seventh seals. Yet, it fits aptly in the sequence of the seals. The opening of the sixth seal brings us to Christ's Second Coming. Facing the impending judgment, the wicked call on the mountains and rocks to fall upon them and hide them from the wrath of God and the Lamb. They ask in panic: "Who is able to stand?" (Rev. 6:17). Revelation 7 provides the answer: those who will be able to stand on the great day of God's wrath are the sealed people of God.

> ¹*After this, I saw four angels standing at the four corners of the earth, holding back the four winds of the earth, so that the wind would not blow upon the earth or upon the sea or on any tree. ²And I saw another angel ascending from the rising of the sun, having the seal of the living God, and he cried with a loud voice to the four angels to whom was given to harm the earth and the sea, ³saying: "Do not harm the earth or the sea or the trees until we have sealed the servants of our God upon their foreheads."*
>
> ⁴*And I heard the number of those who have been sealed, 144,000 sealed from every tribe of the sons of Israel: ⁵from the tribe of Judah 12,000 sealed, from the tribe of Reuben 12,000, from the tribe of Gad 12,000, ⁶from the tribe of Asher 12,000, from the tribe of Naphtali 12,000, from the tribe of Manasseh 12,000, ⁷from the tribe of Simeon 12,000, from the tribe of Levi 12,000, from the tribe of Issachar 12,000, ⁸from the tribe of Zebulun 12,000, from the tribe of Joseph 12,000, from the tribe of Benjamin 12,000 sealed.*

⁹After these things, I looked, and behold, a great multitude, which no one could count, from every nation and tribe and people and tongue, standing before the throne and before the Lamb, clothed in white robes, and palm branches in their hands. ¹⁰And they were crying with a loud voice, saying: "Salvation to our God sitting on the throne and to the Lamb." ¹¹And all the angels were standing around the throne and the elders and the living beings, and they fell on their faces before the throne and worshiped God, ¹²saying: "Amen! Blessing and glory and wisdom and thanksgiving and honor and power and might to our God forever and ever. Amen!"

¹³And one of the elders answered and said to me: "These clothed in the white robes, who are they and from where have they come?" ¹⁴And I said to him: "My lord, you know." And he said to me: "These are the ones coming out of the great tribulation, and they have washed their robes and made them white in the blood of the Lamb. ¹⁵Therefore, they are before the throne of God and serve Him in worship day and night in His temple, and the One sitting on the throne will tabernacle over them. ¹⁶They will not hunger anymore nor thirst anymore, nor will the sun fall upon them nor any heat, ¹⁷because the Lamb who is in the midst of the throne will shepherd them and lead them to springs of the water of life; and God will wipe away every tear from their eyes."

The 144,000 (7:1–8)

The scene begins with four angels at "the four corners of the earth" who are restraining "the four winds" from destroying the earth, the sea, and the trees (Rev. 7:1). The expression "the four corners of the earth" is the ancient way of referring to the four points of the compass. This denotes the global significance of the scene.

In the Old Testament, winds are used as a symbol of destructive forces, which God uses to execute judgments upon the wicked (Isa. 66:15–16; Jer. 23:19–20; Hos. 13:15). Jeremiah referred to the coming judgment against Jerusalem as a strong, scorching wind coming from the wilderness (Jer. 4:11–13). He also envisioned "the spirit [wind] of a destroyer" devastating Babylon (51:1–2). "The four winds" is a well-known concept in the Old Testament (Jer. 49:36). In a vision, Daniel saw the four winds of heaven stirring up the great sea, where the four beasts came from (Dan. 7:2–3). The following passage from the book of Ecclesiasticus shows how the Jews of John's day understood winds as a symbol of divine judgment: "There are winds that have been created for vengeance and in their anger they scourge heavily; in the time of consummation, they will pour out their strength and calm the anger of their Maker."[1]

The blowing winds are associated with God's wrath in Revelation 6:17. They take place during the time of "the great tribulation," mentioned later in the scene (Rev. 7:14). The blowing winds are another way to describe the seven last plagues, which are the fullness of God's wrath (15:1). So the blowing winds represent the seven last plagues that will be poured upon the wicked right before the Second Coming. However, for a certain period of time, these destructive forces are being restrained from harming the earth by divine intervention. They are not released as long as the sealing of God's people continues.

The Sealing of God's People

Next, John sees another angel coming from "the rising of the sun" (Rev. 7:2), an ancient designation of the east. The east in the Bible is regularly associated with God (Ezek. 43:2). Jesus is called the sunrise (Luke 1:78). The sign of the coming of the Son of Man will appear in the east (Matt. 24:27–30). The coming of Christ with His army to fight the battle of Armageddon is referred to in terms of the kings from the east (Rev. 16:12). Thus, saying that the angel comes from the east means that he comes from God Himself.

This angel orders the four angels not to unleash the winds until the sealing of God's people is completed. In ancient times, sealing had a variety of meanings. Documents were sealed to validate their contents or to protect them from tampering. However, the fundamental meaning of sealing was ownership. A seal impression on an object pointed to the owner. This is the symbolic meaning of sealing in the New Testament. According to Paul, the meaning of the seal is that "the Lord knows those who are His" (2 Tim. 2:19). To have the seal with the name of God on the forehead means to belong to Him (Rev. 14:1).

Sealing in the New Testament denotes identification of those who are God's faithful people. God recognizes those who belong to Him and seals them with the Holy Spirit (2 Cor. 1:21–22; Eph. 1:13–14). The presence of the Holy Spirit is a sign of a genuine Christian—the one who has washed his robes and made them white in the blood of the Lamb (Rev. 7:14). To lose the Holy Spirit means to lose sealing: "Do not grieve the Holy Spirit of God, by whom you were sealed for the day of redemption" (Eph. 4:30).

The foregoing passages show that the sealing of God's people in the New Testament is not limited to the time of the end. Sealing the faithful has been taking place throughout history. However, the sealing of God's people reaches a climax at the time of the end. This will be the testing time to distinguish between those who are on God's side and those who are on Satan's side. Those who side with the beast receive the mark of the beast on their foreheads or their right hands (Rev. 13:16–17). However, those who worship God are sealed on their foreheads (14:1).

The faithfulness of those who are sealed has been suitably tested with every generation of Christians. However, the test of faithfulness in the final crisis is to keep God's commandments (cf. Rev. 12:17; 14:12). In particular, the fourth commandment will become the test of obedience to God (cf. 14:7). As the Sabbath was the sign of God's people in biblical times (Exod. 31:12–17; Ezek. 20:12, 20), so it will be the sign of loyalty to God in the final crisis (Rev. 13:16–17).

The sealing described in Revelation 7 is the final ratification of those who belong to God. As such, the seal at the end time functions as a sign of protection. Those who have the seal of God upon their foreheads are protected from the destructive forces of the seven last plagues. These are the ones who are able to stand on the great day of wrath (Rev. 7:3). This concept goes back to Ezekiel 9, regarding the destruction of Jerusalem before the Exile. The prophet saw in the vision a heavenly messenger with a writing case at his side. God ordered him to go through the city and mark the foreheads of the faithful. The Lord then told the executioners to slay all those who did not have the mark on their foreheads. They were explicitly commanded not to touch those who were marked. The sign on the foreheads distinguished those who were on God's side from others who were unfaithful and idolatrous. The seal provided them with protection from the impending judgment (Ezek. 9:1–11).

Just as the marked Israelites were protected in Ezekiel's vision, so God's sealed people are protected from the symbolic blowing of the eschatological winds. The sealing identifies them as God's people and protects them from the harmful effects of the seven last plagues. In this way, the question raised in Revelation 6:17 receives the ultimate answer: those who will be able to stand protected on the day of the divine wrath are the sealed people of God.

The Sealed 144,000 (7:4)

As the vision continues, John hears the number of those who have been sealed as "144,000 sealed from every tribe of the sons of Israel" (Rev. 7:4). This shows that the sealing is completed and the destructive forces of the seven last plagues are to be unleashed. The sealed 144,000 are about to go through the great tribulation.

Who are the 144,000? The context shows that they are God's people living just before the end. Since Revelation is a symbolic book, 144,000 should not be taken as a literal number (cf. Rev. 1:1). In apocalyptic literature, numbers regularly connote a symbolic meaning. The number 144,000 is made of 12 multiplied by 12, giving 144, and then multiplied by 1,000. In the Bible, the number twelve functions as a symbol of the church. In the Old Testament, twelve is the number of tribes in Israel, who are God's people. In the New Testament, it is also the number of the church built upon the foundation of the twelve apostles (Eph. 2:20). In the vision of the New Jerusalem, John observed the names of the twelve tribes of Israel inscribed on the twelve gates of the city and the names of the twelve apostles inscribed on its twelve foundation stones. Thus, 144, made from 12 times 12, stands for the totality of God's end-time people, not a selected group that is separated from the body of Christ.

The number 144,000 is as much symbolic as the 200 million in Satan's army in Revelation 9:16. Both numbers are mentioned in connection with the four angels (Rev. 7:1; 9:15) and in the context of the end time. In both cases, John uses the phrase: "I heard the number of . . ." (7:4; 9:16). This is the only place in the book where the two numbers are referred to in this manner.

The Twelve Tribes of Israel (7:5–8)

Like the number 144,000, the twelve tribes of Israel are not literal for at least two reasons. First, the twelve tribes of Israel do not exist today. During the Assyrian conquest of the northern kingdom of Israel, the ten tribes were taken into captivity (2 Kings 17:6–23). They soon became amalgamated with other nations and disappeared. The two remaining tribes, Judah and Benjamin, were later taken into captivity in Babylon. They later returned to Palestine and were known as Jews in the New Testament era. With the destruction of Jerusalem in AD 70, the Jews were scattered throughout the Roman Empire, and thus, even these two remaining tribes lost their national existence. Judaism today does not represent all twelve tribes.

Second, the list of the twelve tribes in Revelation 7 is not a regular list of the tribes of Israel. For example, Judah is listed as the first tribe instead of Reuben. The obvious reason for this is that Jesus came from this tribe (Rev. 5:5). The tribes of Dan and Ephraim are missing, while Joseph and Levi are included instead. This shows that Revelation 7 does not refer to the historical tribes of Israel. The list here is theological rather than historical.

The reason for the exclusion of Dan is because this tribe was the first to turn to idolatry (Judg. 18:27–32). Later in Israel's history, the tribe of Dan became a center of idolatrous worship, competing with the temple worship in Jerusalem (1 Kings 12:28–31). The Jews of John's day believed that the Antichrist would come out of the tribe of Dan.[2] This is also the reason for the exclusion of Ephraim. This tribe in the Old Testament is the symbol of apostasy and idolatry (2 Chron. 30:1, 10; Hosea 4:17; 8:11). The psalmist describes the people of Ephraim as the ones who "did not keep the covenant of God and refused to walk in His law" (Ps. 78:10).

These are the most likely reasons why Dan and Ephraim are excluded from the eschatological list of Israel's tribes in Revelation 7. The 144,000 are the true Israel that remains loyal to God. These members have washed their robes in the blood of the Lamb (Rev. 7:14). They are sealed and belong to God; they have not "been defiled with women" (14:1–5)—women being a symbol for apostate churches. The unfaithfulness that characterized the tribes of Dan and Ephraim has no place among the sealed people of God. Only those who are faithful to God will be able to stand before God's throne and receive their eternal inheritance (7:14–17).

The twelve tribes in Revelation 7 stand for the whole people of God. The church in the New Testament is referred to in terms of the twelve tribes of Israel (James 1:1). Paul calls the church "the Israel of God" (Gal. 6:16); Christians are Abraham's seed and the heirs of the covenant promises (3:29). The 144,000, consisting of 12,000 from each of the 12 tribes, symbolize God's people right before the end. This is the group that is sealed and is ready to enter the great tribulation of the seven last plagues. They are, however, protected by the seal of God upon their foreheads.

The 144,000 as the Church Militant

In describing God's end-time people standing on the threshold of the great tribulation, Revelation uses the language of war. The 144,000 are portrayed as an army modeled after ancient Israel going to war. Their number is made of twelve times twelve times one thousand. In the Old Testament war scenes, one thousand (Hebrew 'eleph) is a basic military unit (Num. 31:3–6; 1 Sam. 8:12; 22:7). The 144,000 consist of 12 tribes, each having 12 military units of 1,000 and a total of 12,000 soldiers. The 12 tribes, thus, give a total of 144,000 soldiers. So the symbolic number 144,000 symbolizes an army of 144 military units ready to go to battle against Satan and his army of 200 million (Rev. 9:16). Revelation 19:18 shows that Satan's army is also organized into military units of one thousand (the Greek word chiliarchos denotes a commander of 1,000 soldiers; also in 6:15).

Thus, the number 144,000 is a symbolic reference to the church militant, which is organized like ancient Israel into military units about to enter the final and greatest battle in the world's history: the battle of Armageddon (cf. Rev. 16:16). While the symbolic seal identifies them as those who are on God's side in the final conflict, it also protects them from the righteous judgments of God that are about to fall on the wicked.

The Great Multitude (7:9–17)

Having heard the number of God's sealed people, John sees a great multitude that nobody can count, from every nation, tribe, people, and tongue. They are all dressed in white and standing before the Lamb and the throne, praising God and the Lamb for their salvation. Many Christians view the 144,000 as the end-time generation of Christians, who will go through the great tribulation of the seven last plagues and will, as such, assume a special status in God's kingdom. They further assume that, in contrast to the 144,000, the Great Multitude are God's people from all ages.

However, Revelation 7 does not support such an assertion. John makes it very clear that the Great Multitude is also the last generation of God's people. Notice that, in Revelation 7:9, John sees the Great Multitude in white robes before the throne of God. Later, one of the elders explains to him that those in white robes are the ones who have come out of the great tribulation (Rev. 7:14). They have washed their robes in the blood of the Lamb and now stand before the throne of

God, serving Him day and night in His temple (7:15). This shows that the Great Multitude is the last generation of God's people—the ones who will go through the great tribulation of the seven last plagues.

As we interpret this group, we must keep in mind a literary feature used many times in Revelation. This feature is characterized by an "I heard" and "I saw" pattern. Often, John hears about something in the vision. Later, he sees what he has heard about under a different symbol and from a different perspective. For instance, in Revelation 5:5, John hears that the Lion from the tribe of Judah has overcome. However, what he sees a few moments later is the Lamb as slain (Rev. 5:6). The Lion and the Lamb are both symbols of Christ: the Lion shows what Christ did, and the Lamb shows how He did it. Also, in Revelation 17:1, John hears of the great prostitute sitting on many waters. In Revelation 17:3, he sees the prostitute sitting upon the beast. Waters and the beast are both symbols of political and secular powers in the world (cf. 17:15).

This is the situation we find in Revelation 7. John hears that the number of God's sealed people is 144,000. However, when he actually sees them, they appear to him as a great, incalculable crowd. This shows that the 144,000 and the Great Multitude are one and the same group of God's end-time people in different times and circumstances.

To further explain this, in Revelation 7:1–4, the 144,000 are being sealed as the winds are being restrained. The winds are not to be unleashed as long as the sealing is in process. When the sealing is done, the winds are unleashed (Rev. 7:3) and the seven last plagues are poured upon rebellious humanity. The sealed 144,000 must now go through the great tribulation of the seven last plagues. However, John does not see them at this point; he only hears that they have been sealed. When he actually sees them, they are coming out of the great tribulation as a great, incalculable multitude. They stand before God's throne, celebrating the great victory with palm branches in their hands (7:10), and are about to receive their reward (7:15–17).

The 144,000 are portrayed as the church militant, organized into 144 military divisions and entering the final war of this world's history. The Great Multitude, on the other hand, is portrayed as the church triumphant, coming out of that war and celebrating the victory. The war is over, and they are no longer organized into military divisions. They appear to John as a multitude that is impossible to count. The reason that they cannot be counted is not because of their huge number, but because they appear to him as a crowd impossible to count in contrast to the 144,000, who can easily be numbered, because they are organized into 144 units of 1,000.

At this point, we might ask: since the 144,000 are the last generation of believers, what about the Great Multitude? Are they composed of all God's people throughout history? It is important to keep in mind that the purpose of Revelation 7 is to provide the answer to the question raised in Revelation 6:17: "The great day of His wrath has come, and who is able to stand?" The focus of chapter 7 is on the last generation of God's people rather than on God's people in general. God's people in their totality are portrayed in Revelation 19:1–9.

Who Are the 144,000?

We have seen so far that Revelation 7 portrays God's end-time people from two different perspectives. First, they are portrayed as the sealed 144,000 standing on the threshold of the great tribulation of the seven last plagues. As such, they are able to stand on the great day of God's wrath (Rev. 6:17). Second, they are also portrayed as the Great Multitude coming out of the great tribulation. Their earthly journey is over, and they are now standing before the throne of God in His temple. God promises that He "will tabernacle over them" (7:15). By using the language concerning Israel, God tells them that their wilderness experience is over. They will no longer experience hunger, thirst, and the sun's heat (7:16–17). These are part of the plagues during the great tribulation. The Lamb now shepherds them and leads them to springs containing the water of life, where they finally find their homeland. God further promises that He will wipe every tear from their eyes (cf. 21:4).

Remember that Revelation 7 does not explain who the 144,000 are but what they are. All we can know is that they are the last generation of God's saved people. They are the ones who have washed their robes and made them white in the blood of the Lamb (Rev. 7:14). Their salvation is the result of what Christ has done for them, rather than the product of their own holiness and works. "For by grace you have been saved through faith; and that not of yourselves, it is the gift of God; not as a result of works, so that no one may boast" (Eph. 2:8–9).

It is important to keep in mind that Revelation does not support the idea that God has two different groups of saved people on earth. The Bible nowhere teaches that at the time of the end God will have His final generation of saints who will reach a level of holiness unattainable by those who lived before them. The 144,000 are not a select group, separated from the rest of God's people and granted special privileges not available to the rest of the redeemed. The 144,000 are not the only ones who were persecuted; they are not the first to be sealed; they are not the only ones who are redeemed; and they are not the first to be found blameless before the throne. In God's kingdom, all of God's people are, without distinction, promised white robes (Rev. 3:4–5; 6:11; 19:8). This makes them all equal before God. In God's kingdom, there are no clans or ranks; no privileges are available to some and not to others.

In Revelation 14:1–5, we will see some additional characteristics of the 144,000, in the context of the final crisis.

God's people are warned against being involved in "controversy over questions which will not help them spiritually, such as, who is to compose the hundred and forty-four thousand? This those who are the elect of God will in a short time know without question."[3] Yet, we are urged to "strive with all the power that God has given us to be among the hundred and forty-four thousand."[4]

The Seven Trumpets (Part 1)

 Revelation 8:2–13

Revelation 8:2 begins a new vision with seven angels blowing trumpets. At the trumpets' sound, a chain of events is unleashed upon the earth. When interpreting this section, remember the symbolic language of Revelation. As in the other visions, the symbolism of the seven trumpets is rooted in the Old Testament.

Blowing trumpets is a well-known concept in the Old Testament. The life of Israel as a nation was ordered by trumpet blasts. There are several Hebrew words that are translated as "trumpet," two of which are used most frequently in the Old Testament. *Chatsotserah* were trumpets made of hammered metal and were regularly blown by priests to summon the people, to announce religious festivals, as an alarm in times of war, and as a signal for the temple services (see Num. 10:2–10). *Shofar* was a trumpet made from a ram's horn and was used to signal.

Numbers 10:8–10 is the key Old Testament text that unlocks the theological meaning of the trumpets. The passage portrays trumpets as sacred instruments. They were, as a rule, used by priests in different contexts: worship, battles, harvest time, or festivals. They were blown for the purpose of calling on God to remember His covenant with His people. When the priests blew the trumpets over the sacrifices in the temple, God would remember His people and forgive their sins. During the festivals, the trumpet sound was a reminder to God of His covenant promise to be with His people and bless them. In battle, the trumpet sound would remind God to help His people. During the time of King Abijah, the people of Judah found themselves surrounded by an enemy army and "they cried to the LORD, and the priests blew the trumpets" (2 Chron. 13:14). The Lord responded by delivering them from their enemies.

Blowing trumpets went hand in hand with prayer. As the priests blew the trumpets, God's people prayed. As they prayed, God would step in to help them in their distress, whether by defending them from their enemies or by delivering them from their sins. This concept is crucial for understanding the trumpet symbolism in Revelation 8–11.

In the Old Testament, trumpets are also associated with important events in Israel's history, such as the giving of the law at Mount Sinai (Exod. 19:16; 20:18) and the destruction of Jericho (Josh. 6:4–16). Ultimately, the trumpet sound will announce the approach of the Day of the Lord (Isa. 27:13; Joel 2:1; Zeph. 1:16; Zech. 9:14). Similarly, in the New Testament, the trumpet signals the coming of Christ, which will bring deliverance to the faithful and judgment to the unfaithful (Matt. 24:31; 1 Cor. 15:52; 1 Thess. 4:16).

The Prayers of the Saints (8:2–6)

In dealing with this section, we must remember a special literary feature that is repeated several times in the book. As John the Revelator begins a new description of things he sees, he suddenly interrupts it by inserting another scene with different content.[1] The inserted scene is intercalated, or sandwiched, between the opening statement and the remaining part of the vision.

Revelation 8:3–5 is an interlude couched between verses 2 and 6. Verse 2 describes seven angels with trumpets standing before God. It is not until verse 6 that the angels are commissioned to blow their trumpets. Between are verses 3 to 5, which depict a scene that takes place in the sanctuary setting:

> [2]And I saw the seven angels who stand before God, and seven trumpets were given to them. [3]And another angel came, having a golden censer, and stood upon the altar, and much incense was given to him that he might offer it with the prayers of all the saints on the golden altar before the throne. [4]And the smoke of the incense with the prayers of the saints ascended before God from the hand of the angel. [5]And the angel took the censer and filled it with the fire from the altar and cast it to the earth; and there were peals of thunder and sounds and flashes of lightning and an earthquake. [6]And the seven angels who

had the seven trumpets prepared themselves that they might sound.

Here, John observes seven angels with trumpets ready to herald the judgments that will fall upon the earth's inhabitants. Before the angels blow the trumpets, another unspecified angel appears holding a golden censer. He stands upon the altar,[2] which is evidently the altar of sacrifice.[3] The altar of sacrifice was located in the outer court. In Biblical typology, the outer court stands for the earth (cf. Rev. 11:2). This shows that the scene in Revelation 8:3–5 begins on earth.

At the altar, the angel is given "much incense" (Rev. 8:3). He takes the incense into the Holy Place and offers it with the prayers of the saints upon the golden altar before the throne of God. "The smoke of the incense with the prayers of the saints ascended before God from the hand of the angel" (8:4). Afterward, the angel fills the censer with fire from the golden altar and hurls it to the earth. Throwing the censer filled with fire produces "thunder and sounds and flashes of lightning and an earthquake" (8:5). This is the signal for the seven angels to blow their trumpets.

This scene reflects the daily services in the earthly temple.[4] After the sacrificial lamb had been placed upon the altar of sacrifice, the blood was poured out at the base of the altar. The appointed priest would take a golden censer and fill it with coals from the altar. He would then take incense into the temple and offer it upon the golden altar in the Holy Place. Having offered the incense, the priest would come out of the temple and throw the censer down on the pavement between the altar of sacrifice and the entrance of the temple, producing a very loud noise. At that moment, seven priests blew trumpets, marking the end of the daily services.

This hurling the censer filled with fire upon rebellious humanity also mirrors the scene in Ezekiel's vision in which the man clothed in linen takes coals of fire from between the cherubim and hurls them upon Jerusalem because of its sins (Ezek. 10:2). Ezekiel's vision shows that the act of hurling fiery coals upon the earth in Revelation 8:5 denotes judgment.

The symbolic act in Revelation 8:3–5—replicating the daily services in the earthly temple—gives insight into the meaning of the seven trumpets. The incense the angel burns upon the golden altar represents the prayers of God's people (Rev. 5:8; cf. Ps. 141:2). This incense originated from the altar of sacrifices, underneath which, in the fifth seal, the blood of the martyred saints prays to God for judgment "upon those who dwell on earth" (Rev. 6:10). This shows that the incense the angel ministers before God represents the prayers of God's suffering people. Now, judgment will fall on "those who dwell on the earth" in answer to the prayers of the slain saints, found in the fifth seal scene (8:13).

The seven trumpets refer to God's intervention in history in response to the prayers of His oppressed people. The trumpets' sound heralds God's judgment against those who have harmed His people. Yet, they are not God's final word to the wicked. While punitive in purpose, these judgments are mixed with mercy. Their purpose is to give warnings to the earth's inhabitants concerning the Day of Judgment to save them before it is too late.

What time in history do the seven trumpets refer to? The daily services of the earthly temple give us a clue to the beginning of the seven trumpets' sounding. In the earthly temple, the trumpets were sounded after the sacrifice had been offered upon the altar. By following this pattern, the sounding of the seven trumpets began after Jesus's death on the cross. They occur while Jesus intercedes in heaven (8:3–5) and the gospel is preached (10:8–11:14). The trumpets, thus, concern the Christian age—from the cross to the Second Coming, until the seventh trumpet sounds and God establishes His kingdom (11:15–18).

The trumpets cover the same span of history as the seven seals. The two series correspond both structurally and sequentially:

The Seven Seals	The Seven Trumpets
The four horsemen	The first four trumpets
The fifth and sixth seals	The fifth and sixth trumpets
Interlude (Rev. 7)	Interlude (Rev. 10:1–11:14)
The seventh seal	The seventh trumpet

Sequentially, the seals and the trumpets both begin in the first century, following the death of Jesus on the cross and His ascension into heaven. The conclusion of both series brings this book to the time of the end. Structurally, the two series are subdivided into groups of four and three with interludes between the sixth and seventh segments. While the interlude between the sixth and seventh seals describes

God's end-time people, the interlude between the sixth and seventh trumpets describes their experience and role during the end time.

The difference between the two series lies in their focus. While the seals primarily concern those who profess to be God's people, however unfaithful they are to the gospel, the trumpets exclusively concern those who do not profess to belong to God. Yet, God wants both groups to be saved. He wants to win them over before the door of salvation is closed.

The First Four Trumpets (8:7–13)

The prayers of God's suffering people have been heard. The seven angels are ready to blow the trumpets. We are told that the judgments of the seven trumpets affect a third of the earth. In Ezekiel's (Ezek. 5:12–13) and Zechariah's (Zech. 13:8–9) prophesies, judgments against apostate Israel are described as affecting one-third of the nation. In Revelation 12, the tail of the dragon (Satan) sweeps away a third of the stars in heaven, which is a figurative way of saying that a number of the angels joined Satan in his rebellion against God. Also, end-time Babylon splits into three parts under God's judgments (Rev. 16:19). All these verses show that the phrase "a third" in the scene of the seven trumpets refers to one part of Satan's kingdom being affected by divine judgments:

> 7And the first angel sounded his trumpet; and there were hail and fire mixed with blood, and they were hurled down to the earth; and a third of the earth was burned up, and a third of the trees were burned up, and all green grass was burned up.
>
> 8And the second angel sounded his trumpet; and something like a great mountain burning with fire was cast into the sea; and a third of the sea became blood, 9and a third of the creatures which were in the sea, which had life, died, and a third of the ships were destroyed.
>
> 10And the third angel sounded his trumpet; and a great star burning like a torch fell from heaven, and it fell upon a third of the rivers and the springs of water. 11And the name of the star is called "Wormwood"; and a third of the waters became wormwood, and many people died from the waters, because they were made bitter.

> *¹²And the fourth angel sounded his trumpet; and a third of the sun and a third of the moon and a third of the stars were stricken, so that a third of them became darkened and the day did not brighten for a third of it, and the night likewise.*
>
> *¹³And I looked, and I heard a vulture flying in mid-heaven, saying with a loud voice: "Woe, woe, woe to those who dwell on the earth because of the rest of the trumpet sounds of the three angels who are about to sound."*

The seven trumpets herald God's judgments against historical, oppressive powers. They occur in pairs, complementing each other.

The First Trumpet (8:7)

When the first angel blows the trumpet, hail and fire mixed with blood are hurled upon the earth. One-third of the earth and the trees as well as all the green grass is burned up. This scene recalls the seventh plague upon Egypt, which killed humans and animals in the field and destroyed the plants and trees also in the field (Exod. 9:23–25).

In the Old Testament, God used hail mixed with fire, which caused bloodshed, as His means of judgment against the enemies of His people (cf. Isa. 30:30; Ezek. 38:22–23). In the Bible, trees and grass are frequently symbols for God's people.[5] Thus, hail and fire mixed with blood, which destroy the trees and green grass, symbolize God's judgment against apostate believers, who have joined the ranks of God's opponents (cf. Jer. 11:16; Ezek. 20:47).

While addressing the Jewish leaders, John the Baptist stated that every person who does not bear fruit would be cut down like a tree and thrown into the fire (Matt. 3:10; cf. 7:17–19). Jesus used the same symbolism with reference to the inhabitants of Jerusalem: "For if they do these when the tree is green, what will happen when it is dry?" (Luke 23:31). Jesus refers to Himself as the green tree, and those who rejected Him as dry trees. When Jesus is treated in such a harsh way, what will happen to the nation that rejects Him and treats Him harshly? Therefore Jesus was symbolically referring to the destruction of Jerusalem by the Romans, which took place several decades later (cf. 21:20).

Thus, the first trumpet heralds judgment upon those of God's people who were involved in persecuting Christ and the early church. While many Jews accepted Christ, most of them, with their leaders, rejected Him and became opponents of the gospel. As a result, they placed themselves outside the protection offered by the covenant. Now they are the first ones to experience the consequences of rejecting the covenant. Judgment begins with the house of God (1 Pet. 4:17; cf. Ezek. 9). Just as hail and fire were used as God's judgments against the enemies of Israel in the Old Testament, so the sounding of the first trumpet heralds judgment in terms of "hail and fire mixed with blood" against God's people who rejected the covenant and turned into the oppressors and persecutors of Christ's followers (Rev. 8:7). The first trumpet, thus, aptly portrays the demise of the Jewish nation at the destruction of Jerusalem by the Romans in AD 70.

The Second Trumpet (8:8–9)

At the sound of the second trumpet, something resembling a great burning mountain is cast into the sea. A third of the sea turns into blood, killing a third of the sea creatures and wrecking a third of the ships.

Mountains in the Old Testament often represent kingdoms or empires that are under God's judgments.[6] Here, the mountain is described as "great" to denote an essential quality of the empire—it is a great empire. This scene alludes to the prophecy of Jeremiah that refers to Babylon as a "destroying mountain" (Jer. 51:25) to be judged for its cruelty against Judah (51:24). Babylon will be a "burning mountain" (51:25) cast into the Euphrates River to sink and rise no more (Jer. 51:63–64). The same language is used in Revelation 18:21 to describe the demise of end-time Babylon.

Jeremiah's prophecy provides the key to unlocking the symbolism of the second trumpet. In John's day, Babylon symbolically represented the Roman Empire. Because Rome, like Babylon, destroyed Jerusalem and the temple, it was to suffer Babylon's fate.[7] Peter used the term "Babylon" as a cryptic name for Rome (1 Pet. 5:13). The Christians during John's time, who viewed Rome as the new Babylon, could easily identify the symbolic burning mountain of the second trumpet as a prophecy of the Roman Empire's downfall. Turning the sea into blood and destroying the ships echo the first plague against Egypt, which turned the waters into blood and destroyed the fish. The sea in the Bible frequently symbolizes people who are violently opposed to God (Isa. 17:12–13; 57:20; Jer. 51:42). Destroying ships refers to the subjugation of human pride (Ezek. 27:29–32; Rev. 18:17–21). Here again, the phrase "a third" shows that a part of Satan's kingdom is affected by God's judgment.

The scenes of the first two trumpets, thus, herald God's judgments on the two nations involved in putting Jesus to death and persecuting the early church, in an attempt to prevent the spreading of the gospel to the world. The third and fourth trumpets chronologically follow the first two.

The Third Trumpet (8:10–11)

When the third trumpet is blown, a great, blazing star falls from heaven onto a third of the rivers and the springs of water. A third of the waters turn bitter and cause many people to die. Stars in the Bible often represent angels (Job 38:7; Rev. 1:20). The fact that this star is characterized as "great" shows that a particular angel of an exalted rank is referenced here. This points to Isaiah 14:12–15, which depicts Satan as the "star of the morning," fallen from heaven. Later in Revelation, John describes Satan as the head of the fallen angels, who was cast from heaven to earth (12:9).

The star is named Wormwood, after an herb notorious for its bitter and poisonous qualities (Deut. 29:18). The Wormwood star turns the waters bitter, causing many to die. In Jeremiah, when the people of Israel turned away from God and spurned the covenant, they were given wormwood to eat and poisoned water to drink (Jer. 9:13–15; 23:15).

The rivers and springs of water symbolize spiritual nourishment (the Word of God and salvation) for spiritually thirsty people. Satan turns the gospel into "wormwood" by producing false teachings and human traditions. The scene of the third trumpet shows Satan polluting the springs and streams of truth and salvation with human teachings, causing them to have a poisonous and deadly effect.

If the second trumpet concerns the collapse of the Roman Empire, then the third trumpet concerns the time after the Roman Empire. Paul warned early Christians of the approaching apostasy, when false teachers would pervert the gospel and introduce false teachings into the church (Acts 20:26–31; 2 Tim. 4:3–4). He also predicted a great apostasy that would invade the church (2 Thess. 2:1–12). However, the apostasy would not come until the restrainer—the Roman Empire—was removed (2:7).

After the collapse of the Roman Empire, the world was plunged into the Middle Ages. During this period, mainstream Christianity departed from the apostolic gospel and perverted the teaching of the Bible. Corrupted doctrines crept into the church, replacing the Bible with tradition and scholastic teachings. The gospel truth was polluted and perverted into a system of dogmas, with devastating effects. The institutional church promoted sinful practices that were contrary to the Bible. Therefore, the third trumpet describes the medieval apostasy and its consequences—the spiritual death of many who drank from its polluted and poisonous water.

The Fourth Trumpet (8:12)

The plague of the fourth trumpet strikes a third of the sun, moon, and stars, causing darkness on a third of the earth. This scene evokes the ninth plague, which brought darkness upon the land in Egypt (Exod. 10:21–23). In the Old Testament, the darkening of celestial bodies announces the coming of God's judgment (Isa. 13:9–11; Ezek. 32:7–8; Joel 3:15). Darkness is also a symbol of judgment against apostasy (Mic. 3:6).

Light, in the New Testament, stands for the gospel (Col. 1:13; 1 Pet. 2:9). Jesus is the true light; those who believe in Him will not be in darkness (John 8:12; 12:46). Darkness is, thus, the absence of the gospel. When people reject the gospel and choose the darkness, they bring God's judgment upon themselves: "This is the judgment, that the Light has come into the world, and men loved the darkness rather than the Light" (John 3:19).

The fourth trumpet best describes the condition of the world during the period that followed the Middle Ages. The Reformation of the sixteenth century rediscovered the gospel and restored the Bible as the rule of faith and teaching. However, the vibrant generation of reformers was succeeded by a lifeless generation, known for Protestant Scholasticism, which was characterized by theological polemics and controversies. Christianity became less of a personal relationship with Christ and more of a membership in the official church. This situation had a deadly effect upon Christianity.

The Reformation marked the end of religion's dominance over the minds of people and the beginning of the intellectual revolution in Europe during the seventeenth and eighteenth centuries. The Enlightenment period, or the Age of Reason, ended the dominance of Christian faith in the Western world. While this situation led to the rise of rationalism, skepticism, humanism, and liberalism, it ultimately gave birth to secularism. Despite its positive impact on science, politics, religious liberty, arts, and education, secularism's materialistic orientation, denial of supernaturalism, and skepticism toward faith of any kind allowed human reason to replace the Bible's authority. The negative aspects of secularism gradually eroded Christian faith and robbed millions of the hope of salvation.

The fourth trumpet might, thus, describe how the spiritual source of the true light was darkened under the prevailing influence of secularism. The singular effect of the fourth trumpet plague is the partial darkening (one-third) of the spiritual light sources. The deepening of that darkness and its dreadful consequences become evident in the following period, portrayed in the fifth and sixth trumpet scenes.

The Seven Trumpets (Part 2)

 Revelation 9:1–21

Before the fifth angel blows his trumpet, John hears a vulture announcing a triple woe, warning the earth's inhabitants that more severe punishments will come (Rev. 8:13). In the Bible, the vulture is a symbol of impending judgments (Deut. 28:49; Hos. 8:1). Here, the text brings to mind the words of Jesus: "Wherever the corpse is, there the vultures will gather" (Matt. 24:28). The worst is yet to come for the earth's inhabitants.

The Fifth Trumpet (9:1–12)

The description of the plagues heralded by the fifth and sixth angels is more detailed and frightening:

> *¹And the fifth angel sounded his trumpet; and I saw a star fallen from heaven to the earth, and the key of the pit of the abyss was given to him. ²And he opened the pit of the abyss, and smoke came up from the abyss like smoke of a great furnace, and the sun and the air became darkened by the smoke of the abyss. ³And locusts came out of the smoke on the earth, and power was given to them, as scorpions of the earth have power. ⁴And it was said to them not to hurt the grass of earth nor any green thing nor any tree, except the men who do not have the seal of God upon their foreheads. ⁵And it was given to them not to kill them but that they should be tormented for five months; and their torment was as the torment of a scorpion when it stings a person. ⁶And in those days, people will seek death, and they will in no way find it, and*

they will long to die, and death will flee from them.
⁷And the appearance of the locusts was similar to horses prepared for battle, and upon their heads were as crowns of gold, and their faces were like human faces. ⁸And they had hair as the hair of women, and their teeth were as of lions, ⁹and they had breastplates as breastplates of iron, and the sound of their wings was as the sound of chariots of many horses running into battle. ¹⁰And they had tails like scorpions and stingers, and the authority in their tails was to torment the people for five months. ¹¹They have a king over them, the angel of the abyss, whose name in Hebrew is Abaddon, and in Greek, his name is Apollyon.
¹²The first woe has passed; behold, two woes are still to come.

At the sound of the fifth trumpet, a star falls to the earth. This is the same star found in the third trumpet that poisoned the streams and springs of water (Rev. 8:10–11). It is Satan himself, "the prince of the power of the air" (Eph. 2:2). Later in the text, he is identified as the angel of the abyss and the leader of the demonic army (9:11). In Hebrew, his name is Abaddon (destruction) and, in Greek, Apollyon (destroyer).

The star is given a key to open the abyss. When it is opened, John sees smoke composed of locusts arising out of the abyss. These locusts have power like scorpions—a biblical symbol of demons (see Luke 10:17–20). The abyss is the abode of Satan and the fallen angels (Luke 8:31) since their expulsion from heaven (Rev. 12:7–9). They are temporarily confined there until they receive their punishment (2 Pet. 2:4; Jude 6).[1] In the fifth trumpet, however, Christ removes His restraining hand from the demonic forces, giving them more freedom to do their harmful work.

This gigantic cloud of locusts arising from the abyss creates thick darkness in the sky. This is reminiscent of the plague in Egypt where locusts darkened the sky (Exod. 10:15). The scene also echoes the prophecy of Joel in which the locust plague caused the sun, moon, and stars to darken (Joel 2:2, 10). By using the symbol of a locust plague, John describes the supernatural demonic forces that will operate in the world as the end of time nears.

The appearance of the demonic locusts is terrifying. In describing them, John uses eight figurative analogies (Rev. 9:7–10): their appearance is like horses ready for battle; they wear golden crowns; they have human faces and hair like women; their teeth are like those of lions; they have iron-like breastplates; the sound of their wings is like that of battle chariots; and they have tails like scorpions, which they use to sting. This symbolic description of the demonic locusts uses terms similar to those in Joel 2:2–11.

As in Joel, the demonic locusts of the fifth trumpet resemble an army. Yet, they are not a real army. Their meaning is not militant but spiritual. Their weapons are their scorpion-like tails, which they use to afflict people (Rev. 9:10). In the Bible, the tail is a symbol of deception, which Satan uses to turn people away from God and toward himself. Isaiah refers to false prophets deceiving people with their false teachings in terms of "the tail" (Isa. 9:14–15). It is the tail of the dragon that caused one-third of the heavenly beings to rebel against God (Rev. 12:4, 9).

Notice that the demonic locusts first create darkness (Rev. 9:2). Darkness is the opposite of light. The light stands for the gospel; the darkness symbolizes the absence of the gospel (see the fourth trumpet). The demonic locusts of the fifth trumpet obliterate the light of the gospel, replacing it with rationalism and human philosophies that have become the ultimate standard of truth. As a result, Christ has been extinguished from the lives of most people in the world. What follows is spiritual torment and mental anguish of devastating effects. The demonic locusts are not permitted to kill people, only to torment them with their venom. Their torment is clearly spiritual and mental, driving a great number of people into suicidal anguish. People seek death but cannot find it (9:6).

The period allotted to the demonic locusts to torment people is five months (Rev. 9:5). Five months was also the period of the Flood; during this time, Noah and his family were under divine protection, so the floodwaters could not harm them (Gen. 7:24; 8:3). Like Noah and his family, God's people will be protected from the torment of demonic forces. Remember that the trumpet plagues concern those who have rejected the gospel. The demonic locusts are not allowed to harm the grass, any plant, or any tree, which are symbols of God's people (see the first trumpet). These locusts can harm only those who do not have the seal of God on their foreheads (Rev. 9:4), while God's people are protected from the locusts' harmful activities by God's seal.

The fifth trumpet describes the spiritual condition of the world in the aftermath of the Enlightenment, which was characterized by the rise of rationalism, skepticism, humanism, relativism, and liberalism. Ultimately, it gave rise to secularism and its negative effects on Christianity. God-centered theology was replaced by atheistic, human-centered philosophy, which has little or no room for God.[2] This atheistic philosophy has alienated people from God and from each other, creating the agony of emptiness and meaninglessness in their lives. This contrasts with the green grass and trees that are nourished by water.

Although they have separated themselves from God, secular people still have a longing for spiritual values to fill the emptiness in their lives. However, resistance to the transforming power of the gospel provides an opportunity for Satan and his demonic forces to fill this emptiness. The situation in Israel, as described by Amos, best illustrates the spiritual condition in the world today, which the fifth trumpet also symbolizes. When Israel "turned justice into poison and the fruit of righteousness into wormwood" (Amos 6:12), God brought swarms of locusts upon their land. By rejecting the gospel, the people in the world are left defenseless against demonic activities.

The only security for humanity is in Christ and the gospel. Any religion apart from Christ, including one that is based largely on emotions, does not supply the needs of the world. What secular people need today is a clear understanding of the gospel, which alone can fill the emptiness in their lives and protect them from the torment caused by supernatural forces.

The woe of the fifth trumpet is frightening; however, the worst is yet to come as the sixth and seventh trumpets sound.

The Sixth Trumpet (9:13–21)

[13]And the sixth angel sounded his trumpet; and I heard a voice from the horns of the golden altar, which is before God, [14]saying to the sixth angel who had the trumpet: "Release the four angels who are bound at the great river Euphrates." [15]And the four angels, the ones who were prepared for the hour and day and month and year, were released that they might kill a third of humankind. [16]And the number of the army of horsemen was 200 million; I heard the number of them. [17]And thus I saw the horses in the vision and those sitting upon them: having breastplates of fire and hyacinth and sulfur, and the heads of

the horses were as heads of lions, and out of their mouths were coming fire and smoke and sulfur. ¹⁸From these three plagues were killed a third of humankind, from the fire and the smoke and the sulfur coming out of their mouths. ¹⁹For the authority of the horses is in their mouths and in their tails, for their tails are like snakes, having heads, and with them they cause harm.

²⁰And the rest of the people, the ones who were not killed by these plagues, did not repent of the works of their hands, so as not to worship the demons and the idols of gold and of silver and of brass and of stone and of wood, which can neither see nor hear nor walk; ²¹and they did not repent of their murders or their sorceries or their fornication or their thefts.

When the sixth angel blows his trumpet, John hears a voice from the golden altar of incense in the Holy Place of the heavenly temple ordering the sixth trumpet angel to release the four angels bound on the banks of the Euphrates River. The fact that the sixth trumpet scene is initiated from the altar of incense shows that the prayers of God's people are still remembered and that the door of salvation is still open; people have an opportunity to repent and accept Christ and the gospel (Rev. 8:3–4).

The Euphrates River in the Old Testament was the boundary that separated God's people from their enemies (Isa. 7:20; Jer. 46:10). The enemies of God's people came from this great river. The attack by these enemy nations was described in terms of the overflowing Euphrates's waters sweeping the land of Judah (Isa. 8:7–8).

The four angels were prepared to release demonic powers for an appointed hour, day, month, and year to kill one-third of humankind. The divinely appointed time has come for the evil forces to be unleashed. Revelation 9:18–19 shows that the angels are not the ones doing the killing, but the demonic forces are. The demonic forces are not allowed to begin their harmful work until the time appointed by God. At the sound of the sixth trumpet, the restraining angels are ordered to unleash the demonic hordes to kill one-third of humanity.

At this point, a huge army of 200 million cavalry troops appears on the scene. Their number stands in contrast to the 144,000 of God's end-time people (Rev. 7:4). The demonic locusts that inflicted pain on humans in the fifth trumpet have now grown into a huge army that kills humans. In the fifth trumpet, they were not allowed to kill but only afflict people (9:4–6); now, they both kill and afflict those who are alive.

John has trouble describing the demonic cavalry. They appear similar to the horses in the fifth trumpet, yet their power increases. The riders on the horses have fiery red, smoky blue, and sulfurous yellow breastplates that are reflections of the fire, smoke, and sulfur emanating from the horses' mouths (Rev. 9:17). The appearance of the horses is terrifying. Their heads are like those of lions, and out of their mouths come fire, smoke, and sulfur, which kill humans in vast numbers. In the Old Testament, fire, smoke, and sulfur were a means of executing divine judgment (Ps. 11:6; Ezek. 38:22). They were used to destroy Sodom and Gomorrah (Gen. 19:24, 28; Luke 17:29). These will also be used for the destruction of the wicked at the final judgment (Rev. 14:10–11; 20:10; 21:8).

The power of the horses is in their mouths and tails. The tails mirror the tails of the demonic forces in the fifth trumpet (Rev. 9:10). While, in the fifth trumpet, the tails of the demonic forces are scorpion-like, in the sixth trumpet, they are serpent-like and are used to afflict the earth's inhabitants to the point of death. While they afflict people with their serpent-like tails, they kill with their mouths, from which fire, smoke, and sulfur emanate. The mouth in Revelation is a symbol of spiritual weaponry in the end-time battle between Christ and Satan (cf. 16:13–14; 19:15, 21). This shows that the nature of the final crisis is not physical or militant; rather, it is spiritual. It is a battle for the minds and hearts of humanity.

One may observe strong parallels between the sixth trumpet, Revelation 7:1–4, and Revelation 16:12–16. These three passages are linked. First, both the sixth trumpet and Revelation 7:1–4 mention four angels who restrain the plagues, which are about to come upon the earth's inhabitants. Both mention binding and releasing the destructive forces, and both use the phrase, "I heard the number" (Rev. 7:4; 9:16). Also, in both the sixth trumpet and Revelation 16:12–16, we find the Euphrates River, demonic activities, military language, and mouths used as weapons in the end-time conflict.

The parallels between the sixth trumpet and these two passages situate the sixth trumpet at the very time of the end. Similar to Revelation 16:12–16, the sixth trumpet describes the great gathering of Satan's army for the end-time battle of Armageddon. In Revelation 7:1–4, the four angels are holding back the winds of destruction. While the demonic forces are very active in the fifth trumpet by afflicting the earth's inhabitants, their power is still limited and restrained by God (Rev. 9:4–6). However, in the sixth trumpet scene, the supernatural forces are unleashed to do their harmful activities under the governance of Satan, "the angel of the abyss" (9:11).

Thus, the sixth trumpet is clearly at the time of the end, which is characterized by intense preparation for the battle of Armageddon. This is described further in Revelation 16:12–16. The sixth trumpet scene shows that the last crisis will be characterized by intensified demonic activity. People who have rejected the gospel and are without the seal of God are helpless against the demonic powers. Their failure to repent signals the approaching cessation of God's intercession and the gathering for the final battle between Christ and Satan and their armies (Rev. 16:13–16).

It is during these intense demonic activities that God makes a special effort to reach human hearts by offering the everlasting gospel to earth's inhabitants (Rev. 14:6–13). His mercies are still available. He hopes that sin-hardened hearts will respond and make a decisive turnaround.

The purpose of the sixth trumpet plague is to prompt the earth's inhabitants to acknowledge the true God before it is too late. However, the passage's concluding remarks show that the judgment of the sixth trumpet plague does not bring humanity to repentance. Instead, people continue to worship demons and their "idols of gold and of silver and of brass and of stone and of wood" (Rev. 9:20). This passage references the Babylonian gods (Dan. 5:23). Although tormented by demons, the unrepentant continue their ties with their self-made gods. In addition, they do not repent of the fruits of worshiping demons—murders, magic, immorality, and robbery. All these are the characteristics of those who do not follow the Lamb (Rev. 21:8; 22:15).

At this point, the sequence of the seven trumpets is interrupted. Before the seventh trumpet sounds and God establishes His kingdom, a question must be answered: What are God's people doing during this time? Revelation 10:1–11:14 answers this question. Just as the interlude between the sixth and seventh seals describes God's end-time people, the interlude between the sixth and seventh trumpets describes His people's experience and role as the end of this world approaches.

The Mighty Angel with the Scroll

 Revelation 10:1–11

The seven trumpets describe a series of God's interventions in history on behalf of His people. The first two trumpets herald judgment upon those who crucified Christ and persecuted the early church; the third and fourth trumpets call forth judgment upon the apostasy of the medieval and post-Reformation eras; and the fifth and sixth trumpets describe the condition of the secular world in the aftermath of the Age of Enlightenment, which is characterized by extensive demonic activity leading into the battle of Armageddon.

Now, it should be expected that the last angel would blow his trumpet to signal the time of the end. However, before the seventh trumpet sounds, an interlude interrupts the sequence (Rev. 10:1–11:14). This literary feature mirrors the interlude inserted between the sixth and seventh seal in chapter 7. The purpose of this interlude is twofold: first, it is used to describe the condition of God's people during the time of the end (10:1–7), and second, it is used to describe the mission of God's people during that time (10:8–11:14).

> ¹And I saw another strong angel coming down from heaven, clothed in a cloud, and a rainbow was over his head, and his face was like the sun and his feet like pillars of fire, ²and he had in his hand an opened little scroll. And he placed his right foot on the sea and his left on the land, ³and he cried with a loud voice, as a lion roars. And when he cried, the seven thunders uttered their voices. ⁴And when the seven thunders spoke, I was about to write; and I heard a voice from heaven saying: "Seal up the things which the seven thunders spoke,

and do not write them." ⁵And the angel whom I saw standing on the sea and on the land lifted up his right hand toward heaven ⁶and swore by the One who lives forever and ever, who created heaven and the things which are in it and the earth and the things which are in it and the sea and the things which are in it, that there will no longer be time, ⁷but in the days of the sound of the seventh angel, when he is about to sound, then the mystery of God will be completed, as He proclaimed to His servants the prophets.

⁸And the voice which I had heard from heaven spoke to me again, saying: "Go, take the scroll which is opened in the hand of the angel standing on the sea and on the land." ⁹And I went to the angel, telling him to give me the little scroll. And he said to me: "Take and eat it, and it will make your stomach bitter, but in your mouth, it will be sweet like honey." ¹⁰And I took the little scroll from the hand of the angel and ate it, and it was sweet like honey in my mouth; and when I ate it, my stomach was made bitter. ¹¹And they said to me: "You must prophesy again concerning many peoples and nations and tongues and kings."

The Angel with the Scroll (10:1–7)

John sees an angel of magnificent appearance descending from heaven. He is referred to as "another strong angel" to distinguish him from the seven angels who blew the trumpets (Rev. 10:1). The description of the angel resembles the description of Christ found in chapter 1—he is clothed with a cloud, a rainbow is above his head, his face is like the sun, and his feet are like pillars of fire (cf. 1:12–16). These descriptions are all symbolic images that refer to God in the Bible. This angel is closely associated with Christ and comes in the appearance and authority of Christ.

In his hand, the angel holds an opened little scroll. Many recent studies have shown that this scroll is related to the seven-sealed scroll in Revelation 5, which Christ the Lamb alone was worthy to possess and open. The scroll cannot be opened until all the seals are broken. The fact that the scroll in chapter 10 is referred to as "little" suggests that this could be a small portion of the scroll in chapter 5. This little scroll contains the description of the time of the end and the experience of God's people in the world during the last days, as portrayed in Revelation 12–22. Thus, chapters 12–22 of Revelation comprise the content of the little scroll. Christ has disclosed these things to God's people via the angel to prepare them for the coming final crisis of this world's history (cf. 1:1).

The angel places one foot on the land and the other on the sea, indicating the universal scope of the message to be proclaimed. What the angel is about to proclaim has special significance for the whole earth. He makes the proclamation with a loud voice that resembles a lion's roar. In the Old Testament, God's voice is frequently likened to a lion's roar (Hos. 11:10; Amos 3:8). This shows that the proclamation the angel is about to make comes from God and is a special message to His people.

The Seven Thunders (10:3–4)

As the angel starts to speak, John hears the seven thunders (Rev. 10:3). In the Bible, the voice of God is often equated with the sound of thunder (Job 37:5; John 12:28–30). In Psalm 29:3–9, the sevenfold voice of God is referred to as the sound of thunder. The seven thunders stand for the fullness of God's message—seven being the number of fullness. John is about to write what the thunders said, but he is told to seal up what he has heard and not write it down. This is very unusual, because elsewhere in Revelation he is instructed to write whatever is shown to him and not to seal up the messages of the book (Rev. 1:19; 22:10). However, this section is supposed to be kept a secret. The reason for this is that the message was obviously not relevant to God's people.

It is important to remember that "the secret things belong to the Lord our God, but the things revealed belong to us and to our sons forever, that we may observe all the words of this law" (Deut. 29:29). Every prophecy that is profitable for human salvation is revealed in the prophetic word. This is what is recorded in Revelation 12–22, so God's people may know what the future will bring. However, there are some things about the future that God has not revealed to humans, such as when and how the final events will take place. Although John heard these things, he was not allowed to write them in the book. So when studying end-time prophecies, it is important to not venture beyond what God intends to reveal to humans.

Time No Longer (10:5–7)

Now the angel who stands on the land and the sea lifts up his right hand toward heaven. This gesture indicates that he is about to make an oath. With a solemn voice, he swears by the One who is eternal and who created the heavens, the earth, and all that is in them that "there will no longer be time" (Rev. 10:6). And in the days of the sound of the seventh angel, the mystery of God will be completed, as was revealed to His servants the prophets (10:7).

This scene points to Daniel 12:4–10. Daniel was ordered to seal up the words of the scroll until the time of the end. Afterward, there is a question regarding how long it would be before the persecution of the saints is over and the prophesied events take place. In response, the heavenly messenger raises his hands toward heaven and swears an oath by the One who lives forever that the persecution of God's people will last "a time, times, and half a time" (Dan. 12:7). It is after this prophetic time is completed that the end will come (cf. Rev. 6–7). Until this time is fulfilled, God's people must wait patiently (Dan. 12:10).

Revelation 10 clearly echoes Daniel 12, with the exception of the phrase "there will no longer be time," which replaces the phrase "a time, times, and half a time" from Daniel (Dan. 12:7). "A time, times, and half a time" is a symbolic designation of the prophetic period of 1,260 years, which refers to the Middle Ages. During this time, God's people were persecuted by the Antichrist power. As will be explained further in this text, this prophetic period concluded with the events of the French Revolution in AD 1798. As the angel explained to Daniel, the end would come after this prophetic period.

In Revelation 6:10, there is the perennial plea of God's oppressed people: "How long, O Lord, holy and true, will You not judge and avenge our blood upon those who dwell on earth?" They are told to wait for a short time (Rev. 6:11). Now in Revelation 10:6–7, God's people are assured, by means of a divine oath, that "there will no longer be time." The oppression of God's people is over. The rebellion on earth will not continue much longer. God has heard the plea of His people, found in the fifth seal. The end-time events will soon unfold.

The Greek word *chronos*, used here, denotes the duration of a period or a space of time. This is in contrast to *kairos*, which denotes a point in time, as in a fixed, definite period or a season (although the two terms often overlap and are synonymous). The angel's oath provides the church with a strong assurance that God is completely faithful to His promise. There will be no more delay; the time prophesied by Daniel has expired, and the history of this world is nearing its close. God is about to deliver and vindicate His faithful saints and bring this earth's history to its close. Of this time, Ellen White states:

> This time, which the angel declares with a solemn oath, is not the end of this world's history, neither of probationary time, but of prophetic time, which should precede the advent of our Lord. That is, the people will not have another message upon definite time. After this period of time, reaching from 1842 to 1844, there can be no definite tracing of the prophetic time. The longest reckoning reaches to the autumn of 1844.[1]

Although the time of the end prophesied by Daniel is set in motion, the angel warns John that the end is not yet here. It is at the sound of the seventh trumpet that the end will come, when the mystery of God will be complete, as was proclaimed through the prophets (Rev. 10:7) and Daniel, in particular.

The mystery referred to by the angel encompasses the whole purpose of God: to establish His eternal kingdom. This mystery is symbolized by the sealed scroll of Revelation 5 that will be unsealed at the coming of Christ. It is then, as Paul stated, that God will "bring to light the things hidden in the darkness and disclose the motives of men's hearts" (1 Cor. 4:5). This mystery was hidden for ages (Rom. 16:25–26; Col. 1:26–27). Nobody in the entire universe was able to have insight into this mystery (cf. Rev. 5:3; 1 Pet. 1:12). It is only because of Christ's death on the cross that a part of the mystery has been revealed in the gospel (Eph. 1:9; 3:5–12). However, at the Second Coming, the fullness of this mystery will be revealed to the entire universe (Rev. 20:11–15).

The Commissioning of John (10:8–11)

The same voice from heaven that forbade John to write the message of the seven thunders (Rev. 10:4) now directs him to take the opened scroll from the angel's hand. When John does so, the angel orders him to eat the scroll, telling him that it will be bitter in his stomach but sweet as honey in his mouth. As John eats the scroll, it indeed tastes as sweet as honey yet turns sour in his stomach. After eating the scroll, he is told that he must prophesy again concerning many peoples, nations, tongues, and kings. Eating the scroll precedes the proclamation of its message.

John's experience echoes Ezekiel's experience when he was called to prophetic ministry (Ezek. 2:8–3:3). Ezekiel saw in a vision a scroll spread out before him, which he was commanded to take and eat. Upon eating the scroll, the prophet found that "it was sweet as honey" in his mouth (3:3). The Lord then explained to the prophet the bitter experience he would have as he proclaimed God's message to the people of Israel (3:4–11). Jeremiah had a similar experience and exclaimed, "Your words were found and I ate them, and Your words became for me a joy and the delight of my heart" (Jer. 15:16). The Word of God is good news to those who receive it (Pss. 19:10; 119:103). However, it often results in a bitter experience for those who proclaim it.

It is evident that John's bittersweet visionary experience is related to the unsealing of Daniel's end-time prophecies and the proclamation of the mighty angel that "there will no longer be time" (Rev. 10:6–7). The content of the little scroll is related to the prophetic revelation he is commissioned to communicate to God's people (1:1). John faithfully prophesied the revelation he was commissioned to proclaim (1:2, 9). Afterward, he expected the conclusion of earth's history to come with the blowing of the seventh trumpet. But he was told that the end was not yet. Before the end comes, the gospel must continue to be preached throughout the world to many peoples, nations, tongues, and kings (cf. 14:6–7).

It appears that the purpose of Revelation 10 is not just to give a description of John's visionary experience of eating the scroll. Remember that Revelation is a book of prophecy (Rev. 1:3). It is intended to tell God's people about what will happen in the future (1:1; 22:6). Thus, John's visionary experience has a much deeper purpose. John represents the church, commissioned to proclaim the gospel throughout the world during the time between the prophetic period specified in Daniel and the Second Coming. It is during this period that, through the church, God will warn the earth's inhabitants of His judgment (14:6–12). John's visionary experience offers a figurative portrayal of what God's end-time people will experience as they preach the gospel at the end time.

John's experience points to another event that took place at the close of Daniel's prophecy of 1,260 days. Seventh-day Adventists have seen a parallel between John's experience and the Great Disappointment experienced by the Millerites in 1844. Under the leadership of the revivalist William Miller, they mistakenly concluded that the Second Coming would occur in the fall of 1844. The message of Christ's coming was very sweet to them. However, when the date passed without His return, the disappointed Millerites experienced the bitterness of the message they had believed and proclaimed. As a result, many left the movement. Although disappointed and ridiculed, those who stayed found the explanation for their disappointment in John's visionary experience. In John's eating of the scroll, they saw the prophecy of their own experience.

Adventists have seen in Christ's commission to John—to "prophesy again concerning many peoples and nations and tongues and kings"— the commissioning of God's end-time church to proclaim the message of the Second Coming "to those who live on the earth, and to every nation and tribe and tongue and people" (Rev. 14:6). When the gospel message is heard by the whole world, then the end will come and earth's history will conclude (Matt. 24:14).

The Two Witnesses

 Revelation 11:1–19

Remember that Revelation 10:1–11:14 is an interlude between the sixth and seventh trumpets. It describes the experience of the church as it preaches the gospel to a hostile world:

¹And a measuring reed like a staff was given to me, saying: "Rise and measure the temple of God and the altar and those who worship in it. ²And exclude the outer court and do not measure it, for it has been given to the nations; and they will trample the holy city for forty-two months."

³And I will commission My two witnesses, and they will prophesy for 1,260 days, clothed in sackcloth. ⁴These are the two olive trees and the two lampstands standing before the Lord of the earth. ⁵And if anyone wants to harm them, fire comes out of their mouths and devours their enemies; and if anyone would want to harm them, he must be killed. ⁶They have authority to shut heaven, lest it give forth rain during the days of their prophecy; and they have authority over the waters to turn them into blood and to strike the earth with every plague as often as they want.

⁷And when they complete their witness, the beast coming up from the abyss will make war with them and will conquer them and kill them. ⁸And their dead body will be on the street of the great city, which is spiritually called Sodom and Egypt, where also their Lord was crucified. ⁹And those of the peoples and tribes and tongues and nations will behold their dead body for three and a half days, and they will not permit their dead bodies to be placed in a tomb. ¹⁰And those who dwell on the earth will rejoice over them and make merry, and they will send gifts to one another, because these two prophets tormented those who dwell upon the earth. ¹¹And after three and a half days, the breath of life from God entered them, and they stood up on their feet, and a great fear fell on those beholding them. ¹²And they heard a great voice from heaven saying to them: "Come up here!" And they went up to heaven in the cloud, and their enemies beheld them. ¹³And at the same hour there was a great earthquake, and a tenth of the city fell, and 7,000 people were killed in the earthquake; and the rest of the people became afraid and gave glory to the God of heaven.

¹⁴The second woe has passed; behold, the third woe is coming quickly.

The Measuring of the Temple (11:1–2)

In Revelation 10:8–11, John was told that, before the end comes, there would be a final proclamation of the gospel throughout the world. What is the message to be proclaimed? The previous text shows that it is the gospel in connection with the unsealed prophecies of Daniel (Rev. 10:7). Revelation 11:1–2 adds an additional element to this end-time proclamation with a focus on the restoration of the heavenly temple and its services in the context of judgment.

The Measuring of the Temple and the Worshippers (11:1)

John is given a measuring reed and commanded to measure the temple of God, the altar, and the worshippers. Centuries earlier, Ezekiel watched in a vision as a divine person measured the temple and the altar of sacrifice (Ezek. 40–43). In Ezekiel's vision, the temple was measured so it could be restored (39:25–29). The vision was a strong assurance to the people that God was committed to restoring the temple and His people in the Promised Land. The rebuilding of the temple was God's attempt to restore His relationship with Israel (43:7–11). Ezekiel's vision gives us a clue to the meaning of the measuring of the temple in John's vision.

In the New Testament, the temple is sometimes used as a symbol for the church (2 Cor. 6:16; Eph. 2:21; 1 Pet. 2:4–5). However, the concept of the church as the temple does not fit the context of Revelation

11:1–2, because the believers are portrayed not as the temple but as worshipers in the temple. Nor is it the temple in Jerusalem that is in John's vision, because it was destroyed some twenty years earlier. The temple here is the temple in heaven, where Jesus ministers on behalf of His people. The heavenly temple and the activities that take place there occupy a central place in Revelation. John uses the imagery of the earthly sanctuary and temple to refer to the heavenly temple and its furnishings.

The act of measuring the temple with its altar and worshippers is central to Revelation 11:1–2. Some recent studies have cogently shown that in the Old Testament these three elements—the temple, the altar, and the worshippers—are only mentioned together in connection with the Day of Atonement (Lev. 16:16–19, 30–31).[1] The Day of Atonement was the most solemn day in the Jewish sacred calendar. It was a day of measuring, or judgment, when God ultimately dealt with the sins of His people.

Thus, the Old Testament Day of Atonement is the backdrop for Revelation 11:1. In the Bible, the word "measure" figuratively means to evaluate or judge (cf. 2 Cor. 10:12). In the Old Testament, it is used in the context of deciding who would live and who would die (2 Sam. 8:2) or to express God's act of judging His people's sins (Isa. 65:7). In the New Testament, the word is used figuratively for the final judgment (Matt. 7:2).

The purpose of judgment is to determine who serves God and who does not. This judgment must take place prior to the Second Coming, before the righteous receive their reward and the wicked their condemnation (Rev. 11:18; 14:7). The measuring in Revelation 11:1 refers to this pre-Advent judgment. It exclusively concerns God's people—the worshippers in the temple. This measuring parallels the sealing of God's people in Revelation 7:1–4.[2] This shows that the measuring in Revelation 11:1 is meant to decide who will be sealed—namely, who belongs to God and is faithful to Him.

In such a way, Revelation 11:1 shows that the restoration of the heavenly sanctuary lies at the heart of the final gospel proclamation. The restoration of the sanctuary has great significance for God's sovereignty. During the history of sin on earth, God's character and governance have been challenged by Satan. The heavenly sanctuary message is meant to vindicate God's character before the entire universe and restore His rightful rule over the universe. As such, it gives a new dimension to the meaning of the gospel message with regard to the atoning work of Christ and His righteousness as the only means of salvation for the human race.

The Trampling of the Holy City (11:2)

John is further instructed to exclude the outer court of the temple from the measuring. The outer court of the temple in Jerusalem was the place outside the temple building, where the Gentiles were allowed to come—they were not allowed to pass through to the inner court under penalty of death.

Here, in Revelation 11:2, the outer court is excluded from the measuring because it is given to the nations. The Greek word *ethnoi* can be translated as "nations" or "Gentiles." In Revelation, John uses this word to describe those who are not God's people and are hostile to God and the church (Rev. 11:18; 14:8; 16:19). This world belongs to them; this explains why, in the book of Revelation, they are constantly referred to as "those who dwell on the earth" (6:10; 8:13; 11:10; 13:8, 14; 17:2).

Revelation 10:8–11:2 shows that preaching the gospel ultimately divides the world into two groups. Those who accept the gospel are the worshippers in God's temple (Rev. 11:1; 13:6). Those who reject the gospel are excluded from among God's people and relegated to the outer court (11:2). In Ezekiel's vision of the measuring of the temple, no foreigners who were uncircumcised in heart and flesh were allowed to enter the temple (Ezek. 44:9). Likewise, in John's vision, the Gentiles are excluded from the temple and do not belong to the community of believers (Rev. 11:2).

John is told that the nations (or Gentiles) of the earth will trample the holy city for forty-two months. This brings to mind the words of Jesus: "Jerusalem will be trampled under foot by the Gentiles until the times of the Gentiles are fulfilled" (Luke 21:24). Jesus makes the trampling of Jerusalem a symbol of the persecution of God's people by those who are hostile to God and the gospel. Therefore, the trampling of the holy city in Revelation 11:2 symbolically refers to the persecution of God's people by the Antichrist power during the prophetic period of forty-two months (Rev. 13:5–7).

The time period of forty-two months is mentioned several times in Daniel 7 and Revelation 11–13, the sections that describe the persecution of God's people by the little horn and the sea beast respectively. Besides forty-two months (Rev. 11:2; 13:5), this period is also referred to in terms of "a time and times and half a time" (Dan.

7:25; 12:7; Rev. 12:14) and 1,260 days, representing years (11:3; 12:6). These three time designations symbolically refer to the same period in history known as the Middle Ages, when God's people endured severe hardship and oppression by the Antichrist power.

Historicist interpreters have struggled to fit this prophetic period into an exact time frame. The rise of the medieval church to power and dominance was gradual. However, AD 538 should be appropriately taken as the beginning of this prophetic period. By that time, the medieval church had established itself as an ecclesiastical power, and it dominated the Western world throughout medieval times. AD 1798—when the events of the French Revolution brought the church's oppressive political power to its end—marked the conclusion of this prophetic period.

Revelation 13:1–10 provides an additional description of the holy city being trampled by the nations or Gentiles during the prophetic forty-two months. During this period, God's people are portrayed as two witnesses, prophesying in sackcloth (Rev. 11:3–14). These two passages are related and must be studied in connection with each other.

The Two Witnesses (11:3–14)

Revelation 11:3–14 describes the bitter experience of God's people in a hostile world as they bear witness to the gospel during the prophetic forty-two months or 1,260 days when the holy city is trampled by the nations.

The Identification of the Two Witnesses (11:3–6)

The voice from heaven tells John that God will raise two witnesses who will prophesy in sackcloth during the difficult time of the 1,260 days. This is the same prophetic period as the forty-two months, which was allotted to the nations to oppress God's faithful people (Rev. 11:2). The word "prophesy" brings to mind Revelation 10:11, where John was told that he would have to prophesy again concerning many nations. This shows that John's commission to prophesy was extended to the church.

The concept of two witnesses comes from ancient Israel's legal system, which required at least two witnesses to establish something as true (Deut. 19:15; John 8:17). Jesus followed that principle when He sent out His disciples, two by two, to preach the gospel (Mark 6:7; Luke 10:1). The early church continued the same practice (Acts

13:2). The picture of the two witnesses preaching the gospel points to the importance of the gospel proclaimed. Its rejection results in serious consequences.

The two witnesses are dressed in sackcloth—the usual attire of the Israelite prophets (Isa. 20:2; Zech. 13:4). Notice that the two witnesses in Revelation 11:10 are called the two prophets. Furthermore, sackcloth was also the garment of mourning (Gen. 37:34; Esther 4:1–3). The portrayal of the two witnesses prophesying in sackcloth during the prophetic period of 1,260 days points to the difficult time God's people will go through when proclaiming the gospel message to the world (cf. Rev. 6:9). The time of their witnessing corresponds to the three and a half years of Jesus's ministry on earth. Here, there is a description of the bitterness that John tasted after eating the little scroll (10:8–11). God's people often experience painful bitterness, because their witnessing is met with rejection and scorn.

John describes the two witnesses in terms of several Old Testament personalities. First, he describes them as "the two olive trees and the two lampstands standing before the Lord" (Rev. 11:4). Here, John points to Zechariah's vision of the lampstand between the two olive trees (Zech. 4:2–3). Zechariah was told that the two olive trees represented "the two anointed ones" standing by the Lord of the earth (4:14). These two anointed ones were Joshua, the high priest, and Zerubbabel, the governor of Judea. The activity of the two witnesses resembles the roles of Joshua and Zerubbabel. Thus, the two witnesses are portrayed in priestly and royal terms.

Next, John portrays them as Elijah and Moses (Rev. 11:5–6). Elijah closed up the heavens so that it would not rain for three and half years (which equals 1,260 days; 1 Kings 17; cf. Luke 4:25) and, on another occasion, brought down fire from heaven upon the soldiers who came to arrest him (2 Kings 1:9–14). In the same manner, the two witnesses send fire from their mouths upon their enemies and shut up the heavens, so it will not rain during the 1,260 days (or three and a half years). Just as Moses turned water into blood and struck the land of Egypt with all kinds of plagues (Exod. 7–11), the two witnesses also have authority to turn water into blood and to strike the earth with all kinds of plagues.

It is important to remember that the two witnesses are not Moses and Elijah reincarnated. Rather, they are symbolic figures. Their role and ministry resemble the role and ministry of Joshua and Zerubbabel and of Moses and Elijah. The same divine power that accompanied the prophetic activities of Moses and Elijah, the two greatest prophets in Israel's history, accompanies the prophetic ministry of these two symbolic figures in Revelation.

Who are these two witnesses? Their portrayal points to God's people as they bear witness to the Bible and to the gospel in the world. Revelation 11:8 shows that the two witnesses are one entity rather than two (the Greek reads "the dead body of them"). It is, thus, appropriate to see the two witnesses as the people of God in their royal and priestly roles, preaching the Bible as the Word of God (cf. Rev. 1:6; 5:10).[3] It is because of their faithfulness to the Bible that God's people had to go through difficult times during the prophetic period of the 1,260 days or forty-two months during the Middle Ages (6:9; 12:6, 13–14).

The Killing of the Two Witnesses (11:7–10)

After the two witnesses have completed their work during the 1,260 days, "the beast coming up from the abyss will make war with them and will conquer and kill them" (Rev. 11:7). We have already seen that the abyss is the abode of Satan and the fallen angels (Luke 8:31; 2 Pet. 2:4). This passage shows that the beast that wages war against the two witnesses and kills them is an authority controlled and backed by Satan.

A beast is a symbol of a political power (Rev. 13; 17:3–8). Revelation 17 refers to a beast that arises from the abyss during the time of the end (17:8). However, the beast that wages war against the two witnesses and kills them is a dominant political power that steps onto the scene at the end of the prophetic period of 1,260 days. Seventh-day Adventists have rightly identified the killing of the two witnesses with the atheist assault against the Bible and the abolition of religion during the French Revolution. Both events came right at the conclusion of the prophetic 1,260-day period.

The two witnesses lie dead and publicly exposed "on the street of the great city" (Rev. 11:8). The Old Testament gives a long list of the great cities that stood in opposition to God and persecuted God's people. In Revelation, "the great city" refers often to end-time Babylon, which is involved in the final conflict against God and His people. In Revelation 11, the great city is a territory governed by the beast arising from the abyss at the end of the prophetic 1,260 days. This territory has the spiritual characteristics of the great cities mentioned in the Bible which stood in opposition to God. It possesses the wickedness and moral degradation of Sodom (Gen. 19:4–11), the atheistic arrogance of Egypt (Exod. 5:2), and the rebelliousness of

Jerusalem, "where also their Lord was crucified" (Rev. 11:8). Just as Jerusalem rejected Jesus and put Him to death, so this great symbolic city kills the Christian church and the Bible.

The body of the witnesses lies exposed and unburied for three and a half days. This period corresponds to the time Jesus spent in the tomb. The martyrdom and death of the two witnesses are linked to the death of Christ. Their death causes great joy among "those who dwell on the earth" (Rev. 11:10), which is a reference to the wicked (6:10; 8:13; 13:8, 14; 17:2). They are celebrating because "these two prophets tormented those who dwell upon the earth" (11:10). The Word of God always troubles the conscience of those who hear it but are unwilling to surrender themselves to it.

The Resurrection of the Two Witnesses (11:11–14)

After three and a half days, God breathes life into the two witnesses and resurrects them. He also makes them stand erect. The language used here echoes the creation of the first man in Genesis 2:7. This whole scene, however, recalls Ezekiel's vision of the valley of dry bones (Ezek. 37:1–10). The vision was a prophecy of Israel's restoration after the Babylonian exile. Israel was perceived by their enemies to have been defeated and killed. However, God ordered Ezekiel to prophesy, so breath would enter the dry bones. The breath entered into the dead bodies, and they came to life and stood on their feet.

The miraculous restoration of the witnesses to life fills their enemies with awe and great fear. They thought they had silenced the witnesses who tormented their conscience. However, the Word of God ultimately triumphs. Then, in the sight of their enemies, the resurrected witnesses are miraculously taken to heaven on a cloud. This exaltation of the two witnesses from their previous, humiliated position adds to the terror experienced by the earth dwellers.

Historically, one of the outcomes of the French Revolution was a great revival of interest in the Bible, manifested, in particular, by the establishment of the great Bible societies and numerous missionary societies. These were founded to spread the gospel of the Bible. The two witnesses, thus, came back to life, and the stage was set for the widespread preaching of the gospel like never before in history.

The ascension of the resurrected witnesses is accompanied by a great earthquake that strikes a tenth of the great city and kills 7,000 people. A tenth in the Bible symbolizes the smallest part of a whole.[4] The earthquake causes only part of the city to collapse.

Another, more severe, earthquake will strike end-time Babylon, causing its total collapse (Rev. 16:18). The 7,000 people killed represent the totality of the hardened unbelievers—seven being the number of fullness.[5]

The rest of the people are filled with fear and give glory to God. This brings to mind the conversion of King Nebuchadnezzar, who gave glory to God after experiencing divine judgment (Dan. 4:34–37). The word "fear" and the phrase "gave glory to God" sound like a response to the appeal of the first angel in Revelation 14:7: "Fear God, and give Him glory." This suggests that, as a result of the vindication and exaltation of the two witnesses and the earthquake that shook the great city, there are some who will accept the gospel and find faith in Christ. The vindication of the two witnesses parallels the proclamation of the eternal gospel that the first angel gave in Revelation 14. As earth's history approaches its close, the world will, once again, witness a worldwide proclamation of the gospel through the church. This final proclamation will illuminate the earth with the glory of the gospel message (Rev. 18:1).

Revelation 11:3–14 describes the symbolic bitterness and pain God's people experience as they proclaim the gospel message to the world. While the testimony of the symbolic two witnesses applies historically to the Middle Ages, it also applies to the context of the French Revolution. Its significance for God's end-time people goes beyond this temporal and geographical location. It shows that, as in the past, God also has people who are faithful in bearing witness to the gospel in the world today. He uses them as He used Moses during the Exodus, Elijah during Israel's apostasy, and Joshua and Zerubbabel during the postexilic time.

John concludes the section with the statement that the second woe has passed and the third woe is coming. The first and second woes refer to the fifth and sixth trumpets respectively. Thus, the third woe refers to the sounding of the seventh trumpet that will complete God's mystery (Rev. 10:7).

The Seventh Trumpet (11:15–19)

Revelation 10:1–11:14 shows that before the end comes, there will be a mighty proclamation of the gospel to the world. The time has now come for the seventh angel to sound the trumpet, announcing the consummation of all things and the completion of "the mystery of God" (Rev. 10:7):

15And the seventh angel sounded his trumpet; and there were loud voices in heaven saying: "The kingdom of the world has become the kingdom of our Lord and of His Christ, and He will reign forever and ever." 16And the twenty-four elders who were before God, sitting on their thrones, fell on their faces and worshiped God, 17saying: "We give thanks to You, Lord God, the Almighty, who is and who was, because You have taken Your great power and begun to reign; 18and the nations were enraged, and Your wrath came, and the time for the dead to be judged, and to give the reward to Your servants the prophets and the saints and those who fear Your name, the small and the great ones, and to destroy the destroyers of the earth."

19And the temple of God that is in heaven was opened, and the Ark of the Covenant in His temple was seen; and there came flashes of lightning, sounds, peals of thunder, an earthquake, and great hail.

The sounding of the seventh trumpet signals the conclusion of this earth's history. The proclamation of the gospel is complete, and the case of every person is decided. A voice from heaven makes a declaration of the ultimate establishment of God's kingdom on the earth. This rebellious planet—which has been under the dominion of Satan for thousands of years—will finally come back under God's dominion and rule. Here is the fulfillment of the prophecy that Daniel gave to King Nebuchadnezzar: "In the days of those kings the God of heaven will set up a kingdom which will never be destroyed, and that kingdom will not be left for another people; it will crush and put an end to all these kingdoms, but it will itself endure forever" (Dan. 2:44).

It was after His death on the cross and His subsequent ascension to heaven that Christ was recognized as co-ruler with the Father over the universe (cf. Rev. 5:11–14). The usurper, Satan, was cast out of heaven, and Christ was proclaimed the legitimate ruler of the earth (12:10). Christ became the ruler of the universe but not of this world. This rebellious world is still under the dominion of Satan. Christ has to reign as co-ruler with the Father "until He has put all His enemies under His feet" (1 Cor. 15:25). When the usurping powers are subjected, finally "then comes the end, when He hands over the kingdom to the God and Father, when He has abolished all rule and all authority and power. . . . When all things are subjected to Him, then the Son Himself also will be subjected to the One who subjected all things to Him, so that God may be all in all" (15:24, 28). Now, with the sounding of the seventh trumpet, the long-awaited time has come for God to reveal His great power and begin to reign (Rev. 11:17).

Revelation 11:18 contains the second part of the hymn of praise by the twenty-four elders, who are around God's throne. The words of their hymn outline the events that will take place at the seventh trumpet—immediately prior to and after the Second Coming—which are described in detail in the second half of Revelation (Rev. 12–22):

- "The nations were enraged" at God and His people (Rev. 11:18). This echoes Psalm 2, which speaks of the nations raging against the Lord and His Anointed One, and God's wrathful response (Ps. 2:1–2, 12). The nations' rage is the manifestation of the anger of Satan (Rev. 12:17) and his two allies, the sea beast (13:1–10) and the earth beast (13:11–18). They will gather the world's nations for the battle of Armageddon in opposition to God's rule in the world.
- "Your wrath came" (Rev. 11:18). God responds to the nations' anger with His own wrath. The seven last plagues are referred to as the wrath of God (15:1). The wrath of God against the rebellious world is portrayed in detail in Revelation 15–18.
- "The time for the dead to be judged" (11:18). Revelation 20:11–15 describes the resurrected dead standing before the throne of God and being judged. Judgment includes both positive and negative aspects: giving a reward and bringing punishment.
- The positive aspect of the judgment: "To give the reward to Your servants the prophets and the saints and those who fear Your name, the small and the great ones" (11:18). Revelation describes the reward for God's people in terms of the new earth (21–22). The phrase "who fear Your name, the small and the great ones" is derived from Psalm 115:13, which describes believers of all socioeconomic ranks.
- The negative aspect of the judgment: "To destroy the destroyers of the earth" (11:18). The eradication of Satan and his hosts is the final act in the Great Controversy between good and evil (19:11–20:15).

The expression "to destroy the destroyers of the earth" is an allusion to Genesis 6:12–14, which identifies the antediluvians as the destroyers of the earth, who did so by "filling the earth with iniquity" (as stated in the original Hebrew). Therefore, God destroyed the antediluvian destroyers of the earth. Just as in the time of Noah, so

God is going to destroy the end-time destroyers of the earth. This shows that Revelation 11:18 does not refer to ecological concerns of destroying the earth with modern technology but refers to the activities of end-time Babylon that fill the earth with sins, which have "piled up as high as heaven, and God has remembered her iniquities" (Rev. 18:5). This concept is supported by the prophecy of Jeremiah which identifies historical Babylon as the "destroying mountain, who destroys the whole earth." Because of this, Babylon will be destroyed (Jer. 51:25). In Revelation 19:2, end-time Babylon is judged, because it has destroyed (Gr. *phtheiro*) the earth with its immorality.

The seventh trumpet shows that the events of the end will be the final triumph of God's rule in this world. It provides the ultimate fulfillment of the promise to the saints in the fifth trumpet scene who plead: "How long, O Lord, holy and true, will You not judge and avenge our blood upon those who dwell on earth?" (Rev. 6:10). The establishment of God's eternal kingdom and His rule over the world denote the vindication of God's saints in response to their perennial longings and expectations.

Satan tail is to do with deception

The Opening of the Heavenly Temple (11:19)

At the conclusion of the vision, the temple in heaven is opened, enabling John to see the Ark of the Covenant in the innermost part of the temple, known as the Most Holy Place. The appearance of the Ark of the Covenant is accompanied by "lightning, sounds, peals of thunder, an earthquake, and great hail," representing the divine presence (Rev. 4:5; 8:5; 16:18; cf. Exod. 19:16–19; 20:18; Deut. 5:22–23). Mentioning the Ark of the Covenant at the beginning of the new vision is significant for at least two reasons.

First, it refers to disclosing the little scroll's contents, which John received in Revelation 10. This scroll was in the Ark of the Covenant, where the Covenant Book was stored (Deut. 31:24–26). This reveals that Revelation 12–22 contains the contents of the little scroll.

Second, the mention of the Ark of the Covenant reveals that the end-time events described in Revelation 12–16 are related to what is taking place in the Most Holy Place of the heavenly sanctuary. The references to the heavenly sanctuary and its furnishings in the first half of the book (cf. Rev. 4:5; 5:8; 8:3–5) show that the events portrayed in Revelation 1–11 are related to Christ's ministry in the Holy Place of the heavenly sanctuary. Now in Revelation 11:19, the opening of the

Most Holy Place with the Ark of the Covenant points to the beginning of a new phase of Christ's ministry in the heavenly sanctuary, which can best be defined as the pre-Advent judgment (cf. Rev. 14:7).[6] This judgment is introduced in Revelation 11:1–2, and it takes place in heaven at the same time as the preaching of the end-time gospel on earth. When both conclude, there will be a great separation between those who have chosen God and those who are lost. It is at that time that Christ will come to reward every person according to his or her deeds (Rev. 22:12).

In Old Testament times, the Ark of the Covenant was the symbol of God's covenant and His presence with His people. Thus, the reference to the Ark of the Covenant in Revelation 11:19 serves as a reminder to God's end-time people of His covenant promise to be with them, even to the end of the world. He will be with them "always, even to the end of the age" (Matt. 28:20).

the whole of Rev. is symbolic

Satan: A Defeated Enemy

 Revelation 12:1–17

12 onward things to come

Revelation 12 describes a new vision that begins the eschatological portion of Revelation. While the first half of Revelation describes the struggles of the church in a hostile world throughout its history, the primary focus of the second half of the book is on the time of the end and the final events leading to Christ's return. From now on, Revelation focuses on the contents of the open scroll (Rev. 10). God reveals what will happen at the end time, so we might not be surprised.

This section includes three subsections: Satan's attempt to destroy Christ on earth (Rev. 12:1–6); the expulsion of Satan and his angels from heaven (12:7–12); and Satan's efforts to destroy the church (12:13–17):

> ¹*And a great sign was seen in heaven: a woman clothed with the sun, and the moon under her feet, and on her head a crown of twelve stars, ²and she was pregnant and was crying out with birth pains, and she was tormented to give birth. ³And another sign was seen in heaven, and behold, a great red dragon having seven heads and ten horns and upon his heads seven crowns. ⁴And his tail dragged the third of the stars of heaven and cast them to the earth. And the dragon stood before the woman who was about to give birth, so that when she gave birth to her child, he might devour him. ⁵And she gave birth to a son, a male child, who is about to shepherd all the nations with the rod of iron; and her child was caught up to God and to His throne. ⁶And the woman fled into the wilderness, where she had there a place prepared by God, so that they might nourish her for 1,260 days.*

⁷And there was war in heaven; Michael and his angels had to fight against the dragon. And the dragon and his angels fought back, ⁸and he was not strong enough nor was found there a place for them any longer in heaven. ⁹And the great dragon, the ancient serpent, who is called the devil and Satan, the one who deceives the whole world, was cast down to the earth, and his angels were cast down with him. ¹⁰And I heard a loud voice in heaven saying: "Now the salvation and the power and the kingdom of our God and the authority of His Christ have come, because the accuser of our brothers has been cast down, the one who accuses them before our God day and night. ¹¹And they overcame him by the blood of the Lamb and by the word of their testimony, and they did not love their life to the point of death. ¹²For this reason, rejoice, heavens and those who dwell in them; woe to the earth and the sea, for the devil has come down to you, having great anger, knowing that he has little time."

¹³When the dragon saw that he was cast down to the earth, he persecuted the woman that had given birth to the male child. ¹⁴And two wings of a great eagle were given to the woman, so that she might fly into the wilderness, to her place where she was nourished there for a time and times and half a time from the presence of the serpent. ¹⁵And the serpent poured out of his mouth water like a river after the woman, in order to make her flooded by the water. ¹⁶And the earth helped the woman, and the earth opened its mouth and swallowed the river which the dragon had cast from his mouth. ¹⁷And the dragon was angry at the woman and went away to make war with the remnant of her offspring, the ones keeping the commandments of God and having the testimony of Jesus.

The Woman and the Dragon (12:1–6)

Before describing the end-time conflict between Christ, Satan, and their respective followers, John first explains the big picture behind this conflict.

The Woman (12:1–2)

In a vision, John sees a great sign in heaven. Something special and remarkable is shown here (cf. Rev. 12:3 and 15:1). The Greek word *semeion* (sign) denotes a symbolic presentation of a real object. This sign is a woman arrayed with the sun, standing on the moon, and having a garland of twelve stars on her head. She travails in labor and is about to give birth to a child. In using the word "sign" for this woman, John shows that she is not an actual woman but a symbol of a spiritual reality.

A woman in the Bible is a symbol for God's people, whether faithful to God or apostate. In the Old Testament, Israel, as God's covenant people, is often referred to as the wife of God (Isa. 54:5; Jer. 3:20). When Israel was faithful to her covenant with God, she was called a pure and faithful woman. On the other hand, apostate and idolatrous Israel was portrayed as a prostitute.[1] This concept is also carried into the New Testament and applied to the church (cf. 2 Cor. 11:2; Eph. 5:25–32). In Revelation, God's faithful people are represented as a faithful woman (Rev. 19:7–8; 22:17), while a prostitute symbolizes the apostate and unfaithful (chaps. 17–18).

The picture of a beautifully adorned woman in travail brings to mind several Old Testament passages. For one, it echoes the portrayal of Solomon's bride, who is as beautiful as the moon and as pure as the sun (Song of Sol. 6:10). It also reflects the passages depicting Israel as a travailing woman (Isa. 26:17–18; 66:7–9; Jer. 4:31; Mic. 4:10). But above all, the portrayal of a woman enduring the pangs of giving birth to the Messiah is an allusion to Genesis 3:15. Revelation 12 shows the fulfillment of God's promise to redeem fallen humanity through the woman's offspring.

The remarkable woman of Revelation 12 stands as a symbol for the church in both the Old and New Testament. This reality is expressed through her portrayal—clothed with the sun and standing on the moon. The sun, as the source of light, stands for the gospel (2 Cor. 4:6; cf. John 8:12; 12:46). The moon reflects the light of the sun; therefore, the woman stands on the revelation of the Old Testament that reflects the light of the gospel.[2] The twelve stars on her head stand for the twelve tribes of Israel as well as the twelve apostles. In this part of the vision (12:1–5), the woman represents Old Testament Israel bringing the Messiah into the world; however, in verses 6 and 13–17, she represents the Christian church.

The Dragon (12:3–6)

Another sign appears in heaven. This time, John sees a great red dragon that has seven heads with royal crowns and ten horns. In verse 9, John identifies this dragon as Satan, the ancient serpent of Genesis 3 and the archenemy of God and His people. The seven-headed monster was a well-known mythological figure in the ancient world.[3] In portraying the frightening appearance of Satan in terms of this ancient, mythological monster, inspiration wants to impress upon our mind the ferocity of God's archenemy.

The dragon has an earthly manifestation. His seven heads represent the kingdoms in history through which Satan worked to oppose God's plans and purpose in the world and to oppress God's people (see Rev. 17:9–11). The ten horns upon his heads symbolize political authorities (17:12). The seven crowns on the dragon's heads refer to Satan's false claim of lordship over this world (cf. Luke 4:6). This imagery reveals Satan standing behind the Roman Empire, as he tried to destroy the long-awaited Messiah, Jesus Christ.

John adds another identifying characteristic of the dragon. His tail "dragged the third of the stars of heaven and cast them to the earth" (Rev. 12:4). In the Bible, the tail is a symbolic instrument of deception (see discussion on 9:10, 19). As he fell from his exalted position in heaven, Satan seduced and dragged to the earth a great number of heavenly beings, who became evil spirits (Isa. 14:12–15; 2 Pet. 2:4; Jude 6). These fallen angels have been his associates throughout the great cosmic conflict against God and His sovereignty.

In Revelation, Satan is a real enemy, not some imaginary figure. He stands behind all the evil that transpires on earth. In Revelation 12, he is waiting for the Messiah to be born from the people of Israel, so he may destroy him. How long has he been waiting for the birth of the Messiah? Since God announced that there would come the One born from "the woman" who would crush the serpent's head (Gen. 3:15). Since that time, Satan has been waiting for the Promised Child to be born in order to destroy Him.

Eventually, the Messiah is born. He is to rule the nations with an iron rod, in fulfillment of Psalm 2:7–9—a reference to His judicial role (Rev. 19:15). Although Satan desires to kill this child, he is not able to, because the child is taken to heaven, to God's throne (12:5). This refers to Christ's exaltation to the heavenly throne after His ascension to heaven (Eph. 1:20–22; 1 Pet. 3:22). The exaltation of Christ serves to introduce the subsequent scene (Rev. 12:7–12). This event ultimately resulted in the permanent expulsion of Satan from heaven (12:10).

As Christ is taken to heaven, to the throne of God, the woman, who represents the church, finds divine protection in the desert during the prophetic time period of 1,260 days. During this time, she waits for the return of Christ and the establishment of God's eternal kingdom.

War in Heaven (12:7–12)

Revelation 12:7–12 transitions to a new scene in the story. The depiction reveals to us that, at the ascension of Christ and His exaltation to the heavenly throne, a war erupted in heaven. Michael and his angels fought against Satan and his angels. Michael (a name meaning "who is like God?") is the commander of the heavenly host. Elsewhere in the Bible, he is identified as the chief prince (Dan. 10:13, 21; 12:1) and the archangel (Jude 9). He is the one who appeared to Joshua at Jericho as the commander of the heavenly host and is equated with the Lord Himself (Josh. 5:13–15). Thus, the biblical information leads to the conclusion that Michael is an eschatological name for Christ. Here in Revelation 12, Christ leads the heavenly army in fighting Satan. Satan and his angels fight back. However, because they are not strong enough, they eventually lose the battle. As a result, Satan and his forces are expelled from heaven and sent to earth (Rev. 12:9).

When did this war in heaven and the subsequent expulsion of Satan and his angels take place? Clues are given in the anthem heard in heaven following Satan's expulsion (Rev. 12:10–12):

- "Now the salvation and the power and the kingdom of our God and the authority of His Christ have come" (Rev. 12:10). The kingdom of God and the authority of Christ are established after the death of Jesus on the cross.
- "The accuser of our brothers has been cast down, the one who accuses them before our God day and night" (12:10). Satan's accusation could not have taken place at the beginning of the Great Controversy, because humans were not yet created. The Old Testament often pictures Satan accusing God's people before God (Job 1–2; Zech. 3).
- Having been expelled from heaven, Satan realizes that he has a short time left (Rev. 12:12). He recognizes this after Jesus's death on the cross.

- After his expulsion, Satan starts persecuting the church during the prophetic period of 1,260 days (12:13). This period refers to the time of the Middle Ages that started in AD 538 and concluded with the French Revolution in AD 1798.

All this shows that the war and expulsion of Satan from heaven portrayed in Revelation 12:7–9 took place after Jesus's death on the cross and His subsequent ascension to heaven.

Satan was first expelled from heaven at the beginning of his rebellion against God's government. He wanted to take the throne in heaven in order to be "like the Most High" (Isa. 14:14). He stood in open revolt against God but was defeated and cast down to earth. By deceiving Adam, Satan usurped the rule and dominion of this earth (Luke 4:6). Jesus referred to him as "the ruler of this world" (John 12:31; 14:30; 16:11). However, after Satan's expulsion, he still had access to heaven. The book of Job portrays him as attending the heavenly assembly before God and making accusations against Job (Job 1:6–12; 2:1–7). Similarly, Zechariah saw him in a vision, accusing Joshua the high priest before the heavenly court (Zech. 3:1–2).

However, the situation changed with Jesus's death on the cross, when Satan's true character was revealed before the entire universe. At the enthronement ceremony following Christ's ascension to heaven, there was a transference of authority and rule from Satan to Christ when the Father "seated Him at His right hand in the heavenly places, far above all rule and authority and power and dominion, and every name that is named, not only in this age but also in the one to come" (Eph. 1:20–21; cf. 1 Pet. 3:22). It was then that Christ was proclaimed the legitimate ruler over the earth.

This transfer of authority obviously did not take place without resistance from Satan, who once again stood in open revolt against God. At that point, Satan and his associates were forever expelled from heaven. As Ellen White recognized, "The casting down of Satan as an accuser of the brethren in heaven was accomplished by the great work of Christ in giving up His life."[4] Jesus foresaw this event when he stated: "Now judgment is upon this world; now the ruler of this world will be cast out" (John 12:31).

With Satan's expulsion, "the kingdom of our God and the authority of His Christ have come" (Rev. 12:10). Since that time, Satan and the fallen angels have been confined to the earth as a prison, until they receive their punishment (2 Pet. 2:4; Jude 6). Satan no longer has access to the heavenly courts, and he no longer can accuse God's people in heaven.

While the fate of Satan was decided with his expulsion from heaven, his defeat is not yet complete. He still claims lordship over the earth. That is why heaven gives this warning: "Woe to the earth and the sea, for the devil has come down to you, having great anger, knowing that he has little time" (Rev. 12:12). The reference to the earth and the sea points to the global dimension of this warning. Satan's expulsion from heaven affects the whole earth. Particularly significant in this regard is chapter 13, where Satan's two associates arise out of the earth and the sea to cause the earth's inhabitants to side with Satan in the final crisis.

Often, after a person has been humiliated, he pours out his displaced anger upon those closest to him. Similarly, because Satan's authority over the earth was transferred to Christ and because he was expelled from the heavenly courts, he now pours out all his fury on the church. This is what the next section is about.

War on Earth (12:13–16)

The story continues: "When the dragon saw that he was cast down to the earth, he persecuted the woman that had given birth to the male child" (Rev. 12:13). Satan could not harm Christ, but he knows how dear the church is to Him. So Satan now turns against the church that represents Christ on earth. However, the church is given "two wings of a great eagle" to fly to the wilderness, where she is cared for by God for a period of "a time and times and half a time" (12:14) or 1,260 days (12:6).

The language used here comes from Israel's Exodus from Egypt: "You yourselves have seen what I did to the Egyptians, and how I bore you on eagles' wings" (Exod. 19:4). As God cared for Israel during her wilderness years (Deut. 8:15–18), now He cares for the church in the wilderness during the prophetic period of 1,260 days, representing years (AD 538–1798). During this time, the two witnesses bore their witness to the gospel in sackcloth (Rev. 11:3). This is also the period of the persecution of God's people by the Antichrist power, stated in Revelation 13:5, during which Satan incited the established church of Western Europe to persecute those who chose to follow the Bible's teachings rather than tradition. More than 50 million Christians were martyred for their faithfulness to the gospel. During that time, God's faithful people found a refuge in isolated places to escape persecution and the corrupt influences of the institutional church.

In his effort to destroy the woman, "the serpent poured out of his mouth water like a river after the woman, in order to make her flooded by the water" (Rev. 12:15). This torrent of water from the serpent's mouth is reminiscent of the serpent's deceptive words in the Garden of Eden (Gen. 3:1–5). In the same manner, Satan is trying to destroy God's people with a flood of false teaching. In the Old Testament, a flood of water is also often used as a symbol of the enemies of God's people attacking and destroying them (Pss. 69:1–2; 124:2–5; Isa. 8:7–8; Jer. 47:2). In Revelation 17:15, the waters symbolize people and nations in their attack against God's people. The flood of water poured out of the dragon's mouth has two meanings: persecution and false teachings. These are the weapons Satan used against God's people during the prophetic period of 1,260 days in the medieval era.

Providentially, however, the earth rescues the woman by swallowing the waters sent forth by the dragon (Rev. 12:16). Once again, John uses the language of the Exodus. Just as the earth swallowed the Egyptians who were pursuing the Israelites (Exod. 15:12), here the friendly earth swallows the torrent of persecution and false teachings that the dragon used to destroy the woman.

At this point, a new entity is introduced: the earth, friendly to the woman. At the end of the prophetic 1,260 days, a new territory provides protection for the church from Satan's effort to destroy her. Here, the prophecy points to the continent of North America that provided protection and a safe haven to the church at the conclusion of the 1,260-year prophetic period. However, this earth, which initially protected the church, becomes the frontline of the eschatological showdown, giving rise to the political power that becomes Satan's agent in the final crisis (see Rev. 13:11–18).

Satan's Attack on the Remnant (12:17)

Up until now, the dragon has not been able to destroy the woman; however, he does not give up. He regroups to "make war with the remnant of her offspring, the ones keeping the commandments of God and having the testimony of Jesus" (Rev. 12:17). In a nutshell, this passage gives us what comes next in the book. It serves as an introduction to Revelation 13, where Satan prepares for the final battle against God's end-time people.

Satan retreats to prepare for his last attack against God's end-time people. However, he decides not to enter the final battle alone. He associates himself with two allies, portrayed in terms of the sea beast (Rev. 13:1–10) and the earth beast (13:11–18). These three form an unholy triumvirate to fight the final battle against Christ and His faithful remnant.

One might observe that, at the end of time, Satan turns his fury on the remnant of the woman's offspring, not the woman per se. Why? The answer is found in Revelation 17, where the church is no longer a pure woman; she has turned into a prostitute sitting on a scarlet beast and seducing the world away from loyalty to Christ. As the world nears its end, the Christian church will eventually turn from her faithfulness to Christ and serve Satan. This is why, at the end of time, Satan goes after what is left of the true church—the remnant that remains faithful to Christ.

The Greek word *loipoi* literally means "the remaining ones." The term in the Old Testament describes those who have survived destruction to continue as God's faithful people (Isa. 10:20–22; 11:11–12; Jer. 23:3; Zeph. 3:13). Throughout Old Testament times, as the majority of the nation of Israel apostatized, there were people who remained faithful to God (cf. 1 Kings 19:18). John employs the word "remnant" with reference to the Christians who remained faithful to God in the churches of Thyatira and Sardis (Rev. 2:24; 3:2–3). Now in Revelation 12:17, John employs the same word to tell us that at the end of time, as the majority of people in the world side with Satan and his allies, there will be a people who remain faithful to Christ.

This end-time remnant will have two characteristics. The first is its obedience to God in keeping His commandments. Revelation 13 shows that, at the end of time, the first four commandments of the Decalogue will be central to the end-time conflict. Since the issue in the final crisis will concern worship—regarding whom and when we are to worship—the fourth commandment will become a test of loyalty and obedience to God (cf. Rev. 14:7).

The second characteristic of the end-time remnant is that they have the testimony of Jesus. The phrase "the testimony of Jesus" is clarified in Revelation 19:10, where it is equated with "the spirit of prophecy" (cf. Rev. 22:9). The expression "the spirit of prophecy" was used in John's day to designate the Holy Spirit speaking through prophets. Thus, the phrase "the testimony of Jesus" refers to Jesus bearing witness to Himself through His prophets, just as He did through John

(1:2). The prophets' role in the Bible is to bear witness to Christ. Revelation shows that, at the time of the end, God's faithful people will have the prophetic gift in their midst to guide them through those hard times when Satan will make every effort to deceive and destroy them.

God's people must keep in mind that today and in the near future they face a formidable and enraged foe. Satan knows that with the loss of his rule over this world, his fate is decided: he has only a short time left. Paul warns us of the end-time "activity of Satan, with all power and signs and false wonders, and with all the deception of wickedness" (2 Thess. 2:9–10). But Satan is already a defeated enemy. As Christ defeated him in the past, so Christ will also defeat him at the time of the end. White points out the importance of recognizing that our foe has already been defeated:

> There are Christians who think and speak altogether too much about the power of Satan. They think of their adversary, they pray about him, they talk about him, and he looms up greater and greater in their imagination. It is true that Satan is a powerful being; but, thank God, we have a mighty Savior, who cast out the evil one from heaven. Satan is pleased when we magnify his power. Why not talk of Jesus? Why not magnify His power and His love?[5]

The only hope for God's people is found in Christ. Because of what Jesus did on the cross, God's people will be able to overcome Satan by the Lamb's blood and by their faithful witness for Christ and the gospel (Rev. 12:11). We are not to be afraid of the future, because Christ has promised to be with His people forever, even until the end of the age (Matt. 28:20).

The Beast from the Sea

 Revelation 13:1–10

According to Revelation 12:17, at the time of the end Satan is furious against those who have remained faithful to Christ. Revelation 13 describes him preparing for the final attack against Christ's faithful followers in association with two allies: the sea beast and the earth beast.

Regarding this section of Revelation, a word of caution is necessary. So far, this book has discussed the prophecies that were fulfilled in the past. But from now on, this book will deal with the prophecies yet to be fulfilled. In these prophecies, God reveals to us what will happen at the time of the end, so we will not be surprised. However, these prophecies do not tell us how exactly the final events will take place. Jesus warns His followers: "Now I have told you before it happens, so that when it happens, you may believe" (John 14:29; cf. 16:4). Therefore, it is important to be careful not to speculate beyond what the prophecy has revealed. The full understanding of the end-time prophecies will be ultimately possible at the time of their fulfillment, not before. Keep in mind that the purpose of Revelation's prophecies is not to satisfy our curiosity about the future but to move us to readiness.

Satan's End-Time Strategy

At this point in the book, there is a shift in Satan's strategy for trying to win people over to his side. Knowing Satan's end-time strategy will help us not to fall into the snare of his deception. Throughout history, Satan has been attacking the church by means of persecuting force and coercion. But as he begins his final attack against the end-time remnant, his strategy changes from coercion to deception. This shift in Satan's strategy corresponds to the transition from the historical to the eschatological focus of the book. One might observe that the word "deceive" does not occur at all in the historical section of Revelation (Rev. 4–11). But it is used regularly in the eschatological section (12–20) to describe Satan's end-time activities in preparing for the final crisis.[1]

In endeavoring to win the allegiance of the world, Satan will launch a great counterfeit of the true God and His salvific activities in the world. In Revelation 13, a triune league is formed between the dragon and his two allies—the beast from the sea (13:1–10) and the beast from the earth (13:11–18). They form a diabolic triumvirate as an antithesis to the Trinity of the Godhead—the Father, the Son, and the Holy Spirit (1:4–6). Throughout the rest of the book, the members of this satanic triad are inseparably associated with opposing God's activities in the world and deceiving the people in the world to turn them away from God in the final crisis (16:13–14; 19:20; 20:10).

Below is a closer look at each of the members in the satanic triune league.

The Dragon

The dragon is the leader who delegates duties to the other two members of the triad. Revelation portrays him as the counterfeit of God the Father and His work:

God's dwelling place is in heaven (Rev. 4–5).	The dragon's dwelling place was once in heaven (12:7–9).
God has a throne (4–5).	The dragon has a throne (2:13; 13:2).
God is worshiped (4:8–11; 14:7; 15:3–4).	The dragon is worshiped (13:4).
God gives power, His throne, and authority to Christ (2:27; 3:21).	The dragon gives power, his throne, and authority to the sea beast (13:2–4).
God pours out His wrath against rebellious humanity (11:18; 15:1).	The dragon pours out his wrath against God's people (12:12, 17).
God lives and reigns forever (4:9; 5:13; 11:15; 19:6).	The dragon is destroyed forever (20:9–10).

At the time of the end Satan will seek to take God's place in the world and be worshiped, just as he did at the beginning of his rebellion (Isa. 14:12–15). During that time, God urges the earth's inhabitants to worship Him, the One who "made the heaven and earth and sea and fountains of waters" (Rev. 14:7).

The Sea Beast

The sea beast is portrayed as the counterpart of Christ, imitating Jesus and His ministry on earth (Rev. 13:1–10):

Jesus began His ministry coming from water (Luke 3:21–23).	The sea beast comes from water to begin its activities (Rev. 13:1).
Jesus looks like the Father (John 14:9).	The sea beast looks like the dragon, having seven heads and ten horns (Rev. 12:3; 13:1).
Jesus is Michael (Who is like God?; Rev. 12:7).	The beast is addressed as: "Who is like the beast?" (13:4).
Jesus received His authority and throne from the Father (2:27).	The sea beast receives full authority and the throne from the dragon (13:2–4).
Jesus the Lamb has seven horns (5:7).	The sea beast has ten horns (13:1).
Jesus's ministry lasted for three and a half years.	The sea beast's activity lasts for forty-two months or three and a half years (13:5).
Jesus is slain and resurrected (5:6; 13:8).	The sea beast is slain and resurrected (13:3).
Jesus received worship and universal authority after His resurrection (Matt. 28:18).	The sea beast receives worship and universal authority after the healing of the deadly wound (Rev. 13:3–4, 8).
The target of Jesus's salvific activities is "every nation, tribe, tongue, and people" (Rev. 5:9; 10:11; 14:6).	The target of the sea beast's deceptive activities is "every tribe and people and tongue and nation" (13:7; cf. 17:15).

The above comparisons show that at the time of the end there will be a massive counterfeit of Jesus Christ and His salvific activities. The counterfeit will be so great that most people in the world will be deceived (Rev. 13:8).

The Earth Beast

The earth beast is portrayed as the counterfeit of the Holy Spirit and His work in the world (Rev. 13:11–17):

The Holy Spirit is called the Spirit of Truth, guiding people to salvation (John 16:13).	The earth beast is called the false prophet, deceiving people (Rev. 16:13; 19:20; 20:10).
The Holy Spirit directs people to worship Christ (John 16:13–14).	The earth beast promotes the sea beast and directs people to worship it (Rev. 13:12, 15).
The Holy Spirit exercises the authority of Christ (John 16:13–14).	The earth beast exercises the authority of the sea beast (Rev. 13:12).
The Holy Spirit performs miraculous signs (Acts 4:30–31).	The earth beast performs miraculous signs (Rev. 13:13; 19:20).
The Holy Spirit came in fire from heaven at Pentecost (Acts 2:1–4).	The earth beast brings fire from heaven (Rev. 13:13).
The Holy Spirit gives life and the breath of life (Rom. 8:11).	The earth beast gives life and the breath of life to the beast's image (Rev. 13:15).
The Holy Spirit applies the seal of God on the foreheads (2 Cor. 1:22; Eph. 1:13; 4:30; Rev. 7:1–3).	The earth beast applies the mark of the beast on the hands or foreheads (13:16).

The portrayal of Satan's second ally shows that the earth beast will be the key player in the final crisis, imitating the Holy Spirit's work so it may deceive the world.

Throughout the eschatological part of the book, this satanic triad counterfeits God's salvific activities in the world (Rev. 13–20):

Counterfeit Sealing. While God, at the time of the end, seals His worshippers on their foreheads with His name (Rev. 14:1), Satan and his allies mark their worshippers on their foreheads or their right hands with the beast's name (13:16–17). The mark of the beast is, thus, the antithesis of God's seal.

Counterfeit Three Angels' Messages. During those times, God sends to the world's inhabitants the three angels' messages with the everlasting gospel (Rev. 14:6–13). In opposing God, the unholy triumvirate sends to the world three demonic spirits with a false gospel (16:13–14). These three demonic angels are the antithesis of the three angels' messages.

Counterfeit City. God offers to the world's inhabitants the holy city, New Jerusalem, as His answer and solution to all human longings and hopes for ideal life (Rev. 21:2–4). Satan with his associates offers to the world the city of Babylon, based on economical prosperity, power, success, and sensual gratification (17–18). Babylon in Revelation is, thus, the antithesis of the New Jerusalem.

The Beast from the Sea (13:1–10)

As the dragon retreats to prepare for the war against the remnant of the woman's offspring, he stands on the seashore (Rev. 13:1). Although the King James Version reads, "I stood," asserting that John stood on the seashore watching the beast coming out of the water, the early and best Greek manuscripts read "he stood," referring to the dragon.

> *¹And he stood on the sand of the sea. And I saw a beast coming up out of the sea, having ten horns and seven heads, and upon his horns were ten crowns, and upon his heads were names of blasphemy. ²And the beast that I saw was like a leopard, and his feet were like those of a bear, and his mouth was like the mouth of a lion. And the dragon gave him his power and his throne and great authority. ³And one of his heads was as slain unto death, and his mortal wound was healed. And the whole earth marveled after the beast ⁴and worshiped the dragon, because he gave authority to the beast, and worshiped the beast, saying, "Who is like the beast, and who is able to wage war with him?"*
>
> *⁵And it was given to him a mouth to speak great things and blasphemies, and it was given to him to exercise authority for forty-two months. ⁶And he opened his mouth in blasphemies against God, to blaspheme His*

name and His tabernacle, namely, those who dwell in heaven. ⁷And it was given to him to make war with the saints and to overcome them, and authority over every tribe and people and tongue and nation was given to him. ⁸And all those who dwell on the earth will worship him, whose names are not written in the book of life of the Lamb slain from the foundation of the world.

⁹If anyone has an ear, let him hear: ¹⁰if somebody is to go into captivity, into captivity he goes; if somebody kills with the sword, with the sword he must be killed. Here is the endurance and the faith of the saints.

Description of the Beast (13:1–4)

While the dragon is on the seashore, a monstrous beast comes out of the sea. In the Bible, the beast is a symbol of a political power, while the sea symbolizes stormy social and political conditions out of which evil powers come to attack God's people (cf. Dan. 7:2–3).

John describes the beast in the order that its parts are emerging from the water. The beast has ten horns, and upon them are royal crowns of political authority. The ten horns point to Daniel 7, in which the ten horns symbolize the division of the Roman Empire and the nations that sprang up after its demise (Dan. 7:24). The beast also has seven heads with blasphemous names on them. The heads of the beast are the powers used by Satan to persecute God's people throughout history (Rev. 17:9–11). The blasphemous names point to the divine titles the beast claims. This description of the beast mirrors the description of the dragon in Revelation 12:3, which shows that this power is a true representative of the dragon.

As the beast eventually steps out of the water, John sees that its parts resemble a leopard, a bear, and a lion. Thus, the beast combines the characteristics of the four beasts coming out of the sea in Daniel 7:2–8, representing four world kingdoms: Babylon, Medo-Persia, Greece, and Rome (Dan. 7:17). However, John lists them in reverse order, showing that the sea beast is the same as the fourth terrifying beast of Daniel 7, which appeared as a successor of the three kingdoms that came before it (7:7). The fact that the ten horns of the sea beast have royal crowns shows that the power represented by the sea beast appears in history at the time when the nations that sprang up after the demise of the Roman Empire exercised political authority.[2] This clearly corresponds to the little horn of Daniel 7, arising from among the ten horns of the fourth beast (7:23–25).

Power and authority are delegated to the beast by Satan: "The dragon gave him his power and his throne and great authority" (Rev. 13:2). Here is an enthronement scene that copies the enthronement of Christ in Revelation 5. Just as the Father has given His throne and authority to Christ (cf. 2:27; 3:21), so the dragon gives his throne and authority to the beast, investing him as his co-regent and representative on earth. This affirms what was stated before—that this symbolic sea beast is the second member of the false trinity. This ally of Satan wants to take the place of Jesus Christ in the minds and hearts of the people.

John tells us further that, somewhere in history, one of the beast's heads gets a deadly wound, causing the death of the beast. But the mortal wound is eventually healed, and the beast is restored to life (Rev. 13:3). This mirrors the death and resurrection of Jesus Christ—in Greek the same word for slaying the beast is used for the death of Christ the Lamb (5:6). These three phases of the sea beast's existence are defined in Revelation 17:8 in terms of the beast who "was, and is not, and is about to come." This is an antithesis of the divine title: "who is, and who was, and who is coming" (1:4; cf. 4:8).

The resurrection of the beast prompts amazement among the earth's inhabitants. In admiration, they worship both the beast and the dragon standing behind the beast, saying: "Who is like the beast, and who is able to wage war with him?" (Rev. 13:4)—implying that no one is like him or able to do these things. "Who is like the beast?" stands in contrast to "Who is like God?" (Exod. 15:11; Ps. 35:10; Mic. 7:18), referring to the incomparability of God. It also parallels the name of Michael, who defeats the dragon in heaven (Rev. 12:7). In Hebrew, *Michael* means, "Who is like God?" This end-time ally of Satan is a true counterpart of Jesus Christ and His salvific ministry in the final crisis.

Activities of the Beast (13:5–10)

Having portrayed the beast in general terms, John now describes the beast's activities. These are described as the mouth speaking great things and blasphemies during the prophetic period of forty-two months. These activities of the beast echo the activities of the anti-divine power of the little horn coming out of the fourth beast in Daniel 7. The parallels between the two visions show that Daniel 7 and Revelation 13 deal with the same earthly power:

The Little Horn—Daniel 7	The Sea Beast—Revelation 13
Has a mouth speaking great things (7:8; cf. 7:11, 20)	Has a mouth speaking great things (13:5)
Speaks blasphemies against God (7:25)	Speaks blasphemies against God (13:6)
Wages war with the saints and overcomes them (7:21; cf. 7:25)	Wages war with the saints and overcomes them (13:7)
Exercises power and authority for a time, times, and half a time (7:25)	Exercises power and authority for forty-two months (13:5)

First, the sea beast's blasphemies involve the name of God (Rev. 13:5–6). In the New Testament, blasphemy denotes a claim of equality with God (John 10:33; Matt. 26:63–65) or God's prerogatives (Mark 2:7). The sea beast of Revelation 13 claims the titles of God and the prerogatives that belong only to God.

Second, the sea beast's blasphemies are directed against God's tabernacle and those who dwell in it. The dwelling of God is the sanctuary in heaven where Christ ministers on behalf of His people. It is there that the salvation of God's people is worked out. The sea beast denies Christ's mediatorial work in the heavenly sanctuary by substituting it with a human system of offering salvation and forgiveness of sins. The dwellers in heaven are God's people. In Revelation, God's people are already considered the dwellers in heaven (Rev. 14:1; cf. Eph. 2:6, 19), in contrast to the unfaithful, who are regularly referred to as those who dwell on earth. The power of the sea beast was given to it "to make war with the saints and to overcome them" (Rev. 13:7).

Having described the sea beast and its activities, inspiration exhorts people to heed what is being said: "If somebody is to go into captivity, into captivity he goes; if somebody kills with the sword, with the sword he must be killed" (Rev. 13:10). What the text seems to say is that the sea beast will eventually receive retribution proportionate to the harm it has done to God's people. The last word is with Christ, and He will judge the oppressors of His faithful followers (cf. Rev. 19:20–21). This encourages "the endurance and the faith of the saints" (13:10b).

What earthly power does the sea beast represent? The text shows that this power is the successor of the Roman Empire and exercises its authority and power during the prophetic forty-two months or 1,260 days—the same period as the little horn's activities in Daniel 7. The only period that fits aptly into this time frame is the Middle Ages, during which the established church of Western Europe exercised political and religious oppression. Thus, Revelation 13 is a prophecy of the major apostasy in the Christian Church's history.

Several decades prior to the writing of Revelation, Paul foresaw that the apostate power would rise in the Christian church. In Paul's words, this apostate power would take its "seat in the church of God" and exalt itself above God, displaying itself as God (2 Thess. 2:3–4). This apostate power would manifest itself in all the power and appearance of Satan and would come to its end at the Second Coming of Christ (2 Thess. 2:8–9). No doubt, the sea beast of Revelation 13 represents the same apostate power of which Paul spoke.

The rise of the medieval church to power and dominance was gradual. By AD 538, the Christian church had established itself as an ecclesiastical power, and it continued to dominate the Western world throughout medieval times. Thus, AD 538 might mark the beginning of the prophetic period of forty-two months or 1,260 days, symbolizing years. During this period, the state church of Western Europe claimed that the pope was its head, with the position and prerogatives of God. These claims are reiterated in modern times in the statement of Pope Leo XIII: "We [the popes] hold upon this earth the place of God Almighty."[3]

In addition, the atoning ministry of Christ in the heavenly sanctuary was replaced by the claims of the church's priesthood to forgive sins. All those who insisted on living by the Bible, rather than the state religion, experienced persecution and martyrdom. Historians believe that more than 50 million Christians paid with their lives for their faithfulness to the Bible's teachings. Although in modern times of ecumenism and religious tolerance, such statements are regarded as harsh and unfair, the present cannot erase the historical facts and reality.

However, the events of the French Revolution brought the church's oppressive rule to its end. The demise of the papacy under Napoleon in 1798 that inflicted the deadly wound upon the beast marked the conclusion of the 1,260-day prophetic period. The state-instituted religion and the traditional God-centered theology that had dominated the Western world for centuries were replaced by the human-centered and materialistic outlooks of the modern world.

Revelation 13 shows, however, that the religious-political power that Satan used during the Middle Ages, which came to its end with the French Revolution, will rise again and exercise its oppressive power over the world at the time of the end. The healing of the beast's mortal wound will fill the world's inhabitants with awe and admiration: "And all those who dwell on the earth will worship him, whose names are not written in the book of life of the Lamb slain from the foundation of the world" (Rev. 13:8).

At this point, a question arises: What will cause the healing of the beast's mortal wound? The answer is found in the rest of chapter 13, which describes another earthly power appearing on the world scene that will play the key role in reviving the medieval oppressive power and causing the world's inhabitants to acknowledge and accept it.

The Beast from the Earth

 Revelation 13:11–18

Revelation 13:11–18 portrays the time of the end when the healing of the sea beast's deadly wound leads to the admiration of the entire world. Now the focus of the vision shifts to the second of Satan's allies in the final crisis, the one primarily responsible for healing the sea beast's deadly wound. As in the case of the first beast, John first gives a general description of the beast (Rev. 13:11), then moves on to describe its end-time activities (13:12–18):

¹¹And I saw another beast coming up out of the earth, and he had two horns like a lamb, and he spoke like the dragon. ¹²And he exercises all the authority of the first beast before it. And he makes the earth and those who dwell on it to worship the first beast, whose mortal wound had been healed. ¹³And he performs great signs, that he even makes fire come down from heaven to the earth before the people, ¹⁴and he deceives those living on the earth by means of the signs which were given to him to do before the beast, telling those who dwell on the earth to make an image to the beast who had the wound by the sword and came back to life. ¹⁵And it was given to him to give breath to the image of the beast, so that the image of the beast might speak and cause as many as do not worship the image of the beast to be killed. ¹⁶And he causes all—the small and the great, and the rich and the poor, and the free and the slaves—to receive a mark on their right hand or on their forehead, ¹⁷and that no one may buy or sell except the one who has the mark, that is, the name of the beast, or the number of his name.

[18]Here is wisdom: let the one who has understanding count the number of the beast, for it is a human number; and his number is 666.

Description of the Beast (13:11)

John sees another beast appearing on the scene. The primary meaning of the Greek word *allos* is "another of the same kind." The word *therion* denotes a savage beast—it is the same word used for the first beast that arose out of the sea. These two words together show that the earthly power introduced here is of the same kind as the previous one.

There are, however, obvious contrasts between these two beasts. While the first beast arose from the sea, this one arises from the earth. When mentioned together in Revelation, earth and sea represent the whole earth (cf. Rev. 10:2). The fact that one of Satan's allies arises out of the sea and the other from the earth points to the worldwide scope of Satan's end-time activities. This brings to mind the statement heard at Satan's expulsion from heaven: "Woe to the earth and the sea, for the devil has come down to you, having great anger, knowing that he has little time" (12:12).

The reference to the earth and the sea in Revelation 13 also has further significance. The first beast arose from the sea, that is, from the stormy social and political conditions of the world, following the downfall of the Roman Empire. The second beast comes from the earth. This is the same earth that in Revelation 12:14–16 saved the woman (the church) from the flooding waters of the dragon at the conclusion of the 1,260-year prophetic period. This shows that the power represented by the earth beast appears on territory friendly to the church, somewhere after the medieval period.

While the first, sea beast had a long history, the second, earth beast is a new player on the scene. No history of its activities is mentioned. It arises to world power after the sea beast receives the deadly wound. Since the sea beast received the deadly wound during the French Revolution, the earth beast appears on the world's scene after that. The earth beast, thus, functions as an exclusively end-time world power.

Also, while the first beast had a terrifying appearance, the second beast, in contrast, has a harmless appearance. It is lamblike; on its head there are two lamblike horns, in contrast to the sea beast that has ten monstrous horns. The lamb in Revelation is an exclusive symbol of Christ. This shows that this end-time power has a Christlike appearance and is friendly to God's people.

The text shows, however, that this lamblike power displays the satanic spirit; it speaks like the dragon. The dragon-like speaking is a reference to the deceptive and seductive talk of the serpent in the Garden of Eden (Gen. 3:1–5). As the prophets are the mouthpieces of God, so this end-time power is the mouthpiece of Satan. False prophets in the Bible claim to be God's representatives with a message from God; yet, they lead people away from God. The phrase "he spoke like the dragon" is elaborated in Revelation 13:12–17, which describes the lamblike beast as instrumental in inducing the whole world to worship the first beast that received the deadly wound.

What power in the world does this lamblike beast represent? There is only one world power that appeared in history in the post-medieval period that fits the description of the lamblike beast of Revelation 13: the Protestant United States. Revelation 13 shows that the United States of America, which in the post-medieval period provided protection and a safe haven to the church, will play the key role in last-day events.

Activities of the Beast (13:12–13)

Having identified the earth beast, John the Revelator now moves to describe the beast's activities. Here, there is a change in tenses from past to present, bringing us to the closing days of this world's history. The beast begins to exercise "all the authority of the first beast before it" (Rev. 13:12). This end-time earthly power is the true parody of the Holy Spirit. According to the Gospel of John, the purpose of the Holy Spirit is to exercise the authority of Christ, pointing people to Christ (John 15:26; 16:13–14). In the same way, the earth beast exercises all the authority of the sea beast, pointing people to it.

The "authority of the first beast" refers to the coercive power that the medieval church exercised during the prophetic period of forty-two months (Rev. 13:5–8), imposing upon people doctrines and practices that were contrary to the Bible's teachings. Whoever did not condone the teachings of the established church experienced persecution and martyrdom.

By exercising this medieval authority, the earth beast will make the people in the world "worship the first beast, whose mortal wound had been healed" (Rev. 13:12). In doing this, the beast is counterfeiting the Holy Spirit, whose role is to direct worship to Christ. The text shows that making the earth's inhabitants worship the first beast has to do with the healing of this beast's deadly wound; it points to some kind of activities from the earth beast during the time of the end to persuade the people in the world to worship the sea beast.

How will the earth beast achieve this? As the text shows, in an initial phase, this will be achieved by miraculous signs to persuade people (Rev. 13:13–14), while in the final stage, it will be achieved by coercion (13:15–17). The prophecy portrays the beast performing miraculous signs by which it deceives the nations of the earth (13:13). Similarly, Paul foretold Satan's end-time activities that would be accompanied by all sorts of "power and signs and false wonders, and with all the deception of wickedness for those who perish" (2 Thess. 2:9–10). Just as through miraculous signs the Holy Spirit convinced people to accept Jesus Christ and worship Him, so this counterfeit Holy Spirit deceives the people in the world by means of deceptive signs and miracles that persuade them to worship the sea beast.

The greatest of the signs performed is bringing fire down from heaven (13:13). This is reminiscent of the fire the prophet Elijah called down from heaven, which demonstrated that Yahweh was the true God of Israel and the only One to be worshiped (1 Kings 18:38). The lamblike beast, thus, imitates the prophetic role of Elijah. Through the rest of Revelation, it is called the false prophet, working miracles on behalf of the sea beast (Rev. 19:20). By these deceptive miracles, it misleads people into worshiping the sea beast. The Bible warns of false prophets who perform signs and miracles to lead people away from God to worship other gods (Deut. 13:1–3).

The beast's bringing fire down from heaven also counterfeits the day of Pentecost, when tongues of fire came down from heaven upon the disciples (Acts 2:3). All of this shows that bringing fire down from heaven is designed to counterfeit the power of God and to deceive people and persuade them that these miraculous signs are the manifestations of divine power.

The Image of the Beast (13:14–15)

The healing of the sea beast's deadly wound will take place when the medieval religious system is restored. The prophecy shows that the earth beast will play the key role in this process. John goes on to explain how this will happen.

Through miraculous signs, the earth beast deceives the people of the world. The people will accept these deceptive miracles as the manifestation of divine power, primarily because of the beast's lamblike appearance. However, the true nature of the beast is displayed in its dragon-like talk. The beast will persuade the people of the world to make an image of the beast that received the deadly wound. An image is a copy of some reality. The prophecy shows that the world powers will be seduced to create a system of state religion, resembling the one from the Middle Ages. When the civil and political powers join the leading religious organizations to enforce a religion upon people, they will form the image of the beast.

However, as the Old Testament shows, images lack life (Ps. 135:15–17). So here the earth beast plays a decisive role; it gives breath to the image of the beast, making it alive. This portrayal of breathing life into the image recounts Genesis 2:7, where, having created man in His image, God breathed life into him, enabling him to function. Likewise, the earth beast gives life to the sea beast's image, enabling it to function. By using deceptive miracles and political power to enforce its demands for popular worship, the earth beast will persuade the people of the world to acknowledge the sea beast's authority and render their allegiance to it.

This whole scene mirrors Daniel 3, which describes King Nebuchadnezzar ordering the people of his kingdom, on the threat of death, to worship the golden image he erected. Just as in the time of Daniel worshiping the golden image was enforced by a legislative decree, so at the time of the end the demand for popular worship will be supported by civil power, forcing the whole earth to worship the sea beast.

Revelation 13 indicates here that the Protestant United States will have the leading role in healing the sea beast's deadly wound. It tells us that the religiopolitical system that Satan used during the Middle Ages will rise again in the closing days of this earth's history to win and control the worship and conscience of the world's people. This prophecy points to the revival of medieval intolerance at the time of the end (Rev. 13:15). The lamblike beast will side with the sea beast to establish a religious union and enforce an institution that characterized medieval Christianity in both Western Europe and the Eastern hemisphere. The earth beast's impact will be worldwide.

The Mark of the Beast (13:16–17)

Those who succumb to the pressure applied by this institution will receive a mark with the beast's name on their right hand or their forehead (Rev. 13:16). All classes of human society are commanded to receive the mark of the beast. To receive the mark of the beast means to belong to the beast and worship it. The mark of the beast is, thus, an antithesis of God's seal (14:1). Just as the seal identifies those who belong to God, so the mark of the beast identifies those who belong to and worship the beast.

While the sealing signifies the Holy Spirit's working presence in human hearts (Eph. 1:13–14; 4:30), the mark of the beast counterfeits the work of the Holy Spirit. The people with the mark of the beast have been brought into this religious system, and they ever serve it with their minds and hearts—some willingly, others reluctantly.

Placing the mark on the right hand or forehead evokes Deuteronomy 6:8, where Moses instructed the Israelites to bind God's law as a sign upon their hands or their foreheads—the injunction that Jews have taken literally by wearing phylacteries to show their belonging and obedience to God.[1] This suggests that the mark on the forehead has to do with impressing God's law upon the minds and behavior of His people. In contrast, receiving the mark of the beast on the right hand or the forehead stands as refusing God's commandment—the exchange of obedience to God for obedience to the beast.

Revelation shows that the central issues in the final crisis will be worship and obedience to God by keeping His commandments (Rev. 14:12). The whole world will be divided into two camps: those who worship God and those who worship the beast. While God's true worshippers are characterized by keeping His commandments (12:17; 14:12), the beast's worshippers are characterized by their refusal to keep God's commandments.

Revelation shows that the first four commandments of the Decalogue—the ones that concern a person's relationship with God and worship—will become the standard of loyalty to God in the final crisis. Satan's end-time activities are portrayed in the book as a well-planned attack on these four commandments:

- The sea beast's demand for worship (Rev. 13:15) is a direct attack on the first commandment: "You shall have no other gods beside Me."
- The earth beast raises up an image of the sea beast to be worshiped (13:14–15), which is a direct attack on the second commandment:

"You shall not make for yourself an image. . . . You shall not worship them or serve them."

- The beast's blasphemy of God (13:5–6) is a direct attack on the third commandment: "You shall not take the name of the Lord your God in vain."
- The mark of the beast (13:16–17) is a direct attack on the fourth commandment: "Remember the Sabbath day, to keep it holy."

Revelation 14:6–12 clearly indicates that the Sabbath commandment, in particular, will be the litmus test of one's faithfulness and obedience to God.[2] The appeal of the three angels' messages to worship and obey the true God rather than to worship the beast and receive the mark of the beast is clearly done in the context of the Sabbath commandment (Rev. 14:7; 14:9). The Sabbath in the Bible concerns proper worship and relationship with God. As the Sabbath is the distinctive sign of God's faithful people's obedience, so the mark of the beast is the sign of obedience to the beast (cf. Exod. 31:12–17; Ezek. 20:12, 20). The mark of the beast, thus, substitutes human commandments for God's commandments. The most obvious evidence of this is substituting the human-established false Sabbath—namely, Sunday, the first day of the week—for the seventh-day Sabbath.

Yet, observance of Sunday does not itself mean having the mark of the beast. Sunday keeping will become "the mark of the beast" only when people have a clear understanding of the issues involved in choosing a day of worship.[3] That time still lies ahead in the future. In the present, Christ's followers must not label any individual or group as having the mark of the beast. Sunday keeping today does not make any person lost for the gospel, just as Sabbath keeping does not make any person a genuine Christian. The time is coming, however, when the mark of the beast will become the issue. At that time, every person in the world will have to take his or her stand for or against God.

Revelation does not explain what the mark of the beast will be like and how exactly it will be applied. Remember that, as in the case of any unfulfilled prophecy, the mark of the beast will be understood at the time of its fulfillment. While it is clear that the mark of the beast is not a visible sign on people, we have to wait for its final realization. Ellen White notes that, in regard to the mark of the beast, much is not "yet understood nor will it be understood until the unrolling of the scroll."[4]

Revelation 13:17 shows that the climax of the end-time drama includes economic sanctions against those who refuse to worship the beast's image (Rev. 13:17). People in the world will be deceived by the demonic activities (16:13–14). Refusal to worship the beast will be treated as an act of disloyalty, with the penalty of death. All of this is a result of Satan's longtime desire to be the sole owner of this world—something that cannot be realized as long as those who refuse to acknowledge his rule over this world remain. However, this scenario will be concluded with the coming of Christ with power and glory. He will defeat the satanic triune league and their forces and defend His faithful people, bringing them to their eternal homeland (19:11–21; Dan. 12:1).

The Number 666 (13:18)

Revelation 13 concludes with a call to the reader to figure out the number of the beast, which is 666. For this, a special wisdom and understanding are needed. The wisdom here does not refer to a brilliant intellectual ability but to the divine discernment imparted by the Holy Spirit. "The LORD gives wisdom," wrote Solomon; "from His mouth come knowledge and understanding" (Prov. 2:6; cf. Dan. 2:21). James tells us that if we ask God for wisdom, He will readily give it to us (James 1:5).

The reference to wisdom and understanding in Revelation 13:18 clearly points to Daniel 12. Here, Daniel was told to seal his book—the part that described the persecution of God's people—until the time of the end, when it will be unsealed. The wise will get an understanding of those prophecies and "be purged, purified and refined, but the wicked will act wickedly; and none of the wicked will understand" (Dan. 12:10).

Revelation 13:18 reflects on this passage from Daniel. God's end-time people will need divinely imparted wisdom to discern the deceptive character of the beast and to be protected from the end-time deception (see Rev. 17:9). However, all those who lack this wisdom will become victims of the end-time deception (cf. 2 Thess. 2:10–12; Rev. 13:8).

Vicarius Filii Dei

Throughout Christian history, many attempts have been made to determine the identity behind the number 666. A popular method has involved the use of *gematria*, a technique in which the letters of the alphabet are associated with numbers. Before the invention of Arabic numbers, letters of the Hebrew, Greek, and Roman alphabets had numerical values. For instance, A stood for 1, B for 2, C for 3, etc. Using *gematria*, the numerals from a person's name or title have been added to make the number 666. As a result, many different proposals have been put forward. Almost every generation of Christians has applied the number 666 to its own time.

In the seventeenth century, the German classical scholar Andreas Helwig applied the numerical value of the number 666 to the Latin inscription *vicarivs filii dei* (spelled Vicarius Filii Dei in English, meaning Vicar of the Son of God), assuming it to be the title of the papacy. Uriah Smith popularized this view among Adventists in his commentary on Revelation, making the further claim that the title was inscribed on a papal crown. It is interesting that Ellen White never referred to Vicarius Filii Dei in her writings to interpret 666,[5] though she clearly identified the beast of Revelation, and his number, with the papacy.[6]

Applying the Latin phrase *vicarivs filii dei* to 666 is problematic for several reasons. First, there is no documented evidence, despite the claims, that the phrase has ever appeared on the papal tiara or miter. Although in the past, some popes were occasionally referred to as Vicarius Filii Dei, there is no evidence that this has ever been an official papal title. Second, nowhere in Revelation is *gematria* used as the method of calculation. Numbers in Revelation regularly have symbolic meanings. When, for example, in the following passage (Rev. 14:3), the 144,000 are described as having the name of God on their heads, this does not call for a mathematical calculation but for the spiritual understanding of the name.

Third, the text does not specify the language that the name of the beast is written in. In Revelation, when a name has a special meaning, the language is regularly specified as either written "in Hebrew" (9:11; 16:16) or "in Greek" (9:11). Latin is not used in Revelation, and there is no indication that 666 could be decoded in this language. If the meaning of the beast's name should be decoded by using the numerical value of its letters, the language would be specified, as it is in all other cases in the book.

Fourth, Revelation 13 clearly shows that the number 666 applies exclusively to the time of the end, not before. The number is identified with the sea beast after the healing of its mortal wound, and during the time that the lamblike beast causes the earth's inhabitants to receive the sea beast's mark, which consists of its name or its number. God's people are called to figure out the meaning of this number, so they may perceive the true nature of the beast and avoid being deceived by it. Applying 666 to particular historical figures or to the medieval

Latin inscription *vicarivs filii dei* does not fit the end-time context in which the beast's worshippers will receive the mark of the beast.

Meaning of the Number 666

What, then, is the meaning of the number 666? Revelation defines 666 as a human number. The Greek phrase *arithmos anthropou* can be translated as "the number of a man" or "the number of humanity." It is obvious that the latter meaning is true here. This is similar to Revelation 22:17, where *metron anthropou* clearly means "human measurement." The beast of Revelation 13 does not refer to a certain person who will appear during the time of the end; rather, the chapter refers to a religiopolitical system that opposes God.

The best way to understand 666 is from a spiritual perspective. Seven in the Bible is the divine number that expresses God's perfection. Being one short of seven, six represents humanity falling short of the divine perfection. This is based on the fact that humans were created on the sixth day—a day prior to the completion of the full week of seven days. Humans find their purpose only in the number seven by acknowledging God as their Creator and Redeemer.

Thus, 666 refers to humanity apart from God. Such an understanding is further affirmed by 1 Kings 10:14, the only other text in the Bible that mentions 666. It states that King Solomon's annual income was 666 talents of gold. King Solomon was once faithful to God. However, right after this statement, he turned away from God as he started accumulating gold in his palace, multiplying chariots and horsemen, and taking many foreign wives for himself. This was clearly a violation of God's instruction to the Israelite kings, as recorded in Deuteronomy 17:16–17. The purpose of this law was to keep Israelite kings from pride and from being exalted above their brothers (Deut. 17:20).

In disobeying the divine instruction, King Solomon completely turned away from God, became filled with pride and arrogance, and served images of other gods, leading his people away from God. Thus, 666 expressed the sum of all his successes and achievements apart from God. Solomon credited himself, instead of God, for all his achievements and prosperity. Even the temple that he built to God's glory became a token of his own pride and arrogance.

In light of this Old Testament background, the beast's number in Revelation 13 refers to the human system that has turned away from God and is in Satan's service. As such, this rebellious system opposes God, exalts itself above God, and claims the titles and prerogatives of

God. It demands worship from the world's people in place of Christ (Rev. 13:6–8; cf. 2 Thess. 2:4). As stated earlier, this is a clear reference to apostate Christianity that, like Solomon, was once faithful to God but eventually turned away from Him. At the end time, this system, also like Solomon, will lead people away from God to Satan's side and will persecute those who remain faithful to God and keep His commandments (Rev. 13:15).

The Number of Babylon

It is significant that 666 refers to the sea beast in association with the lamblike beast and the dragon. The number 666 consists of a triple six, expressed in Greek as *hexakosioi hexekonta hex*. This trifold six (Gr. *hex*) identifies the satanic triune league—the dragon, the sea beast, and the earth beast—as the counterfeit of the Trinity of God specified in Revelation 1:4–6. This satanic triad comprises the end-time religious system called Babylon after ancient Babylon in the Old Testament—the earthly power that stood in opposition to the religion of the true God and tried to control the world. From its beginning, Babylon stood as an incarnation of godless power in opposition to God. In Isaiah 14:12–14, the king of Babylon is a symbol of Lucifer and his behavior.

The meaning of 666 is found in the fact that six is the number of Babylon. The ancient Babylonian counting system was based on the sexagesimal system, which categorized numbers by six and sixty. We still use the Babylonian measurement for angles (90, 180, and 360 degrees) and time (sixty seconds, sixty minutes, and twenty-four hours). In addition, the number six in Babylon had a religious significance; it was the number of chief gods in the Babylonian pantheon. This explains why King Nebuchadnezzar's statue was sixty cubits high and six cubits wide (Dan. 3:1).

Much of the language in Revelation 13:14–18 echoes Daniel 3, where Nebuchadnezzar enforced image worship upon people: the image, the number six, worshiping the image, the death threat, and the universality of the scene (Dan. 3:1–6). It becomes obvious that Daniel 3 is the backdrop of the scene in Revelation 13:14–18. Revelation 13 tells us that the story of Daniel 3 will be repeated at the time of the end on a worldwide scale. People will have to make their choice: to worship the image or to remain faithful to God.

This is the context that defines the theological meaning of 666 as the Babylonian number—the number of rebellious humanity—in

Revelation. This number refers to the end-time system that will cause the people in the world to side with Satan and worship the beast with the now-healed wound. All who receive the mark of the beast side with the system that, like the Babylon of old, exalts itself above God and tries to take God's place in the world (cf. 2 Thess. 2:3–4).

But this system is nothing more than a human institution counterfeiting God yet falling short of the divine character. God's message to this system is the same as it was to the Old Testament king of Tyre who claimed to be God: "You are a man and not God" (Ezek. 28:9). Such an identification of this end-time Antichrist power and system requires divine wisdom and discernment rather than intellectual cleverness and calculation.

God's Final Message to the World

 Revelation 14:1–20

evelation 12–13 provide a sketch of the end-time scenario in the context of the Great Controversy between Christ and Satan. The purpose is to warn about Satan's final effort to deceive the world and seduce God's people into a false form of worship. Revelation 14 talks about God's response to Satan's deceptive activities by preaching the gospel in which He calls people in the world to leave Babylon and worship Him as the only true God. Preaching the end-time gospel will divide the world into two camps: those who respond and worship God and those who reject that message and side with the satanic trinity.

The Victorious 144,000 (14:1–5)

As the result of Satan's intensive activities in the closing days of earth's history, the whole world is deceived to follow and worship the beast (Rev. 13:8–17). However, during those perilous times, God has a true remnant of those who remain loyal and obedient to Him until the end. These are portrayed as gathered together on Mount Zion. In contrast to those who have the mark of the beast on their forehead or their right hand, these people are portrayed as the victorious 144,000, standing with Christ the Lamb and having Christ's name and His Father's name written on their foreheads. They belong to Christ and remain faithful to Him.

> ¹*Then I looked, and behold, the Lamb was standing on Mount Zion, and with Him 144,000, having His name and the name of His Father written on their foreheads. ²And I heard a voice from heaven, like the sound of many waters and like the sound of loud thunder, and the voice which I*

heard was like the sound of harpists playing on their harps. ³And they sang a new song before the throne and before the four living creatures and the elders; and no one could learn the song except the 144,000 who had been purchased from the earth. ⁴These are the ones who have not been defiled with women, for they have kept themselves chaste. These are the ones who follow the Lamb wherever He goes. These have been purchased from among men as first fruits to God and to the Lamb. ⁵And no lie was found in their mouth, for they are blameless.

The New Song (14:1–3)

This group of saints is the same one spoken of in Revelation 7. Their number is symbolic, denoting the totality of God's end-time people. They are protected by the seal on their foreheads, which enables them to stand on the great day of God's wrath. They have been the objects of Satan's furious rage (Rev. 12:17). Now, they stand on Mount Zion. In the Old Testament, Mount Zion stands as the center of God's rule on earth (Ps. 48:1–3; Mic. 4:7). It is the place where God's people are secure from their enemies. Here, in Revelation 14, the 144,000 are gathered under Christ's banner and are ready to battle Satan and his forces.

John hears them singing "a new song" (Rev. 14:3). This is the song of deliverance sung by Israel after passing through the Red Sea (Exod. 15). It will be sung again by those who have gone through the final crisis (Rev. 15:3). These people now stand victoriously on Mount Zion, worshiping Christ the Lamb.

Nobody else is able to learn the new song except the 144,000, because it reflects their own experience. These people have a close association with Jesus. They have His and His Father's names written on their foreheads. God's name stands for His character; these redeemed saints reflect God's character in their lives. They have washed their robes in the blood of the Lamb. They have gone through the tribulation of the last days (Rev. 7:14), experiencing the full rage of Satan (12:17). Their tribulation experience is similar to the one Jesus experienced during the last days of His earthly ministry. They faced the end-time coalition of the political, secular, and religious powers that were against them. They stood firm in the midst of Satan's deceptive activities.

Their loyalty has been severely tested; however, they victoriously withstood the end-time deception. They preached the gospel in spite of the difficulties they faced from the hostile world (Rev. 14:6–12).

And they were delivered in the final crisis, like no other people in history (Dan. 12:1). This is why no other group of people is able to learn this song.[1]

Characteristics of the 144,000 (14:4–5)

Some characteristics of the 144,000 are listed. First, they are virgins, for they did not defile themselves with women. This defilement must be taken metaphorically. Adultery in the Bible is a regular symbol for unfaithfulness to God; those who turn away from God commit spiritual fornication. Paul used this metaphor to refer to Christians: "I betrothed you to one husband, so that to Christ I might present you as a pure virgin" (2 Cor. 11:2). Revelation talks about the great prostitute Babylon and her daughters—apostate churches (Rev. 17:5)—who seduce people into illicit relationships with them (17:1–5; 18:3, 9).

In Old Testament times, before going into battle, Israelite soldiers were required to keep themselves pure and not have relationships with women (Deut. 23:9–11; 1 Sam. 21:4–5). The Dead Sea Scrolls show that some Jewish groups believed that this regulation also applied to the great eschatological war against the forces of darkness.[2] The 144,000 are portrayed as military troops in battle against Satan and his army (cf. Rev. 7:4–8). As such, they have not spiritually defiled themselves with women—Babylon and her daughters—but have kept themselves chaste for Christ. They have remained faithful to their one Husband: Christ.

These people "follow the Lamb wherever He goes." They put Christ first and choose to keep their relationship with Him, no matter the cost. They remain unwavering in their faithfulness to Him, in contrast to the majority of the world who follow the beast. Nobody and nothing can separate them from Christ's love.

The 144,000 are the ones who "have been purchased from among men as first fruits to God and to the Lamb" (cf. Rev. 14:4). In ancient Israel, the first fruit belonged to God as the best fruits of the harvest. In the Bible, the term is used metaphorically to describe God's people (in their totality) and to distinguish them from the rest of the world's people (Jer. 2:3; James 1:18). The 144,000 are purchased by Christ's blood and are the first fruits from the harvest, brought to Mount Zion (cf. Rev. 14:14–16).

Their final characteristic is that "no lie was found in their mouth, for they are blameless" (Rev. 14:5). Here, Zephaniah's prophecy is fulfilled: "The remnant of Israel will do no wrong and tell no lies, nor will a deceitful tongue be found in their mouths" (Zeph. 3:13). The lie spoken of in Revelation 14:5 denotes more than a common untruthfulness. The truthfulness of the 144,000 stands in contrast to Satan's end-time deceptions (2 Thess. 2:9–11; Rev. 13:14). While most people in world choose to believe the lie, God's end-time people will receive the love of the truth and be saved (2 Thess. 2:10–11).

The 144,000 are blameless. The Greek word *amōmos* (blameless) does not denote a moral, sinless status but rather the fidelity of the 144,000 to Christ. This is not an exclusive characteristic of the last generation of saints. In the Old Testament, Abraham and Job were blameless but not sinless (Gen. 17:1; Job 1:1). Two thousand years ago, Christians were called to be holy and without blemish before God (Eph. 1:4; 5:27; Phil. 2:15; Col. 1:22; Jude 24).

In the Bible, to be blameless means to walk with God as Noah and Abraham did (Gen. 6:9; 17:1). In contrast to most of the world's people who renounce their loyalty to God, the 144,000 reflect the true character of Christ. They have washed their robes and made them white in the blood of the Lamb. As such, they are found "spotless and blameless" before God (2 Pet. 3:14).

The Three Angels' Messages (14:6–13)

The previous section provides God's end-time people with a firm assurance of Christ's promise to be ever with them and to sustain them during the great eschatological showdown. During these hard times, God's people are delegated with a special message to deliver to the world—pictured in terms of three vocal angels flying in mid-heaven with special messages for the earth's inhabitants:

> *6And I saw another angel flying in mid-heaven, having an eternal gospel to preach to those who live on the earth, and to every nation and tribe and tongue and people; 7and he said with a loud voice, "Fear God, and give Him glory, because the hour of His judgment has come; worship Him who made the heaven and the earth and sea and springs of waters."*
>
> *8And another angel, a second one, followed, saying, "Fallen, fallen is Babylon the great, she who has made all the nations drink of the wine of the passion of her immorality."*

> ⁹*Then another angel, a third one, followed them, saying with a loud voice, "If anyone worships the beast and his image and receives a mark on his forehead or on his hand, ¹⁰he also will drink of the wine of the wrath of God, which is mixed in full strength in the cup of His anger; and he will be tormented with fire and brimstone in the presence of the holy angels and in the presence of the Lamb. ¹¹And the smoke of their torment goes up forever and ever; they have no rest day and night, those who worship the beast and his image and whoever receives the mark of his name." ¹²Here is the perseverance of the saints, who keep the commandments of God and their faith in Jesus.*
>
> ¹³*And I heard a voice from heaven, saying, "Write, 'Blessed are the dead who die in the Lord from now on!'" "Yes," says the Spirit, "so that they may rest from their labors, for their deeds follow with them."*

The Greek word *angelos* (angel) means "messenger." In the Bible, angels often represent persons in God's service (Mal. 2:7; Matt. 11:10). Revelation 14:12 clearly links the three angels to God's end-time people, carrying God's warning message to the world.

The First Angel's Message (14:6–7)

The first angel is seen with an eternal gospel to proclaim to every person on earth. The gospel is good news. The fact that the gospel the angel proclaims is specified as "eternal" shows that this is the gospel of the Bible, which is about God saving humans. The gospel contains both salvation and judgment. It is good news for those who accept it, because they are saved, but it means judgment for those who reject it.

The proclamation of the end-time gospel is worldwide; it is to be proclaimed to "every nation and tribe and tongue and people" (Rev. 14:6). This brings to mind the commission of John to prophesy "concerning many peoples and nations and tongues and kings" (10:11). This affirms the notion that the three angels represent God's end-time people, entrusted with the preaching of the gospel. This preaching is significant, because at the time of the end, the beast will exercise its Satan-delegated authority over "every tribe and people and tongue and nation" (13:7). Just as Satan's deceptive activities are worldwide, so is the end-time proclamation of the gospel. This is the preaching of the gospel pointed to by Jesus in His Sermon on the Mount of Olives (Matt. 24:14).

The angel proclaims the message with "a loud voice" (Greek *phōnē megalē*, from which the word "megaphone" comes). This message is urgent: it concerns the eternal destiny of every person on earth. It is God's call to the earth's inhabitants to repent. This call is expressed with a triple imperative: to fear God, to give Him glory, and to worship Him as the Creator.

"Fear God, and give Him glory" (Rev. 14:7). In Revelation, God's end-time people are the ones who fear God (11:18; 19:5). To fear God in the Bible means to take Him seriously and acknowledge Him for who He is. It implies respect and reverence for God. Fearing God denotes a right relationship with Him and a full surrender to His will (Gen. 22:12; Job 1:8–9). It results always in right doing. Those who fear God keep His commandments (Deut. 5:29; 13:4; Eccles. 12:13).

Fearing God and giving Him glory go together (Rev. 11:13; 15:4). While the former designates a right relationship with God, the latter denotes obedience to God. The person who fears God lives a life of glorifying God. Humans glorify God by keeping His commandments. Jesus states: "My Father is glorified by this, that you bear much fruit" (John 15:8). God's end-time people in Revelation are characterized by their close relationship with Jesus Christ and by keeping His commandments (Rev. 12:17; 14:12).

The reason for fearing God and giving Him glory is because "the hour of His judgment has come" (Rev. 14:7). This echoes the words of Solomon: "Fear God and keep His commandments . . . . For God will bring every act to judgment . . . whether it is good or evil" (Eccles. 12:13–14). Paul states that we all have to appear before the judgment seat of Christ to be recompensed for what we have done (2 Cor. 5:10).

The judgment here is the pre-Advent judgment, which takes place prior to the Second Coming—in contrast to the final judgment, which takes place after the millennium (Rev. 20:11–15). Its purpose is to decide who is in a right relationship with God and who is not. Those decisions are made before Jesus comes. This pre-Advent judgment takes place at the same time as the end-time gospel is preached. When the preaching of the gospel is done and the pre-Advent judgment is concluded, there will be the final separation between those who are for the kingdom and those who are lost (Rev. 14:14–20). Then Jesus will come to bring His reward to every person, according to his or her deeds.

Judgment is not a popular religious concept among Christians today. Yet, judgment is a part of the gospel. It is good news for the faithful and obedient, but it is a bad news for the unfaithful. When the judgment is done, the destiny of every person is decided (Rev. 22:11). There is not a second chance, for the offer of salvation is no longer available. To God's people, judgment means vindication and salvation, but to the others, it means condemnation. It is to the latter that the messages of the three angels are directed, calling them to worship the living God. Sinners still have an opportunity to repent and turn to God. God does not want anyone to perish; rather, He wants all to come to repentance (2 Pet. 3:9).

"Worship Him who made the heaven and the earth and sea and springs of waters" (Rev. 14:7). This exhortation echoes the call of Paul and Barnabas to the people in Lystra to turn "to a living God, who made the heaven and the earth and the sea and all that is in them" (Acts 14:15). Worship is central in the final conflict between Christ and Satan. At the time of the end, people in the world fall into two groups: those who fear and worship God and those who fear and worship the beast. A clear line is drawn between the two groups.

It is important to keep in mind that the end-time test is not a denial of worship but a denial of who is worshiped. While most of the world's people reject the truth and choose to follow and worship the beast, God's people choose to worship and serve God wholeheartedly.

True worship in the Bible is associated with a correct day for worship. The call to worship God who made the heaven and the earth and the sea and the springs of waters reflects the fourth of the Ten Commandments. The editors of *The Greek New Testament* from the United Bible Societies show in the margin that this statement from Revelation 14:7 is a direct quotation from Exodus 20:11.[3] This shows that the first angel's call to worship God the Creator is given in the context of Sabbath observance. This is a call to worship God, who created this earth in six days and proclaimed the seventh day holy (Gen. 2:1–3). The seventh-day Sabbath is a special sign of our relationship with God (Exod. 31:13; Ezek. 20:12, 20). It is a memorial of both creation (Exod. 20:11) and redemption (Deut. 5:15).

The first angel's message shows that, at the time of the end, the truth about God the Creator will be once more proclaimed to the world. The people will be called to return to worshiping the true God. This message counters Satan's deceptive activities that are intended to pull the world into false religion and into serving the counterfeit god (2 Thess. 2:4).

The Second Angel's Message (14:8)

The second angel follows the first; this shows that the two messages are related. While the first message calls the earth's people to fear and worship God the Creator, the second message announces the fall of Babylon the Great—the counterfeit god—who has made all the nations drink the wine of the passion of her immorality.

The symbol of Babylon in Revelation is rooted in the historical Babylon as the power that opposed God and oppressed His people. From its very beginning, Babylon in the Bible is characterized by arrogance and rebellion against God (Gen. 11:1–9). Isaiah 14:12–15 equates Babylon with Satan and his attempt to make himself equal to God. The expression "Babylon the great" echoes the boasting of King Nebuchadnezzar (Dan. 4:30). This boasting was met with the announcement of divine judgment over this power. Babylon was to meet its end.

The end-time Babylon in Revelation is symbolic of the satanic trinity—Satan, the sea beast, and the earth beast. This satanic league will unite apostate religious powers under its auspices; these are referred to as Babylon's daughters (Rev. 17:5). These daughters will put themselves into the service of Satan in opposition to God and His people (see 13:11–18). This apostate religious confederacy is characterized by the pride and arrogance of historical Babylon. Like Babylon of old, it exalts itself above God, seeking to take God's place.

Revelation 17 pictures end-time Babylon as a prostitute making all nations drink her wine and seducing them into illicit relationships with her (Rev. 17:1–5; 18:3). Jeremiah speaks of Babylon "intoxicating all the earth. The nations have drunk of her wine; therefore the nations are going mad" (Jer. 51:7). In Revelation 13:11–18, the satanic trinity deceives and seduces the people in the world to worship the beast and its image. The seduced nations will associate with end-time Babylon for economic security (18:3, 9–19). The medieval system of the state religion will be restored, and the mortal wound of the beast will be healed. The newly established religious-political union will enforce false religion, controlling people's consciences and conduct. The world's people will be coerced to worship the beast and receive the mark of the beast.

The second angel's message provides an assurance to God's people that this wicked system will not last long. It is already fallen and will soon come to its end, just like the Babylon of old (cf. Isa. 21:9; Jer. 51:8). The twofold repetition of the word "fallen" points out that

Babylon will certainly end. This collapse of the end-time Babylon is portrayed in Revelation 18.

The Third Angel's Message (14:9–11)

The third angel follows; his message builds on the previous two. While the two other messages call the people to fear and worship the true God and announce the doom of Babylon as the false system, the message of the third angel gives a serious warning to those who choose to worship the beast and its image and receive the mark on their forehead or on their right hand.

This angel uses drastic language. All who choose to drink of Babylon's wine will have to "drink of the wine of the wrath of God, which is mixed in full strength in the cup of His anger" (Rev. 14:10). Drinking wine from the Lord's cup in the Old Testament is a frequent symbol of God's wrath (Job 21:20; Ps. 75:8; Isa. 51:17–23).[4] In ancient times, wine was often diluted with water to reduce its strength. Undiluted wine was mixed with various herbs and spices to increase its intoxicating strength. The mixed, undiluted wine represents God's wrath being fully executed, without His mercy. The psalmist applies this metaphor to divine judgment: "For a cup is in the hand of the LORD, and the wine foams; it is well mixed, and He pours out of this" (Ps. 75:8).

Drinking this undiluted cup of God's wrathful wine is portrayed in Revelation 15–16 as the seven last plagues. The seven last plagues are spoken of as the cup of the wine of God's fierce wrath, poured out on those who worship the beast and receive the mark of the beast (Rev. 16:1, 19). In pouring out the seven last plagues, "the wrath of God is completed" (15:1).

All who worship the beast's image and receive the mark of the beast will be tormented with eternal fire before the angels and the Lamb. The smoke of the fire will ascend forever and ever. And these people will not have rest day and night.

This is a well-known image in the Bible. Fire and sulfur in the Old Testament are a symbol of judgment (Gen. 19:24; Isa. 34:8–10). The concept of eternal fire and smoke ascending forever also comes from the Old Testament. Isaiah prophesied that Edom would be destroyed by fire and sulfur and become a burning pitch: "It will not be quenched night and day; its smoke will go up forever," and it will never rise again from its ruins (34:9–10). Jude described the fate of Sodom and Gomorrah as suffering "the punishment of eternal fire" (Jude 7). It seems clear that these texts do not talk about endless burning. Neither Sodom and Gomorrah nor Edom are burning today in modern Jordan. However, the effects of the fire that destroyed them last forever. The same is true regarding the eternal fire in Revelation; it does not denote endless burning but burning long enough to make the consumption complete—until nothing is left to burn.

The Old Testament prophets used the destruction of Sodom and Gomorrah as the model for destroying ancient Babylon (Isa. 13:19; Jer. 50:40). The same language is employed in Revelation 14 to describe the fate of end-time Babylon. The grotesque and fearful language used points not to an eternal burning and suffering but to total annihilation. Those who choose to worship the beast and its image and receive the mark of the beast will receive eternal punishment, thus sharing the fate of Babylon the Great (Rev. 19:3; 20:10).

The vivid language used in the third angel's message is intended to stir up the people's senses and to move them to stand firm in the face of Satan's end-time deception, rendering their allegiance to the true God. Fear is expelled by a greater fear. As the beast of Revelation 13 uses fear to compel the world's people to choose false religion and receive the mark of the beast, Revelation uses here a stronger fearful language to dispel that fear. There is something greater to fear: "Do not fear those who kill the body," Jesus said, "but are unable to kill the soul; but rather fear Him who is able to destroy both soul and body in hell" (Matt. 10:28). Those who respond to the call and choose God can escape the fate of the satanic trinity and their followers (Rev. 20:11–15).

The End-Time Saints (14:12–13)

The three angels' messages conclude with a positive statement. It points to the saints' endurance; these saints are entrusted with preaching the end-time gospel message (Rev. 14:12). These are the same people spoken of in Revelation 12:17, who are the object of Satan's furious rage and attack. They are characterized by their unswerving faithfulness to Christ and to keeping God's commandments. The word "here [is the perseverance of the saints]" shows that their endurance is primarily because of their faithful preaching of the end-time gospel which counters Satan's deceptive activities.

These saints are promised that, if they suffer physical hardship and persecution even to the point of death (cf. Rev. 12:11), they will receive rest. They will rest from their labors, and their good works will follow them. This promise contrasts with the threat to those who worship the beast and receive the mark of the beast—they will never have rest (14:11). The eternal destiny of God's people is secured with Christ, who promised to always be with them, until the very end of the age (Matt. 28:20).

The Two Harvests (14:14–20)

When the end-time gospel preaching is finished and the pre-Advent judgment is concluded, the destiny of every person will be decided. This section describes the great separation between those who had a relationship with God and those who followed the beast, portrayed in terms of two harvests. Another set of three angels appears on the scene, coming from the temple in heaven to gather the wheat into the storehouses (14:14–16) and the grapes to be trodden on in the winepress (14:17–20):

> *¹⁴Then I looked, and behold, a white cloud, and sitting on the cloud was one like a son of man, having a golden crown on His head and a sharp sickle in His hand. ¹⁵And another angel came out of the temple, crying out with a loud voice to Him who sat on the cloud, "Put in Your sickle and reap, for the hour to reap has come, because the harvest of the earth is ripe." ¹⁶Then He who sat on the cloud swung His sickle over the earth, and the earth was reaped.*
>
> *¹⁷And another angel came out of the temple in heaven, and he also had a sharp sickle. ¹⁸Then another angel, the one who has power over fire, came out from the altar; and he called with a loud voice to him who had the sharp sickle, saying, "Put in your sharp sickle and gather the clusters from the vine of the earth, because her grapes are ripe." ¹⁹So the angel swung his sickle to the earth and gathered the clusters from the vine of the earth and threw them into the great winepress of the wrath of God. ²⁰And the winepress was trodden outside the city, and blood came out from the winepress, up to the horses' bridles, for a distance of 1,600 stadia.*

The Wheat Harvest (14:14–16)

John sees a cloud, and upon it sits One who looks "like a son of man" (Rev. 14:14). This scene echoes the phrase "like a son of man" from Daniel's vision (Dan. 7:13–14). There is no doubt that Jesus Christ is referred to here (cf. Matt. 24:30; 26:64; Rev. 1:7). The preaching of the gospel has ended, the intercession in heaven is concluded, and the destiny of every person is decided. Christ is now about to bring judgment upon the earth. He wears the crown of victory (Gr. *stephanos*) on His head, and in His hand, He has a sharp sickle to reap the harvest. As Jesus said, when the grain is ripe, God immediately sends the sickle, because the harvest is ready (Mark 4:29). He also made clear that this harvest would take place at the end of this earth's history (Matt. 13:39).

Another angel comes from the temple and from the presence of God. He brings a message to Jesus that the harvest may start: "Put in Your sickle and reap . . . because the harvest of the earth is ripe" (Rev. 14:15). This also mirrors Joel's prophecy of judgment on nations: "Put in the sickle, for the harvest is ripe" (Joel 3:13). In response, Christ swings the sickle upon the earth, and the harvest is reaped.

Here is a symbolic portrayal of a great gathering of God's people at the end of this earth's history. The sealing of God's people is done. Now is the harvest time. Jesus explained that the reapers are angels (Matt. 13:39). Before Christ comes, He will send His angels to gather His elect people from all parts of the earth and store them in His barn (Matt. 13:30–31). These gathered saints are the 144,000, the "first fruits" of the harvest (Rev. 14:4). They are pictured in Revelation 15:2–4 as being in the presence of God and are securely protected from being harmed by the seven last plagues. They are about to experience the transformation of their mortal bodies (1 Cor. 15:51–54) and be joined by the resurrected saints; then they will be taken up in the air to meet Jesus, who is coming in power and glory (1 Thess. 4:17).

The Grape Harvest (14:17–20)

The wheat harvest is followed by the grape harvest. Another angel comes from the temple in heaven with a sharp sickle. Then an angel who has authority over fire comes from the altar. This angel could be the one who ministered the incense, representing prayers of God's people, upon the altar of incense before God, and who concluded the service by hurling the censer filled with fire upon the earth, symbolizing God's judgment upon rebellious humanity (Rev. 8:3–5). He now gives a signal to the angel with the sickle to swing the sickle and gather the clusters, for the grapes are ripe.

The angel swings the sickle and places the grapes into the winepress of God's wrath to be crushed (cf. Rev 19:13). The grapes are trodden outside the New Jerusalem; in this city, nothing unclean is to enter

(21:27). Blood comes from the winepress, rising to the horses' bridles and flowing for 1,600 stadia (184 miles or 300 kilometers), which is the approximate length of Palestine from north to south. The symbolic meaning of this number is obtained by the multiplication of four times four hundred, being a number of the earth (Isa. 11:12; Rev. 7:1; 20:8). This hyperbolical distance points to the severity and worldwide scope of God's wrath. The entire world looks like a battlefield as a result of the harm caused by the seven last plagues (19:17–21). Trampling the grapes is described in the following section as pouring the seven last plagues (15–16).

Again, vivid language is used to warn those who read Revelation about how serious the choice they make is. Fear is expelled by a greater fear. The only way to escape the destiny of the satanic trinity and the beast's worshippers is to worship and serve the true God.

The Seven Last Plagues

 Revelation 15:1–16:11

Revelation 14 concludes with the great gathering of the two harvests: God's people are pictured as the wheat gathered into Christ's barn (cf. Matt. 13:30), while the unrepentant are pictured as grapes to be trodden in the winepress of God's wrath. Chapters 15–16 build on this scene: the victorious saints are gathered before God's throne (Rev. 15:1–4), while the rebellious ones are trodden in the winepress of God's wrath (15:5–16:21).

The Meaning of the Plagues (15:1–8)

Revelation 15 introduces a new scene. Seven angels appear, each with a bowl filled with seven plagues to be poured upon rebellious humanity. However, before they pour out the plagues, the chapter provides some vital information regarding the meaning and timing of the plagues:

> *¹Then I saw another sign in heaven, great and marvelous: seven angels who had seven plagues, which are the last, because in them, the wrath of God is finished.*
> *²And I saw something like a sea of glass mixed with fire, and those who had been victorious over the beast and his image and the number of his name standing on the sea of glass, holding harps of God. ³And they sang the song of Moses, the bond-servant of God, and the song of the Lamb, saying, "Great and marvelous are Your works, O Lord God, the Almighty; righteous and true are Your ways, King of the nations! ⁴Who will not fear, O Lord, and glorify Your name? For You alone are*

holy; for all the nations will come and worship before You, for Your righteous acts have been revealed."

⁵After these things, I looked, and the temple of the tabernacle of testimony in heaven was opened, ⁶and the seven angels who had the seven plagues came out of the temple, clothed in linen, clean and bright, and girded around their chests with golden sashes. ⁷Then one of the four living creatures gave to the seven angels seven golden bowls full of the wrath of God, who lives forever and ever. ⁸And the temple was filled with smoke from the glory of God and from His power; and no one was able to enter the temple until the seven plagues of the seven angels were finished.

The Timing of the Seven Last Plagues

Revelation 16:1–11 tells us that the seven last plagues are reserved exclusively for those who rejected God and received the mark of the beast. These plagues are specified as "the last" (Rev. 15:1). They are last, because they follow the seven trumpet plagues. The trumpets were preliminary judgments, anticipating more severe judgment plagues yet to come. Although there are similarities in the language between the trumpet plagues and the last plagues, the two series are not the same. There are significant differences between them.

First, during the trumpet plagues, the gospel is preached throughout the world (Rev. 10:8, 11–14) and the mediatory ministry of Christ goes on in heaven (8:3–5). However, the last plagues are poured out after the preaching of the gospel is finished and the intercession in the heavenly sanctuary is concluded (14:6–13). The book clearly shows that.

Second, Revelation 15:8 illustrates that the temple in heaven became "filled with smoke from the glory of God and from His power; and no one was able to enter the temple." This language is derived from both the dedication of the tabernacle in the wilderness during Israel's Exodus (Exod. 40:34–35) and from Solomon's temple (1 Kings 8:10–11). On both occasions, the cloud of God's glory filled the building, so the priests could not enter to minister before God. With the absence of the priests, there was no intercession in the temple. Revelation 15:8 reflects this idea, telling us that before the seven plagues are poured on rebellious humanity, Christ's mediatory ministry in heaven will be concluded. The door of opportunity will ultimately close, and the destiny of every person will be decided (Rev. 14:14–20).

Third, the trumpet plagues are restricted in scope and effect. They affect only a part of Satan's kingdom—the phrase "a third" is constantly repeated in the text (Rev. 8:7–12; 9:15, 18). No restriction is linked to the seven plagues. They are evidently global in scope. Note the statement: "Every living thing in the sea died" (16:3).

Last, the seven trumpets cover a long span of history, from the first century until the Second Coming. Relatively long periods are linked to them (Rev. 9:5, 15; 11:2, 11). However, no prophetic time frame is specified regarding the seven plagues. The plagues affect humanity at the end of history for a relatively short period prior to the Second Coming. Actually, the seven last plagues occur within the seventh-trumpet time frame:

Intercession and the Preaching of the Gospel in Progress	First Trumpet
	Second Trumpet
	Third Trumpet
	Fourth Trumpet
	Fifth Trumpet
	Sixth Trumpet
Intercession No Longer	Seventh Trumpet SEVEN PLAGUES

The battle at Jericho in Joshua 6 is illustrative of this point. The Israelites marched around the city for six days, once each day, while the priests blew their trumpets. Then, on the seventh day, they marched seven times. As the priests blew the trumpets, the city walls collapsed. This event best illustrates the relationship between the trumpets and the seals. The seven last plagues are a part of the seventh trumpet. They are poured out as God's response to the anger of the nations (Rev. 11:18). The seventh plague causes the collapse of Babylon the Great (16:17–21).

The Fullness of God's Wrath

The seven last plagues are identified as the last, because in them, God's wrath is completed (Rev. 15:1). Revelation 14:9–10 shows that the plagues are the manifestation of the fullness of God's wrath. Those who worship the beast and its image and receive the mark of the beast on their forehead or on their right hand have to "drink of the wine of the wrath of God, which is mixed in full strength in the cup of His anger" (Rev. 14:10). Up until now, God's wrath has always been mixed with mercy. His judgments were always designed to bring sinners to repentance. But now, the time has come for all who have spurned God's grace to experience the fullness of divine wrath.

In the Bible, divine wrath is defined as God's reaction to the choices people make. When people turn away from God, God gives them over to their choice (cf. Rom. 1:26–28). Yet, He never gives up on them. His grace is at work to win them back to Him. The Bible is replete with such cases.

As stated earlier, the seven last plagues are last, because they are preceded by the seven trumpet plagues, representing God's judgment on His people's oppressors. Although punitive in purpose, the trumpet plagues are diluted with mercy. They are intended to wake up rebellious humanity and bring sinners to repentance. These judgments are executed while the gospel is preached to reach those people under divine judgment and to bring them to God.

But the seven last plagues are pictured as the expression of God's wrath in its undiluted fullness. They are not intended to bring anyone to repentance, because the opportunity for repentance has passed, the preaching of the gospel is concluded (Rev. 14:14–20), the pre-Advent judgment is finished, and intercession in heaven is no longer available (15:8).

The Purpose of the Plagues

What, then, is the purpose of the seven last plagues? First, they are redemptive. Just as God sent the plagues on Egypt to deliver His people and to take them to the Promised Land (Exod. 7–12), so here, God sends the seven last plagues to defeat His enemies and to deliver His people from those who want to destroy them. In addition, these plagues are to bring His people into His kingdom.

Second, the last plagues are punitive (Rev. 15:1; 16:2). They fall on those who chose to follow the satanic trinity and harm God's people. Now these people will experience the righteous judgments of God. In Revelation 6:9–11, the martyred saints are pictured as crying to God for vindication. Their cry is representative of the perennial plea of all of God's suffering people throughout history. God told them to wait for a while. The partial answer to their prayers came with the seven trumpet judgments. Now, with the pouring out of the seven last plagues, their prayers are ultimately answered and God's people are vindicated.

Third, the seven last plagues are intended to bring rebellious humanity to the realization of the consequences of their own choices and actions. In Revelation 13, the people of the world have chosen to follow Babylon—the satanic trinity—which seduced them with false promises and hopes. As God withdraws His protection from the world—portrayed in the symbol of releasing the destructive winds (Rev. 7:1)—the seven last plagues are poured upon the earth with a devastating effect. Now, the people are forced to consider the consequences of their choices. Yet, they do not repent. This brings us to the final point.

Like the Egyptian plagues, the seven last plagues are intended to disclose the hardness of the hearts of those who rejected the gospel and chose to side with the satanic trinity (cf. Exod. 7:1–5). There is no second chance offered. They have willingly chosen to follow the satanic trinity and receive the mark of the beast in spite of God's clear warning (Rev. 14:9–11). As severe as the last plagues are, they do not move these people to repentance. Just as each of the Egyptian plagues increased the hardness of the hearts of Pharaoh and his officials, so each plague coming upon the worshippers of the satanic trinity hardens their hearts into an even greater hatred toward God and His people (16:9–11).

Literal or Symbolic?

An important and difficult question arises as to whether the plagues are literal or symbolic. Revelation's language is often symbolic, which seems obvious when interpreting the seals and the trumpets. However, the situation seems different with the seven last plagues. The fact that the first five plagues inflict intense physical pain and suffering, causing people to curse God, shows that these plagues are literal (Rev. 16:8–11). This is affirmed in Revelation 7:16, which states that the 144,000 will not hunger or thirst anymore and that neither the scorching sun nor the heat will again affect them. All these are clearly the trials of the seven last plagues, which are literal.

However, when we come to the sixth plague, which leads to the battle of Armageddon, the language is obviously symbolic and spiritual. The language of the seventh plague, which talks about the fall of end-time Babylon, seems to blend literal and symbolic meaning.

It is important to remember that the seven last plagues are a prophecy yet to be fulfilled. The true nature will be fully understood when it is fulfilled. Whether literal or figurative, the seven last plagues will expose the impotence of the satanic trinity to help suffering humanity and will vindicate God and His government.

The Victorious Saints (15:1–4)

Before the angels pour the plagues upon the beast's worshippers, there is an interlude, which describes those who chose not to worship the beast and receive its mark as standing upon an expanse resembling a sea of glass (Rev. 15:2–4). They are pictured with harps in their hands, singing the song of Moses and the Lamb.

There is no doubt that this group of the redeemed is the same one in Revelation 14:1–5. While earlier they showed faithfulness to God (in contrast to those who rejected the gospel and sided with the satanic trinity), here, they are protected by God (in contrast to the beast's worshippers, who experience the seven last plagues' harmful effects). Since the seven last plagues are portrayed similarly to the plagues that struck the Egyptians during the Exodus, the victorious saints are appropriately pictured as the Israelites at the Red Sea, celebrating the great victory and praising God for their great deliverance.

This is not to say that God's people will be in heaven during the outpouring of the seven last plagues. They will be on earth when Jesus comes, and they will be taken to meet Jesus coming in power and glory (1 Thess. 4:13–17). Although they are protected from the harmful effects of the plagues, Revelation 7:16 clearly shows that they will, in a certain measure, suffer hunger, thirst, and the scorching heat of the sun during the plagues' trial. But before the plagues are poured out, God's people are assured that He will be close to them during this difficult time. He will care for them as much as He cared for Elijah during the severe famine in Palestine (1 Kings 17).[1]

The First Five Plagues (16:1–11)

With the conclusion of Christ's mediatory ministry, the sealing of God's people is concluded, and the door of opportunity to switch sides is permanently closed. The winds that have been held back are now unleashed to blow, and the seven last plagues are poured upon the earth:

> *[1]Then I heard a loud voice from the temple, saying to the seven angels, "Go and pour out on the earth the seven bowls of the wrath of God."*

²So the first angel went and poured out his bowl on the earth; and it became a loathsome and malignant sore on the people who had the mark of the beast and who worshiped his image.

³The second angel poured out his bowl into the sea, and it became blood like that of a dead man; and every living thing in the sea died.

⁴Then the third angel poured out his bowl into the rivers and the springs of waters; and they became blood. ⁵And I heard the angel of the waters, saying, "Righteous are You, who are and who were, O Holy One, because You judged these things; ⁶for they poured out the blood of saints and prophets, and You have given them blood to drink. They deserve it." ⁷And I heard the altar, saying, "Yes, O Lord God, the Almighty, true and righteous are Your judgments."

⁸The fourth angel poured out his bowl upon the sun, and it was given to it to scorch men with fire. ⁹Men were scorched with fierce heat; and they blasphemed the name of God, who has the power over these plagues, and they did not repent so as to give Him glory.

¹⁰Then the fifth angel poured out his bowl on the throne of the beast, and his kingdom became darkened; and they gnawed their tongues because of pain, ¹¹and they blasphemed the God of heaven because of their pains and their sores; and they did not repent of their deeds.

A voice from the temple in heaven—the place where intercession was previously taking place—commands the seven angels to pour out the plagues upon those who sided with the satanic trinity and received the mark of the beast (Rev. 16:1). This voice comes from the Holy Place in the heavenly sanctuary, where the prayers of the oppressed saints were offered (8:4). Their prayers are now ultimately answered. The time has come for God to vindicate His faithful people and bring His righteous judgments upon those who harmed them.

The first angel pours out his bowl on the earth, and painful and malignant sores strike those who have the mark of the beast. This disease is described as painful and incurable boils, covering the entire body (Deut. 28:35; Job 2:7). A plague of this kind struck the Egyptians during the Exodus (Exod. 9:10–11). The victims of this plague are exclusively those who have the mark of the beast and worship the beast's image. The first plague, thus, carries out the threat of the third angel's message: those who have the mark of the beast and worship the beast and its image must now drink mixed, undiluted wine from the cup of God's wrath (Rev. 14:9–10). God's sealed people are not affected by this plague.

The second angel pours out his bowl into the sea, which becomes like the blood of a dead man. Every living thing in the sea dies. The third angel pours out his bowl into the rivers and the springs of water. All the water on earth immediately turns into blood. Without water to drink, rebellious humanity will not survive.

The reason given for these plagues is because "they poured out the blood of saints and prophets, and You have given them blood to drink" (Rev. 16:6). In response, a voice comes from the altar, saying, "Yes, O Lord God, the Almighty, true and righteous are Your judgments" (16:7). This is the altar of burnt offering, spoken of in the fifth seal, under which God's people prayed for God to vindicate them and to judge those who oppressed them. Now, the voice from the altar affirms that their prayers are finally answered with these plagues; God is beginning to judge these oppressors. Justice is finally dispensed.

The fourth angel pours out his bowl upon the sun. An intense heat scorches people, causing unbearable pain. The unbearable pain, however, does not move them to repentance. Nothing will make them change their actions. They have hardened their hearts to such an extent that they cannot turn around. Instead, they curse and blaspheme the name of God, who executes these plagues, and they refuse to repent. In doing this, they follow in the footsteps of the beast, who blasphemes God's name (Rev. 13:6).

While the first four plagues affected the population in general, the fifth plague strikes the beast's throne, bringing total darkness over the earth. This scene mirrors the ninth plague of Egypt, which struck the whole land with intense darkness (Exod. 10:21–23). It is Satan who delegated the throne and authority to the sea beast (Rev. 13:2). With the support of the earth beast, the sea beast exercises its authority over the earth, deceiving and coercing the world's people to side with the satanic trinity. But even the seat of Satan's authority cannot withstand the force of these plagues.

The authority of the sea beast is now undermined, and the beast suffers great humiliation before the people. As the world's people gnaw their tongues in pain, they become more enraged. They begin to realize the impotence of the unholy trinity to protect them from the effects of the plagues. They feel deceived. However, as in the case of the pharaoh in Egypt, the terror and pain of the plagues increasingly harden their hearts. They have set their minds against God. They continue to curse and blaspheme God for their pain and sores and further refuse to repent (Rev. 16:11). They are ready to turn their anger against God's people. In this way, the world's people become fertile soil for the final deception, which Satan will use to draw the entire world into the great battle between God and Satan. This final deception is portrayed in the sixth plague scene (16:12–16).

The Battle of Armageddon

 Revelation 16:12–21

The seven last plagues are poured exclusively upon those who have chosen to side with the satanic trinity and receive the mark of the beast. While the first five plagues are literal, the last two are clearly symbolic and spiritual. The sixth plague brings us to the very threshold of the great battle of Armageddon, which will take place at the closing period of this earth's history. The seventh plague concludes the scenario; it pictures the demise of end-time Babylon—the enemy of God and His faithful people.

The Sixth Plague (16:12–16)

¹²The sixth angel poured out his bowl on the great river, the Euphrates; and its water was dried up, so that the way would be prepared for the kings from the East. ¹³And I saw coming out of the mouth of the dragon and out of the mouth of the beast and out of the mouth of the false prophet, three unclean spirits like frogs; ¹⁴for they are spirits of demons, performing signs, which go out to the kings of the whole world, to gather them together for the war of the great day of God, the Almighty. ¹⁵("Behold, I am coming like a thief. Blessed is the one who stays awake and keeps his clothes, so that he will not walk about naked, and men will not see his shame.") ¹⁶And they gathered them together to the place which is in Hebrew called Armageddon.

The sixth angel pours out his bowl upon the Euphrates River, drying up its water to prepare the way for "the kings from the East"

(Rev. 16:12). This scene is symbolic. Here, Old Testament language from ancient Babylon's fall is used to describe the final battle between the satanic trinity with the beast's worshippers and Christ with His end-time people.

The Euphrates River was already introduced in the sixth trumpet in connection with the final battle, involving evil forces (Rev. 9:24). In the Old Testament, the Euphrates was the boundary that separated Israel from its enemies: Assyria and Babylon (Isa. 7:20; Jer. 46:10). These enemy nations came against God's people from this great river. Their attacks are often compared to the overflowing waters of the Euphrates, sweeping over the land of Judah (Isa. 8:7–8). The Euphrates River flowed through Babylon and was important to the city. It nourished crops and provided water for people. Without the Euphrates River, Babylon could not exist.

Babylon was introduced in Revelation in the second angel's message (Rev. 14:8). The meaning of end-time Babylon as the key player in the final conflict is rooted in the historical Babylon of the Old Testament. Babylon is pictured as the oppressor of God's people. It conquered Judah and took the people into captivity. The Euphrates River was also the place where God's people were held in Babylonian captivity (cf. Ps. 137).

In Revelation, Babylon is a symbol of religious powers united against God and His people in the closing days of this earth's history. Revelation 17:1–2 pictures Babylon as a prostitute sitting on many waters, seducing the earth's nations. "Many waters" is another reference to the Euphrates (cf. Jer. 51:13). Revelation 17:15 explains that the waters or the Euphrates, upon which end-time Babylon dwells, symbolizes worldwide civil, secular, and political powers. This also shows that these world powers, for a time, will put themselves into the service of this end-time apostate religious confederacy arrayed against God and His people. Just as ancient Babylon was sustained by the Euphrates, so this end-time religious confederacy exists with the support of the civil, secular, and political world powers. At a certain point, however, these symbolic waters supporting Babylon will somehow dry up.

The Drying Up of the Euphrates (16:12a)

The book of Daniel describes God's people when they were captives in Babylon. In BC 539, Cyrus the Great from Persia came with his armies and besieged the city. Because of Babylon's strong fortifications and abundant supply of water and food, the people felt that the city was impregnable. However, on the night the leaders were having a drinking party in the palace of King Belshazzar, the city was captured by the Persian army (Dan. 5). Ancient historians state that the Persians diverted the Euphrates River and entered the city through the dried riverbed, taking the city by surprise.[1] Because of Babylon's overthrow, God's people were allowed to return to their homeland.

The capture of ancient Babylon by Cyrus the Great is the background for the sixth plague scene. As in the case of ancient Babylon, so here the symbolic drying up of the Euphrates River results in the collapse of end-time Babylon—the enemy of God and His people. This scene must be understood symbolically, because as stated earlier, the Euphrates in Revelation represents the world's civil, secular, and political powers, giving their support to Babylon (Rev. 17:15). While Babylon has all the nations behind itself (18:3), those powers will eventually withdraw their support and turn against Babylon, causing its fall (17:15–17). This is how the Euphrates's drying up should be understood.

A question arises: Why do the civil, secular, and political world powers have a sudden change in attitude toward Babylon? Up to the fifth plague, the world's people have focused their hope on Babylon for protection. As they experience the upheavals in nature, they hope that Babylon will protect them. However, as they observe the fifth plague striking the very seat of the beast's authority, the disillusioned people realize the impotence of Babylon to protect them from the plagues' effects (Rev. 16:10). Feeling deceived, and filled with hostility, they are united as they turn against Babylon and destroy it (17:17).

Yet, the pain caused by the plagues does not soften their hearts. As the world's people gnaw their tongues in pain, they get angrier; they continue to curse God and refuse to repent (Rev. 16:11). They are now ready to turn their anger against God's people. In such a way, they become fertile soil for the intense demonic activities which draw the entire world into the great battle of Armageddon (16:12–16).

The Kings from the East (16:12b)

The reason for the Euphrates's drying up in Revelation, and the subsequent collapse of end-time Babylon, is to prepare the way for "the kings from the East" or from the rising of the sun. Here again, John uses language that is modeled after the conquest of ancient

Babylon in the Old Testament. The "kings from the East" or from the rising of the sun is an allusion to Cyrus the Great and his armies, who overthrew ancient Babylon, which was the oppressor of God's people. Cyrus the Great is referred to by Isaiah as God's messiah (Isa. 45:1), who would come "from the rising of the sun" (41:25). His conquest of Babylon delivered God's people from captivity and returned them to their homeland (44:28; Jer. 50:33–38).

Revelation uses this historic event to portray the final battle between Christ and Satan. Similar to how the dried Euphrates prepared the way for Cyrus the Great and his forces to conquer ancient Babylon, the symbolic dried Euphrates also prepares the way for the coming of "the kings from the East" (Rev. 16:12b). As in the case of ancient Babylon, the overthrow of end-time Babylon brings ultimate deliverance to God's end-time people and prepares the way for their entrance into the New Jerusalem.

Who are the "kings from the East" in this text? Revelation clearly shows that they are Christ and His army of saints, engaged in the final battle: "These will wage war against the Lamb, and the Lamb will overcome them, because He is the Lord of lords and King of kings, and those who are with Him are the called and chosen and faithful" (Rev. 17:14). In Revelation 19:14–16, as Jesus returns, He leads the armies of heaven "clothed in fine linen, white and clean" (19:14). This is the dress of the Lamb's bride and represents the righteous acts of God's people (19:7–8).

Some think that these "kings from the East" are heavenly angels. Jesus makes it clear that at His coming He will be accompanied by heavenly angels (Matt. 24:30–31). In the Bible, however, angels are never referred to as kings, while in Revelation, God's people are called kings and priests (Rev. 1:6; 5:10). Elsewhere in the book, the end-time saints are pictured as an army of 144,000 warriors under the leadership of Jesus Christ, fighting evil forces (7:1–8; 14:1–5). This shows that the final battle of this earth's history will involve Christ and His faithful people on one side and the satanic trinity and their followers on the other.

The Three Frog-like Demons (16:13–14)

The drying of the Euphrates River shakes the satanic trinity—the dragon, the sea beast, and the earth beast, which is referred to as the false prophet. At this point, Satan and his two associates gather the whole world for the final deception. Proceeding from the mouths of the satanic trinity are three frog-like, demonic spirits going out to the leaders of the world "to gather them together for the war of the great day of God, the Almighty" (Rev. 16:13–14). These three demons coming from the mouths of the satanic trinity are the very "breath" of the satanic trinity in the last deception.

The frog-like spirits are reminiscent of the frog plague in Egypt (Exod. 8:1–15). The frog plague was the last plague of Moses that Pharaoh's magicians were able to duplicate and use to influence Pharaoh to persist in his opposition to God, rejecting God's message through Moses. In light of this Old Testament background, the three frog-like demons of the sixth plague are Satan's last attempt to counterfeit God's work. They are portrayed as the counterpart to the three angels in Revelation 14. The satanic trinity sends them out with a false gospel to persuade the world's secular and political authorities and powers to side with them against God and His people in preparation for the great day of God Almighty.

Thus, these frog-like demons are Satan's powerful agents, who will entice the earth's people into the final battle. This situation recalls the "deceiving spirit" which enticed King Ahab to refuse the message sent to him from God and to instead go into battle (1 Kings 22:21–23). Satan is determined to win the victory in the final crisis, and he enables the demonic spirits to perform miraculous signs. Their method of persuasion is deception. Miraculous signs are a part of Satan's end-time deception to persuade people to side with the satanic trinity rather than the true God (Rev. 13:13–14). Ellen White admonishes Christians:

> Fearful sights of a supernatural character will soon be revealed in the heavens, in token of the power of miracle-working demons. The spirits of devils will go forth to the kings of the earth and to the whole world, to fasten them in deception, and urge them on to unite with Satan in his last struggle against the government of heaven. By these agencies, rulers and subjects will be alike deceived. Persons will arise pretending to be Christ Himself, and claiming the title and worship which belong to the world's Redeemer.[2]

The activities of the demonic trinity result in great success. The nations of the world are deceived again, and they submit their powers to Satan against God's people. Now, the stage is set for the final battle.

The Laodicean Warning (16:15)

John the Revelator interrupts, for a moment, the description of the demonic activities to draw the earth's people into the final battle and inserts the words of Jesus, exhorting His people not to lose their focus on Him in the midst of the Great Deception: "Behold, I am coming like a thief. Blessed is the one who stays awake and keeps his clothes, so that he will not walk about naked, and men will not see his shame" (Rev. 16:15). This statement points to the true nature of the final battle. It shows that the final battle is not military but spiritual. It is the battle for the minds and hearts of people.

God's people must take seriously what is soon to take place. By means of deceptive miracles, evil forces will win the allegiance of the earth's people. They will exert much effort to deceive even God's people. That is why God's people must be spiritually awake, watchful, and ever ready to face the Great Deception (cf. 1 Thess. 5:1–8).

Jesus's exhortation to His followers to stay awake and keep their garments on (so they do not walk around naked and so people do not see their shame) echoes a practice in the temple of Jerusalem. At night, the temple captain would check the guards of the temple gates. If any guard was caught asleep at his post, his clothes were stripped off and burned, and he was sent away naked, in disgrace.[3] By alluding to this practice, Christ urges His followers to be spiritually alert. They must be like temple guards or soldiers, dressed and on the alert. With a similar admonition to His followers, Christ concluded His speech on the Mount of Olives: "Be on the alert . . . in case he should come suddenly and find you asleep. What I say to you, I say to all, 'Be on the alert!'" (Mark 13:35–37).

Jesus's admonition in Revelation 16:15 reiterates His earlier appeal to the church of Laodicea to clothe themselves with white garments, so the shame of their nakedness will not be exposed (Rev. 3:18). Garments in Revelation symbolize uncompromising loyalty and faithfulness to Christ (3:4–5; 6:11; 7:9, 13–14; 19:8). They are the requirement for participation to meet Christ when He comes the second time (19:7–9; Matt. 22:11–14).

On the other hand, nakedness denotes a compromising attitude toward Babylon under its deceptive delusion (cf. Rev. 17:2; 18:3). In defeating Babylon, God will make it "desolate and naked" (17:16), as a token of the severe humiliation of a defeated army (cf. Isa. 20:4). Those who compromise with Babylon will also be humiliated and shamed. Only those clothed spiritually with the robe of Christ's righteousness will be able to stand firm at "the hour of trial that is about to come on those who dwell on the earth" (Rev. 3:10).

Gathering for Armageddon (16:16)

The deceptive, demonic miracles will achieve success beyond any prediction or expectation. In refusing the true gospel, people will believe the lie accompanied by the deceptive miracles (2 Thess. 2:9–12). The world powers will gather at the place which is called in Hebrew *Armageddon*, meaning "the Mountain of Megiddo." In the Old Testament, Megiddo was a fortress-city, located in the Plain of Esdraelon, at the foot of the Carmel Ridge, and between the Mediterranean Sea and the Sea of Galilee. The city stood on the great highway from Egypt to Damascus, providing a natural passage for the invasion of Palestine. As such, the city was an important strategic site.

The Plain of Esdraelon (or the Valley of Jezreel) was known for many famous battles in ancient times. In the Old Testament, the city of Megiddo witnessed many decisive battles in Israel's history. At Megiddo, Barak and Deborah defeated Sisera and his army (Judg. 5:19–21), Gideon won the victory over the Midianites (6:33), Saul was defeated by the Philistines (1 Sam. 31), Ahaziah was shot by Jehu (1 Kings 9:27), and Josiah was killed by the pharaoh (2 Kings 23:29–30).

Once again, Revelation uses familiar language from Israel's history to depict the final conflict between God and the forces of evil. The religious and secular powers are unified and organized into an army under the satanic trinity's leadership for the battle on the great day of God. They are portrayed in Revelation 9:16 as demonic forces which number 200 million—in contrast to the 144,000 saints. This is reminiscent of Psalm 2:2: "The kings of the earth take their stand and the rulers take counsel together against the LORD and against His Anointed."

The Mountain of Megiddo was Mount Carmel, situated close to Megiddo. Mount Carmel was the site of one of the most significant battles in Israel's history, involving the prophet Elijah and the prophets of Baal (1 Kings 18). The issue to be resolved on Mount Carmel was who the true God was: the Lord or Baal (18:21). The fire that came from heaven to the earth demonstrated that the Lord was the only true God to be worshiped (18:38–39). In the final battle, however, the earth beast brings fire down from heaven to counterfeit God's work and to deceive the whole world (Rev. 13:13–14).

The issue to be resolved in the final battle is the same one that Satan introduced at the beginning of the Great Controversy—namely, who is the legitimate ruler of the universe. Keep in mind that Armageddon is not a military battle fought in Palestine or elsewhere in the Middle East. Rather, it is a spiritual battle between Christ and His followers and the forces of darkness. It is the battle for the minds of people. As Paul stated, "The weapons of our warfare are not of the flesh, but divinely powerful for the destruction of fortresses. We are destroying speculations and every lofty thing raised up against the knowledge of God, and we are taking every thought captive to the obedience of Christ" (2 Cor. 10:4–5). The outcome of the final battle will be like that of the Carmel conflict—God's ultimate triumph over the forces of darkness.

Revelation 16:12–16 does not portray the actual battle but only the great gathering of the religious and political powers to Armageddon. The actual battle follows the sixth plague and is described in Revelation 16:17–19:21. John later sees "the beast and the kings of the earth and their armies gathered to make war" against Christ coming from heaven and accompanied by His army of the saints (Rev. 19:19; cf. 17:14). The battle will conclude with the defeat of the beast and his armies (19:20–21) by the legitimate King of kings and Lord of lords (19:16).

The Seventh Plague (16:17–21)

17Then the seventh angel poured out his bowl upon the air, and a loud voice came out of the temple from the throne, saying, "It is done." 18And there were flashes of lightning and sounds and peals of thunder; and there was a great earthquake, such as there had not been since man came to be upon the earth, so great an earthquake was it and so mighty. 19The great city was split into three parts, and the cities of the nations fell. Babylon the great was remembered before God, to give her the cup of the wine of His fierce wrath. 20And every island fled away, and the mountains were not found. 21And huge hailstones, about one hundred pounds each, came down from heaven upon men; and men blasphemed God because of the plague of the hail, because its plague was extremely severe.

The last of the seven angels pours his bowl upon the air. At that moment, a loud voice issues out of the temple from God's throne announcing, "It is done" (Rev. 16:17). God's throne is located in the heavenly temple (4–5). The throne signifies God's rule and His sovereign authority over creation. In Revelation, this throne stands in opposition to the throne of Satan (2:13; 13:2) and the throne of the beast (16:10). The fact that this loud voice comes from the throne of God suggests that God Himself is speaking. This is the same voice that, in Revelation 16:1, commissioned the seven angels to pour out their bowls.

In the New Testament, the pronouncement "It is done" is made three times by Jesus. The first time He cried, "It is done," on the cross of Calvary, announcing the victory over Satan and the beginning of the time of the end (John 19:30). Here, in Revelation 16, the same voice of Christ proclaims the conclusion of earth's history and the final victory over Satan and his evil powers. Once again and for the last time, "It is done" will proclaim the eradication of sin and the glorious beginning of God's everlasting kingdom on earth (Rev. 21:6).

The pronouncement "It is done" is followed by "flashes of lightning and sounds and peals of thunder" (Rev. 16:18). In Revelation, these phenomena are always associated with the throne of God (cf. 4:5; 8:5; 11:19). Also, a severe earthquake, unlike any before in history, occurs (16:18). Earthquakes in the Old Testament are regularly associated with the visitation of God's final judgment upon the earth and are referred to as the Day of the Lord. This earthquake shatters Babylon, splitting it into three parts. End-time Babylon is made up of the union of the satanic trinity in the alliance with the religious world powers. The satanic trinity's union is shattered; it splits into three parts: the dragon, the sea beast, and the earth beast.

The breakup of end-time Babylon leads to the unavoidable collapse of "the cities of the nations" (Rev. 16:19). The nations discussed here denote the civil, political, and secular world powers that supported end-time Babylon and frustrated God's work on earth. Revelation 16:12 shows that these powers withdraw their support from Babylon. Now, these powers that supported Babylon collapse as well. Babylon and those who identified themselves with it are about to experience the fullness of divine judgment.

Thus, Babylon the Great is remembered before God. Babylon has to drink "the cup of the wine of His fierce wrath" (Rev. 16:19). In Revelation 18:5–6, God remembers Babylon's iniquities and punishes her with "the cup which she has mixed," making a double portion for her. Also, in Revelation 14:10, all who worship the beast and his image and receive the mark are threatened and will drink "of the wine of the wrath of God, which is mixed in full strength in the cup of His anger." Now, God gives Babylon—"who has made all the nations drink of the wine of the passion of her immorality" (14:8; cf. 17:2; 18:3)—"the cup of the wine of His fierce wrath" (16:19). This same cup is also given to all who sided with her.

The earthquake of the seventh plague submerges all islands and mountains into the sea. At the opening of the sixth seal, the earthquake moves mountains and islands from their places (Rev. 6:14). The author of Hebrews points to the final shaking of creation "so that those things which cannot be shaken may remain," namely, the kingdom of God (Heb. 12:26–28).

Finally, the passage states, "And huge hailstones, about one hundred pounds each, came down from heaven upon men" (Rev. 16:21). It is not clear if these hailstones are literal or symbolic. In the Old Testament, hailstones are used as judgment against Israel's enemies (Josh. 10:11; Ezek. 38:22). In the same way, these hailstones are used as weapons of judgment upon the enemies of God's end-time people.

As with other plagues, these hailstones do not change the wicked, who respond by cursing God and refusing to repent of their evil deeds (Rev. 16:9, 11, 21). The plagues do not make anyone repent; rather, they reveal what is in their rebellious hearts. Probation has closed, and intercession is no longer available (cf. 15:8). It is impossible for even this "extremely severe" plague to change their attitude toward God and cause them to return to Him (16:21).

The Woman and the Beast

 Revelation 17:1–18

Revelation 14:8 announced the fall of end-time Babylon, and 16:19 pronounced its collapse. Chapters 17–18 describe how this will happen. Previously in Revelation, a new character introduced in a vision is first described in general terms. This convention is also used in Revelation 17–18. Before describing the demise of end-time Babylon (Rev. 18), Revelation 17 describes this end-time apostate religious system as a prostitute riding on the beast, seductively deceiving the earth's inhabitants:

> *¹Then one of the seven angels who had the seven bowls came and spoke with me, saying, "Come here, I will show you the judgment of the great prostitute who dwells on many waters, ²with whom the kings of the earth committed acts of immorality, and those who dwell on the earth were made drunk with the wine of her immorality."*
>
> *³And he carried me away in the Spirit into a wilderness; and I saw a woman sitting on a scarlet beast, full of blasphemous names, having seven heads and ten horns. ⁴The woman was clothed in purple and scarlet and adorned with gold and precious stones and pearls, having in her hand a gold cup full of abominations and of the unclean things of her immorality, ⁵and on her forehead a name was written, a mystery: "Babylon the great, the mother of harlots and of the abominations of the earth." ⁶And I saw the woman drunk with the blood of the saints and with the blood of the witnesses of Jesus.*
>
> *When I saw her, I wondered greatly. ⁷And the angel said to me, "Why do you wonder? I will tell you the*

mystery of the woman and of the beast that carries her, which has the seven heads and the ten horns. ⁸The beast that you saw was, and is not, and is about to come up out of the abyss and go to destruction. And those who dwell on the earth, whose names have not been written in the book of life from the foundation of the world, will wonder when they see the beast, that he was and is not and will come.

⁹"Here is the mind which has wisdom. The seven heads are seven mountains on which the woman sits, ¹⁰and they are seven kings; five have fallen, one is, the other has not yet come; and when he comes, he must remain for a short time. ¹¹The beast, which was and is not, is himself also an eighth and is one of the seven, and he goes to destruction.

¹²"The ten horns which you saw are ten kings who have not yet received a kingdom, but they receive authority as kings with the beast for one hour. ¹³These have one purpose, and they give their power and authority to the beast. ¹⁴These will wage war against the Lamb, and the Lamb will overcome them, because He is Lord of lords and King of kings, and those who are with Him are the called and chosen and faithful."

¹⁵And he said to me, "The waters which you saw, where the harlot sits, are peoples and multitudes and nations and tongues. ¹⁶And the ten horns which you saw, and the beast—these will hate the harlot and will make her desolate and naked and will eat her flesh and will burn her up with fire. ¹⁷For God has put it in their hearts to execute His purpose by having a common purpose and by giving their kingdom to the beast, until the words of God will be fulfilled. ¹⁸The woman whom you saw is the great city, which rules over the kings of the earth."

The fall of end-time Babylon is announced two times in the book, without actually describing it (Rev. 14:8; 16:9). This is done in Revelation 17, which describes this end-time apostate religious system and gives the reasons for its fall (17:1–11). The rest of the chapter gives further information on the sixth and seventh plagues concerning the Euphrates River drying up—the powers on the earth withdrawing their support from this apostate religious system and turning against it (cf. 16:12–21).

The Great Prostitute (17:1–6)

One of the seven angels with the bowls invites John to witness the judgment of "the great prostitute" (Rev. 17:1). This prostitute is later identified as "Babylon the great, the mother of harlots" (17:5). In Revelation, Babylon stands for "a short-lived coalition of dragon, beast, and false prophet. Each has its own history but, at end-time, they join together in deception and coercion."[1] Her daughters are the world's religious powers that will unite with the satanic trinity, forming a religious confederacy in the closing days of this earth's history. This explains why the destruction of Babylon is described as splitting it into three parts (16:19). The breakup within this satanic triumvirate causes the demise of this end-time religious confederacy.

Babylon Dwells on Many Waters (17:1b–2)

The angel states that the prostitute Babylon "dwells on many waters" (Rev. 17:1b). Jeremiah 51:13 shows that "many waters" refers to the Euphrates River. The angel later explains to John that these waters symbolize the civil, secular, and political world powers (17:15). That Babylon as the end-time union of religious authorities is pictured as sitting on the worldwide powers shows that, at the time of the end, these two entities are distinct—something that was not the case in the past. Throughout history, and through the Middle Ages, political powers and the established religious authority went hand in hand. Nations were governed by religiopolitical powers. Revelation 13:1–10 portrays the medieval church, led by the papacy, as a religiopolitical power, dominating the Western world during the prophetic 1,260-day period. However, at the time of the end, these two entities will be distinct, yet they will work together for a common purpose.

Just as ancient Babylon depended on the Euphrates River for its existence, so end-time Babylon will depend on the civil, secular, and political world powers to enforce its plans and purposes. This end-time religious confederacy will form an alliance with the governing world powers; these powers will put themselves into the service of this apostate religious system, which will work against Christ and His faithful people during the end-time crisis.

Two groups are specified as being seduced by Babylon in the final crisis. The first are "the kings of the earth," portrayed as committing adultery with the prostitute Babylon (Rev. 17:2). These are the governing political world powers. Their adultery is not literal. In the Old Testament, the language of fornication is used frequently to describe Israel aligning itself with pagan nations (Isa. 1:21; Jer. 3:1–10; Ezek. 16; 23). Ezekiel charged Judah: "You have played the harlot with the nations" (23:30). The adulterous relationship between "the kings of the earth" and the prostitute Babylon symbolizes an illicit union between the end-time religious confederacy and the world's governing political leaders in the final crisis (Rev. 17:2).

The second group mentioned are "those who dwell on the earth," who are spiritually drunk with the wine of Babylon's immorality (Rev. 17:8; cf. 14:8). This is the general populace—not the world's leaders. While the world's leaders commit adultery with the prostitute Babylon, the rest of the earth's people are intoxicated by Babylon's deceptive teachings and activities, which entice people to worship the beast (14:8; 18:3). When people are drunk, they cannot think soberly; when the effects of drunkenness are over, there is a realization of their bad decisions and actions. However, this comes too late.

Both groups are equally deceived and have put themselves under the control of Babylon for political and economic benefits. Revelation tells us that, at the time of the end, the world will once again be united, and religion will dominate in the way it did during the Middle Ages. The time will come when the world's people will realize the bad choices they made and will turn against Babylon; however, it will be too late.

The Prostitute Riding the Beast (17:3–6)

John was told that the prostitute Babylon sat on many waters. Now, he is carried in a vision into the wilderness, where he sees a woman sitting on a scarlet beast (Rev. 17:3). While the prostitute represents the end-time union of religion, the beast symbolizes the worldwide confederacy of political powers. The prophecy tells us that, at the end of time, the political powers on earth will put themselves into the service of end-time Babylon. Babylon sitting on the beast means that this religious system will dominate the political powers during the end-time crisis.

The woman is pictured as extravagantly dressed in purple and scarlet and lavishly adorned with ornaments of gold and precious stones. She has an inscription on her forehead: "Babylon the great, the mother of harlots" (Rev. 17:5). In ancient times, prostitutes wore scarlet clothing and lavish ornaments for seduction (Jer. 4:30). The scarlet color of the woman's dress corresponds to the scarlet color of the beast, which she sits upon (Rev. 17:3). Scarlet is also the color of blood and oppression; this corresponds appropriately to the character of this religious system, which is "drunk with the blood of the saints and with the blood of the witnesses of Jesus" (17:6). Purple is used for royal attire (Judg. 8:26; Esther 8:15; Dan. 5:7), and it fits the prostitute's claim to be a queen (Rev. 17:7).

The prostitute's dress is meant to seduce. It also evokes the attire of the high priest in the Old Testament, which included purple, scarlet, and gold (Exod. 28:5–6). Her forehead inscription resembles the inscription "Holy to the Lord" on the mitre of the high priest (28:36–38). Also, the cup in her hand reflects the drink offering in the sanctuary (30:9; Lev. 23:13). Her description strikingly resembles the New Jerusalem (Rev. 21). All this suggests that the Babylon of chapter 17 refers to an end-time religious system rather than a political power. With its historic Christian appearance, this end-time religious system becomes Satan's powerful tool to deceive and seduce the world into apostasy during the end-time crisis.

Although she appears in religious garb, Babylon is a prostitute and the mother of prostitutes, seducing the world away from God. She is drunk with the blood of the saints, who died because of their witness to Jesus Christ (cf. Rev. 6:9). This religious system, which makes all people drunk with its false teachings, is itself drunk with the blood of Christ's followers. This clearly links end-time Babylon to the beast of Revelation 13, which represents medieval apostate Christianity in Western Europe, led by the papacy, which was responsible for the deaths of millions of Christians, who were persecuted for their faithful witness to the gospel. The time is coming, however, when God will judge this "great prostitute" and avenge "the blood of His servants from her hand" (17:1; 19:2).

In Revelation 17:6, John is greatly astonished at this prostitute. His reaction denotes his recognition of the prostitute. He sees her in the desert (17:3) and recognizes her as the woman who fled into the wilderness to escape the persecution of the dragon during the 1,260-day prophetic period of the Middle Ages (12:13–14). This suggests that this end-time opponent of God's people was once Christ's faithful church. This explains why, at the time of the end, Satan is filled with great animosity against the remnant of the woman's offspring rather than the woman (12:17). The church that, in the past, was faithful to

God will, at the time of the end, turn into an enemy of God's faithful remnant—those who keep God's commandments and have the testimony of Jesus.

The Scarlet Beast (17:6–13)

In response to John's amazement, the interpreting angel discloses to John the "mystery" of the scarlet beast that carries the prostitute Babylon and what role it will play at the end of time.

The Resurrected Beast (17:6–8)

As previously established, the prostitute Babylon symbolizes the end-time union of religious authorities, and the beast symbolizes a worldwide political union. These two are inseparable, for the prostitute derives her character and power from the beast. As the medieval church used political power to control the minds and beliefs of people, so Babylon will use the world's governing political powers at the time of the end.

The scarlet beast is identified as the one that "was, and is not, and is about to come up out of the abyss" (Rev. 17:8). The phrase "was, and is not, and is about to come up" is, first, a parody of the divine name Yahweh—"who was and who is and who is coming"—in Revelation 4:8 (cf. 1:4, 8). Second, this tripartite formula further shows that the beast has passed through three phases of its existence: past, present, and future.

First, the beast "was"—it existed in the past. There are clear links between this scarlet beast and the sea beast in Revelation 13, which recovered from its deadly wound. Both beasts are full of blasphemous names and have seven heads and ten horns (Rev. 17:3, 7). This shows that the "was" phase of the beast refers to its activities during the prophetic period of 1,260 days (cf. 13:5). Then, with its deadly wound, the beast came into its "is not" phase (13:3). In other words, it disappeared for some time, yet it survived.

Finally, when the deadly wound is healed, the beast will come to life again in full satanic rage against God's faithful people during the end time (Rev. 12:17). The resurrection of the beast will prompt the admiration of "those who dwell on the earth, whose names have not been written in the book of life from the foundation of the world" (17:8b). This reiterates Revelation 13:8, which links the scarlet beast carrying the prostitute Babylon with the medieval religious system.

All of this points to the sea beast with seven heads and ten horns in Revelation 13:1–8.

Revelation 17, thus, describes the sea beast of chapter 13 after the healing of its deadly wound. It is upon this resurrected beast that the end-time prostitute Babylon sits. Thus, this end-time religious system, which will play a key role in the final conflict, is a continuation of the religiopolitical power that harmed and oppressed God's people during the 1,260-day prophetic period. Revelation thus states that religion will once again dominate and control politics, as it did during the Middle Ages—albeit for a short time. But there is a noticeable difference between the medieval period and the time of the end. While the sea beast, representing the medieval church, was a religiopolitical power, the scarlet beast is exclusively a political power. Religious and political powers are distinct at the end of time.

The Seven Heads of the Beast (17:9–11)

At this point, a call is made for wisdom. The wisdom here is the same spoken of in connection with 666 as the number of the beast (Rev. 13:18). This wisdom refers to spiritual discernment rather than brilliant mental and intellectual ability—such discernment is only imparted by the Spirit (James 1:5). Only through this divinely imparted wisdom will God's end-time people be able to discern the true character of this satanic power.

The angel explains that the existence and activities of the beast are identified with its heads. Throughout history, the beast has ruled and been active through its heads. "The seven heads are seven mountains on which the woman sits" (Rev. 17:9). The Greek word *oros* means "mountain" and not "hill," as some translators suggest, thereby trying to show that the city of Rome, situated on seven hills, can be viewed in the text. However, neither literal hills nor mountains are correct here, because the angel immediately explains to John that these seven mountains actually symbolize "seven kings" (17:10). The waters, the mountains, the beast, and the kings are symbols used to describe the political powers that provide support for end-time Babylon—the apostate religious system—in its work of persecuting God's people.

These are not individual kings, however. In the Bible, "kings" is another expression for kingdoms or empires (Dan. 2:37–39; 7:17). Mountains often represent world powers or empires (Jer. 51:25; Dan. 2:35). Thus, the seven mountains, which the prostitute Babylon sits upon, stand for seven successive empires that have dominated the world throughout history and through which Satan has worked to oppose God.[2] These empires have shared the common traits of religiopolitical governance and coercion, which were used to persecute and destroy God's people.

The angel further explains to John that five of these world empires have fallen, one is, and the seventh one was not yet active at the time of John. Remember that the angel explains the meaning of these kingdoms to John from his own temporal perspective, not ours. In such a way, the "one is" kingdom is the Roman Empire of John's time. The five that have fallen are thus the empires that ruled the world and harmed God's people prior to John's time:

- **Egypt** was the world power that enslaved and oppressed Israel, seeking to destroy it.
- **Assyria** destroyed and scattered the ten tribes of Israel.
- **Babylon** destroyed Jerusalem and took Judah into exile.
- **Persia** almost annihilated the Jews at the time of Esther.
- **Greece** oppressed and tried to destroy the Jews through Antiochus IV Epiphanes.

The seventh kingdom that "has not yet come" was still a future manifestation from John's perspective, arising after the fall of the Roman Empire. The best interpretation is that the seventh head is the sea beast of Revelation 13, which represents the medieval church, headed by the papacy, that dominated the Western world during the Middle Ages and oppressed God's people.

The seventh kingdom is said to remain for a short time. The Greek adjectival word for "a short time" used here is *oligon*, meaning "short" or "little." This word is different from *micron*, used in Revelation to indicate "a shortness of time" (see Rev. 6:11; 20:3). In contrast, *oligon* does not indicate a length of time; rather, it is used in a qualitative sense. For instance, Revelation 12:12 states that after being cast out of heaven, Satan realized that "he has little time." This "little time" does not indicate a length of time, for it has been almost two thousand years since his expulsion from heaven. Rather, it indicates that Satan realized that his time was limited, just as a person who is sentenced to death realizes that he or she has only a little time, despite the fact that the execution might be many years later.

This same meaning applies to Revelation 17:10. That the seventh kingdom must remain for a short time does not point to the length of its existence; rather, the doom of this kingdom is determined by God ("it must remain"), and it will come to its end. It will receive a deadly wound, which took place during the French Revolution in 1798.

The angel also explains that there would be an eighth power to come at the time of the end. Although this eighth power is one of the seven heads, it is a new power. But which of the seven heads is also the eighth power? Most likely it is the seventh head, which experienced the deadly wound but revived after its wound was healed. This seventh head will reappear as the eighth head and exercise political power the way it did during the Middle Ages. It is through this eighth head that the scarlet beast, carrying the prostitute Babylon, works. Now, we live in the era of the seventh head, but the eighth head with its ten united kingdoms has no power yet. It will appear on the worldwide scene during the time of the end and impose its apostate religious system on the earth's inhabitants.

The Ten Horns of the Beast (17:12–13)

The angel explains that the ten horns of the scarlet beast represent the ten kings who will receive dominion with the beast during the time of the eighth head. The book doesn't explain exactly who these ten kings are. Because this passage is about a prophecy that is yet to be fulfilled, only the future will reveal the full identity of these end-time powers.

All that can be learned from the text is that the ten kings (meaning kingdoms) compose a very powerful confederacy of the world's nations. They are exclusively end-time powers. Their number denotes the totality of the world's nations, and they will put themselves under the control of the satanic trinity. They are evidently the governing political powers spoken of in Revelation 17:2, who are involved in the adulterous relationship with Babylon. These world powers will render their allegiance to the beast, something that will last for only a short time—one hour in prophetic terms. The beast will use them to enforce its plans and purposes.

At this point, once again, the book briefly describes the battle of Armageddon—introduced in Revelation 16:12–16 and concluded in 19:11–21.

The Battle of Armageddon (17:14–18)

Induced by Babylon, the worldwide political powers will engage in war with the Lamb (Rev. 17:14). This shows that the final battle is not a military battle in the Middle East between Jews and various Muslim nations but between Satan with his confederacy and Christ with His faithful people. The final battle is spiritual rather than political and military. Babylon's aim is to defeat Christ and destroy God's people, but this end-time religiopolitical confederacy will be the loser. The battle will conclude with the triumph of Christ and the ultimate destruction of the worldwide confederacy that loyally supported Babylon. The outcome of the final battle is described in more detail in Revelation 19:11–21.

In the final stage, the picture suddenly and dramatically changes. The ten horns and the beast (the political powers) turn against the prostitute Babylon (the false religious system). The political and secular powers that enabled Babylon to dominate the world withdraw their support and, enraged, turn against her. This withdrawal of support from Babylon is pictured in the sixth plague as the Euphrates River drying up (Rev. 16:12). As chapter 16 indicates, the deceived political powers have become disillusioned because of Babylon's impotence to protect them from the plagues (16:10–11). They feel deceived and, filled with antagonism and hostility, attack her and bring her to ruin.

In his description of this scene, John again employs Old Testament language used for the judgments that fell upon adulterous Jerusalem (Jer. 4:30; Ezek. 16:35–41; 23:22–29). The disillusioned political powers will make the prostitute Babylon "desolate and naked and will eat her flesh and will burn her up with fire" (Rev. 17:16). This savage act is driven by extreme hostility and hatred (cf. Ps. 27:2; Mic. 3:3). Burning by fire was the punishment for a high priest's daughter who was involved in prostitution (Lev. 21:9). This is a further indication that the prostitute Babylon denotes a religious system that was once true to God but, at the time of the end, will turn away from Him and become unfaithful.

The scene concludes with a reminder that God is in control and that the wicked may go no farther than God allows them: "For God has put it in their hearts to execute His purpose by having a common purpose and by giving their kingdom to the beast, until the words of God will be fulfilled" (Rev. 17:17). The actions of the deceived political powers, in fact, carry out God's judgment upon Babylon. In this way, the end-time crisis will ultimately conclude God's purposes.

The angel reminds John that the great prostitute, who seduced the world's people and who is about to be judged, is the great city that rules over "the kings of the earth" (17:18). The prostitute Babylon, sitting on the beast, and the great city Babylon, dwelling on the Euphrates, are the same entity. They symbolize the same end-time apostate religious system that opposes God. Divine judgment is now set in motion against this religious system. This judgment is described in the following chapter in terms of the ancient city of Babylon, which became wealthy through economic trade.

Judgment on Babylon

Revelation 18 continues the theme of the destruction of Babylon from the previous chapter. This apostate religious system has filled up her cup of abomination and is about to receive the cup of the wine of God's wrath (Rev. 16:19). While, in chapter 17, the judgment on this end-time apostate religious system is pictured in terms of the prostitute's execution (according to the Mosaic law), in chapter 18, it is portrayed as a wealthy commercial city sinking into the sea:

¹After these things, I saw another angel coming down from heaven, having great authority, and the earth was illumined with his glory. ²And he cried out with a mighty voice, saying, "Fallen, fallen is Babylon the great! She has become a dwelling place of demons and a prison of every unclean spirit and a prison of every unclean and hateful bird. ³For all the nations have drunk of the wine of the passion of her immorality, and the kings of the earth have committed acts of immorality with her, and the merchants of the earth have become rich by the wealth of her sensuality."

⁴I heard another voice from heaven, saying, "Come out of her, my people, so that you will not participate in her sins and receive of her plagues; ⁵for her sins have piled up as high as heaven, and God has remembered her iniquities. ⁶Pay her back even as she has paid, and give back to her double, according to her deeds; in the cup which she has mixed, mix twice as much for her. ⁷To the degree that she glorified herself and lived sensuously, to the same degree give her torment and mourning; for she says in her heart, 'I sit as a queen, and I am not a widow and will never see mourning.' [8]For this reason, in one day her plagues will come, pestilence and mourning and famine, and she will be burned up with fire; for the Lord God who judges her is strong.

[9]"And the kings of the earth, who committed acts of immorality and lived sensuously with her, will weep and lament over her when they see the smoke of her burning, [10]standing at a distance because of the fear of her torment, saying, 'Woe, woe, the great city, Babylon, the strong city! For in one hour your judgment has come.'

[11]"And the merchants of the earth weep and mourn over her, because no one buys their cargoes anymore— [12]cargoes of gold and silver and precious stones and pearls and fine linen and purple and silk and scarlet and every kind of citron wood and every article of ivory and every article made from very costly wood and bronze and iron and marble [13]and cinnamon and spice and incense and perfume and frankincense and wine and olive oil and fine flour and wheat and cattle and sheep and cargoes of horses and chariots and slaves and human lives. [14]The fruit you long for has gone from you, and all things that were luxurious and splendid have passed away from you, and men will no longer find them. [15]The merchants of these things, who became rich from her, will stand at a distance because of the fear of her torment, weeping and mourning, [16]saying, 'Woe, woe, the great city, she who was clothed in fine linen and purple and scarlet, and adorned with gold and precious stones and pearls; [17]for in one hour such great wealth has been laid waste.' And every shipmaster and every passenger and sailor and as many as make their living by the sea stood at a distance [18]and were crying out as they saw the smoke of her burning, saying, 'What city is like the great city?' [19]And they threw dust on their heads and were crying out, weeping and mourning, saying, 'Woe, woe, the great city, in which all who had ships at sea became rich by her wealth, for in one hour she has been laid waste!'

[20]"Rejoice over her, O heaven, and you saints and apostles and prophets, because God has pronounced judgment for you against her."

²¹Then a strong angel took up a stone like a great millstone and threw it into the sea, saying, "So will Babylon, the great city, be thrown down with violence and will not be found any longer. ²²And the sound of harpists and musicians and flute-players and trumpeters will not be heard in you any longer; and no craftsman of any craft will be found in you any longer; and the sound of a mill will not be heard in you any longer; ²³and the light of a lamp will not shine in you any longer; and the voice of the bridegroom and bride will not be heard in you any longer; for your merchants were the great men of the earth, because all the nations were deceived by your sorcery. ²⁴And in her was found the blood of prophets and of saints and of all who have been slain on the earth."

In describing God's judgment on end-time Babylon, John employs language used by Isaiah and Jeremiah in their descriptions of ancient Babylon's fall.

The Fall of Babylon Announced (18:1–3)

The chapter begins with the appearance of another angel coming from heaven with great authority and glory that illuminates the whole earth (Rev. 18:1). His radiating glory outshines the seductive glory of Babylon. He proclaims with a loud voice: "Fallen, fallen is Babylon the great!" This proclamation reiterates the message of the second angel in Revelation 14:8. As shown earlier, Babylon stands for the end-time apostate religious system allied with the worldwide governing powers. The glorious appearance of the angel and his loud voice are intended to draw the attention of the earth dwellers to God's call to leave this apostate religious system and turn to God before it is too late.

Babylon is referred to as fallen, because its fall has already happened. The repetitive phrase "fallen, fallen" points to the certainty of Babylon's fall. This was language used by Isaiah concerning ancient Babylon (Isa. 21:9). The collapse of end-time Babylon is as certain as the collapse of ancient Babylon. Like Babylon of old, this end-time religious system has become the habitation of demons, unclean spirits, and unclean birds (cf. Isa. 13:19–22; Jer. 50:39). John employs the Old Testament description of ancient Babylon's fate to describe the doom of this end-time apostate religious system.

According to Revelation 18:3, Babylon is judged and charged on three grounds: religious, political, and economic. The first charge is that Babylon has intoxicated the earth's inhabitants with its corrupt teachings and doctrines, leading them away from the true God and toward worshiping the beast (cf. Rev. 14:8; 17:2). The second charge is that this apostate religious system has seduced the kings of the earth—the worldwide governing political powers—into an adulterous relationship for political and economic gain (cf. 17:2). The third charge against Babylon is that it made the earth's merchants wealthy by its extravagant wealth and luxury. The economic aspect of Babylon's activities was hinted at earlier in Revelation 13:16–17. This shows the economic motivation for the end-time religious and political union. "The great men of the earth" have secured for themselves economic status and benefits by their association with end-time Babylon (18:23).

Call to Separate from Babylon (18:4–8)

Before Babylon is judged, a voice from heaven addresses God's people in Babylon. There are many sincere, God-fearing people who are in Babylon for different reasons. Many of them are deceived by the "form of godliness" (2 Tim. 3:5) of this false religious system. As shown earlier, Babylon appears to have a religious pedigree and plays the role of Christ on earth. Some people are in Babylon without being aware of it. Whether knowingly or unknowingly, they are identified with it. Their situation evokes the story of Lot in Sodom. Although Lot did not participate in the sins of Sodom, he was identified with it (Gen. 19). Just before the city was destroyed, he was exhorted to break off all ties with it, so he could escape the fate of the city and its inhabitants.

In a similar way, God sends His final appeal to His people to cut all ties with this apostate religious system to escape its fate: "Come out of her, my people, so that you will not participate in her sins and receive of her plagues" (Rev. 18:4). This call echoes the prophet Jeremiah's appeal to the Jews in Babylon: "Flee from the midst of Babylon, and each of you save his life! Do not be destroyed in her punishment, for this is the LORD's time of vengeance; He is going to render recompense to her" (Jer. 51:6; cf. 50:8; 51:45). God does not want anyone in Babylon to perish. This is the last opportunity for people to turn to God and escape the fate of Babylon and all those who are associated with it. As Revelation 19:1–10 shows, many in Babylon will respond to the call.

If those who are in Babylon refuse to separate themselves from this apostate religious system, they are charged with participating in the sins of Babylon and will consequently share in its fate (Rev. 18:4). The sins of Babylon are innumerable. They have accumulated to the point that they reach up to heaven (18:5), just like the crimes of ancient Babylon: "For her judgment has reached to heaven and towers up to the very skies" (Jer. 51:9). God will not forget Babylon's unrighteous acts (cf. Rev. 16:19). He is coming to bring retribution upon this apostate religious system for what it has done to God's people: "'I will repay Babylon and all the inhabitants of Chaldea for all their evil that they have done in Zion before your eyes,' declares the LORD" (Jer. 51:24).

The punishment of Babylon will fit its crime (Rev. 18:6–8). This arrogant apostate system exhibits self-glorification and self-sufficiency: "I sit as a queen, and I am not a widow and will never see mourning" (18:7). This arrogant boasting mirrors the self-glorification of ancient Babylon: "You said, 'I will be a queen forever.' . . . Who says in your heart, 'I am, and there is no one besides me. I will not sit as a widow'" (Isa. 47:7–8). In glorifying itself, Babylon assumes the prerogatives of God (Rev. 14:7; cf. 15:4; 19:1). This arrogant self-glorification and self-sufficiency are the basis for the condemnation and punishment of this end-time apostate religious system. "Repay her according to her work," wrote Jeremiah. "According to all that she has done, so do to her; for she has become arrogant against the LORD, against the Holy One of Israel" (Jer. 50:29). Babylon will be judged according to its sins. The judgment will demonstrate that God is strong and that He will bring this apostate religious system to its end (Rev. 18:8).

Lament over Babylon (18:9–20)

Babylon's fall brings great sorrow to those who cooperated with this end-time religious system for personal benefit and gain. The rest of the chapter describes three mournful lamentations of those who have suffered personal loss as a result of Babylon's collapse (Rev. 19:9–19). They are expressed in the form of ancient funeral dirges. Each begins with "Woe, woe, the great city" and ends with "for in one hour" (18:10, 16–17a, 19). These lamentations conclude by calling heaven and the faithful to rejoice over Babylon's destruction (18:20).

The first group lamenting Babylon's collapse is "the kings of the earth, who committed acts of immorality and lived sensuously with her" (Rev. 18:9–10). These are the worldwide governing political powers spoken of in Revelation 17:2, who have put their authority and influence into the service of this apostate religious system by enforcing its corrupt teachings and policies. This end-time religious system acted through them to control the world's inhabitants. These people were seduced by Babylon's copious wealth and luxury, and Babylon additionally promised them safety and security. These political rulers finally realize that they were deceived. They turn against Babylon in their rage, carrying out its destruction (17:16), even though they realize that Babylon's destruction means their own loss of power and wealth.

The second group of mourners is comprised of "the merchants of the earth," who have profited economically from their commercial activities with this end-time apostate religious system (Rev. 18:11–17a). These "great men of the earth" (18:23) have grown prosperous and rich by selling and distributing Babylon's corrupt goods. Verses 12–13 give a catalog of Babylon's luxurious and costly goods, which are similar to those mentioned in the dirge over Tyre (Ezek. 27:5–24).

The third group is comprised of ship captains and sailors, who transported Babylon's goods for the merchants in the previous group (Rev. 18:17b–19). Both have acquired wealth by cooperating with Babylon. Their lament mirrors the lament over Tyre's fall in Ezekiel's vision (Ezek. 27:29–32). Now the two groups mourn as they stand at a distance, watching the city burn. Their mourning is not caused by Babylon's doom per se but by their selfish motives. The collapse of Babylon means they will no longer profit from its wealth and luxury. In its fate, they see their own destiny.

Yet, there is a fourth group. While the fall of Babylon brings sorrow to those who have cooperated with this apostate religious system, it brings joy to God's people. As the fall of ancient Babylon was good news for Israel, so the fall of end-time Babylon is good news for God's end-time people. To them, the destruction of Babylon means deliverance from oppression: "Rejoice over her, O heaven, and you saints and apostles and prophets, because God has pronounced judgment for you against her" (Rev. 18:20).

This call for rejoicing mirrors the words of Jeremiah with regard to the fall of ancient Babylon (Jer. 51:48–49). End-time Babylon is deemed responsible for inducing the world's governing powers to attack God's people and shed their blood (Rev. 18:24). The judgment upon the end-time apostate religious system is God's act of salvation for His oppressed and persecuted people. The rejoicing called for in Revelation 18:20 is further portrayed in Revelation 19:1–10.

The Fall of Babylon Recounted (18:21–24)

The conclusion of the vision provides a symbolic demonstration of Babylon's overthrow. John watches a strong angel taking a millstone-like stone and hurling it into the sea with the comment: "So will Babylon, the great city, be thrown down with violence and will not be found any longer" (Rev. 18:21). This picture reflects the scene from Jeremiah 51:59–64 that describes the prophet tying a stone to a scroll containing the judgments that will fall on Babylon and throwing it into the Euphrates. The scene concludes with the declaration: "Just so shall Babylon sink down and not rise again because of the calamity that I am going to bring upon her" (Jer. 51:64). Here, the judgment of historical Babylon is similar to the judgment of end-time Babylon.[1] The fall of this end-time apostate religious system is as certain as the overthrow of historical Babylon. Its fall is total and complete: no more music and no everyday business or domestic activities, such as craftsmanship and food production (Rev. 18:22). Never again will light shine in it nor the sound of nuptial festivities be heard (18:23).

The purpose of Revelation 18 is to assure God's wandering people on earth, especially those living at the end time, that evil will not last forever. Babylon, the apostate religious system, has severely harmed and shed the blood of God's faithful people: "In her was found the blood of prophets and of saints and of all who have been slain on the earth" (Rev. 18:24). This apostate system has become drunk with the blood of the saints (17:6). Revelation 6:9–10 pictures a perennial cry of God's suffering people, pleading for vindication and justice: "How long, O Lord, holy and true, will You not judge and avenge our blood upon those who dwell on the earth?" With Babylon's overthrow, the prayers of God's suffering people are finally answered. Jeremiah declared: "Babylon must fall for the slain of Israel" (Jer. 51:49, RSV). "'I will repay Babylon and all the inhabitants of Chaldea for all their evil that they have done in Zion before your eyes,' declares the LORD" (51:24).

The readers of Revelation are reminded over and over again that God will judge the evil in the world. He is with His people, even when they suffer unjustly. His people, however, must patiently wait, for evil in the world will not last forever. The time is coming when evil will finally be defeated and never rise again. This will secure the eternal deliverance of God's people and bring them to their long-awaited home.

The Two Suppers

 Revelation 19:1-21

Revelation 19 wraps up the end-time scenario with the conclusion of the battle of Armageddon. The scene shifts from the mourning of Babylon's supporters to a jubilant celebration of God's people over the demise of this end-time religious system (Rev. 19:1–10). The chapter concludes with the description of the battle of Armageddon, showing Christ coming as the warrior king to fight the evil forces on behalf of His people (19:11–21).

The Wedding Supper of the Lamb (19:1–10)

Revelation 19:1–10 functions as an interlude between the description of Babylon's judgment (Rev. 17–18) and the conclusion of the battle of Armageddon (19:11–21):

> *¹After these things, I heard something like a loud voice of a great multitude in heaven, saying, "Hallelujah! Salvation and glory and power to our God, ²because His judgments are true and righteous; for He has judged the great prostitute, who destroyed the earth with her fornication, and He has avenged the blood of His servants from her hand." ³And they said a second time: "Hallelujah! Her smoke ascends forever and ever!" ⁴And the twenty-four elders and the four living beings fell down and worshiped God sitting on the throne, saying, "Amen! Hallelujah!" ⁵And from the throne, a voice came, saying, "Praise our God, all His servants, those who fear Him, small and great."*
>
> *⁶And I heard something like a voice of a great multitude and like a voice of many waters and like a voice of*

strong thunders, saying, "Hallelujah, because our Lord God, the Almighty, has begun to reign. ⁷Let us rejoice and be glad and give glory to Him, because the wedding of the Lamb has come, and His wife has prepared herself; ⁸and it was given to her to clothe herself in fine linen, bright and clean, for the fine linen is the righteous deeds of the saints." ⁹And he said to me, "Write: 'Blessed are those who are invited to the wedding supper of the Lamb.'" And he said to me, "These are the true words of God."

¹⁰And I fell before his feet to worship him. And he said to me, "See that you do not do this; I am a fellow servant of you and your brothers, who have the testimony of Jesus. Worship God! For the testimony of Jesus is the spirit of prophecy."

Rejoicing over the Fall of Babylon (19:1–6)

In Revelation 18:20, God's people are called to rejoice over the destruction of end-time Babylon. The first half of chapter 19 describes the response to this call in terms of the jubilant celebration of the redeemed saints, celebrating the victory over Babylon. To describe this joyful scene, John puts together many passages from different parts of Revelation and combines them into one coherent theme. The description of the entire scene echoes the description of the throne-room scene in Revelation 4.

John hears a great multitude in heaven exclaiming: "Hallelujah! Salvation and glory and power to our God" (Rev. 19:1). This scene echoes the shouts of the Great Multitude in Revelation 7: "Salvation to our God sitting on the throne and to the Lamb" (7:9–10). Now in Revelation 19, these redeemed saints are portrayed as praising God for His righteous judgment on Babylon, who "destroyed the earth with her fornication" (cf. 17:1–6). Here, what was announced in Revelation 11:18 is fulfilled: the destroyers of the earth will be destroyed. Babylon and its supporters, as the destroyers of the earth, are finally obliterated.

With the destruction of Babylon, God has avenged the blood of His people. This end-time apostate religious system is found responsible for shedding the blood of God's faithful people (Rev. 18:24). The fifth seal scene pictures the martyred saints' perennial plea, asking God to avenge their blood and vindicate them (6:10). Now, with Babylon destroyed, their prayers are ultimately answered.

No doubt these saints are at the center of the rejoicing multitude portrayed in Revelation 19. Their rejoicing, however, should not be regarded as vengeance but gratitude to God for saving His people. Their salvation has been possible only with the overthrow of the enemy power, which freed God's people from Babylon.

The smoke from the overthrown Babylon "ascends forever and ever" (Rev. 19:3). Here what was announced earlier in Revelation 14:11 is fulfilled. The smoke ascending "forever and ever" is another way of saying that Babylon will never again rise, as Edom of old never did (cf. Isa. 34:8–10). Destroying the oppressor of God's people will be definite and irreversible.

In celebrating the total victory over their enemy, the redeemed saints are joined by the twenty-four elders (who represent the entire church) and the four living beings (who represent the angelic hosts). They fall down together before the throne and worship God, praising Him, saying, "Amen! Hallelujah!" This jubilant celebration reaches its climax with the exclamation: "Hallelujah, because our Lord God, the Almighty, has begun to reign." This exclamation reiterates the announcement at the seventh trumpet: "We give thanks to You, Lord God, the Almighty, who is and who was, because You have taken Your great power and begun to reign" (Rev. 11:17). The destruction of end-time Babylon marks the beginning of God's reign over the earth in the fullness of His power and authority.

The Wedding Supper Announced (19:7–9)

At this point, the scene shifts to what seems to be the focus of the entire book: the long-awaited joining of Christ with His people, referred to as "the wedding of the Lamb" (Rev. 19:7). Everything in Revelation moves toward this climactic moment. Now, there is a proclamation that this special event is about to take place. This calls for rejoicing and celebration. The bride has made herself ready. Now, it is time for the bridegroom to come and for the wedding to take place.

This scene reflects the ancient Jewish wedding practice. The prospective groom would go to the house of the bride-to-be's father for the betrothal. After the groom paid the dowry, the groom and the bride were considered legally married, although they could not yet live together. The groom would then return to his father's house to prepare the place where he and his bride would live. The bride stayed at her father's house to prepare herself for the wedding. When the preparations were complete, the groom would come back to the bride's father's house, and the wedding feast would take place. Afterward, he would take his bride to the place he had prepared, where they would live together.

In a similar manner, Christ left His Father's house in heaven to come to the earth to betroth His bride—the church. After paying the dowry with His life at Calvary, He returned to His Father's house to prepare a place for His bride. He promised to come back and take His bride to Himself (John 14:2–3). His bride remained on the earth, preparing herself. At the end of history, Christ will come back, and the long-awaited wedding will take place. He will finally be united with His bride, the church, and He will take her to His Father's house. Revelation 19:7–9 points to this joyous event.

Revelation uses the metaphor of the bride to describe God's people during the interval between the two comings of Christ. During this period, His people prepare themselves for that long-awaited event. According to Paul, when Christ comes, He desires to see His church without "spot or wrinkle or any such thing; but that she would be holy and blameless" (Eph. 5:27). Here, in Revelation 19:7–8, Christ's bride is ready for the wedding. She is arrayed in "fine linen, bright and clean" (Rev. 19:8). Her clothing contrasts sharply with the purple and scarlet dress and lavish adornment of the prostitute Babylon (17:4). The bride consists of God's people, who do not partake in Babylon's sins. They kept themselves undefiled from the impurity of Babylon and were totally faithful to Christ. Now, they partake in the Lamb's wedding supper.

The clothing of Christ's bride represents "the righteous deeds of the saints" (Rev. 19:8). This does not mean, however, that God's people are to wear their own deeds. The text states that the bride "was given" bright and clean linen to dress in, representing the righteous deeds. Elsewhere in Revelation, Christ supplies the robes of God's people (3:18; 6:11), which are washed in the Lamb's blood (7:14; 22:14).

The bride has readied herself with the clothing Christ gave her. This illustrates both the human responsibility and the divine activity in human lives. Paul points to the relationship between the two: "Work out your salvation with fear and trembling; for it is God who is at work in you, both to will and to work for His good pleasure" (Phil. 2:12–13). The righteous deeds of God's people are the result of divine activity in their lives. These righteous deeds are the external reflection of the gospel's outworking. "I will rejoice greatly in the

LORD," said Isaiah, ". . . for He has clothed me with garments of salvation, He has wrapped me with a robe of righteousness, as a bridegroom decks himself with a garland, and as a bride adorns herself with her jewels" (Isa. 61:10).

In this scene's conclusion, the angel urges John to write: "Blessed are those who are invited to the wedding supper of the Lamb" (Rev. 19:9). Revelation portrays the experience of God's end-time people from two different perspectives: they are both the bride and the invited guests at the wedding supper. While the former points to the long-awaited union with Christ, which will soon take place, the latter reminds God's people that they must respond to the call and prepare themselves for that great day.

At this point, it is important to remember that Revelation 19 does not describe the actual wedding of the Lamb; it only announces that the time for that long-awaited event has finally come. The wedding event will take place when God's people are in the New Jerusalem, referred to as "the bride, the wife of the Lamb" (Rev. 21:9). The New Jerusalem and God's people are equated, because in that city, God's people will finally unite with their Lord for eternity.

The Spirit of Prophecy (19:10)

Filled with awe about what he has just heard, John falls at the angel's feet to worship him. However, the angel restrains him, explaining: "I am a fellow servant of you and your brothers, who have the testimony of Jesus. Worship God!" This echoes the statement of Jesus in addressing Satan in the desert: "You shall worship the Lord your God, and serve Him only" (Matt. 4:10). The central issue in the final crisis will be worship. The first angel's message warns us that the true God to be worshiped is the One "who made heaven and the earth and sea and springs of waters" (Rev. 14:7).

The angel explains that the community of believers, which John is a part of, are the ones "who have the testimony of Jesus." This repeats what is stated in Revelation 12:17, where the end-time remnant of the woman's offspring is identified as the ones who keep the commandments of God and have the testimony of Jesus.

What is the testimony of Jesus? The angel explains to John that it is "the spirit of prophecy" (Rev. 19:10). John had no difficulty understanding this, because in his day, the expression "the spirit of prophecy" was widely used in reference to the Holy Spirit speaking through prophets (22:9).[1] Thus, the testimony of Jesus refers to the special message that Jesus sends to His people through individuals called by God to be prophets. In Revelation 1:1–2, the testimony of Jesus means the things to take place in the future, which were shown to John in a vision and which he recorded in Revelation.

Revelation shows that the prophetic ministry will continue among God's people until the time of the end. What was true of God's people in all times will continue to be true at the end time: God's people will possess the prophetic gift. In the final crisis, when the whole world will turn away from God, God's faithful people will not be alone. They will experience Christ's voice speaking to them through the gift of prophecy, as a token of His special care for them. Through prophecy, Christ will provide special guidance, so they will not be lost. The hope of God's end-time people is found in their faithfulness to Jesus's testimony through this prophecy.

Conclusion of the Final Battle (19:11–21)

Having described the great celebration over Babylon's destruction, the book next describes the conclusion of the battle of Armageddon. The battle of Armageddon has been introduced two times in the book; however, it is in Revelation 19:11–21 that the description of the actual battle is given:

> *11And I saw heaven opened, and behold, a white horse, and the One sitting upon it was called faithful and true, and in righteousness He judges and wages war. 12His eyes are like a flame of fire, and on His head are many crowns; He has a name written on Himself, which nobody knows except Himself, 13and He is clothed in a robe dipped in blood, and His name is called the Word of God. 14And the armies who are in heaven were following Him on white horses, clothed in fine linen, white and clean. 15And from His mouth proceeds a sharp sword, that with it, He may smite the nations, and He will rule them with a rod of iron, and He treads the winepress of the wine of the anger of the wrath of God, the Almighty. 16And He has on His robe and on His thighs a name written: King of kings and Lord of lords.*
>
> *17And I saw an angel standing in the sun, and he cried with a loud voice, saying to all the birds flying in the sky:*

> *"Come, gather for the great supper of God* [18]*that you may eat the flesh of the kings and the flesh of the commanders of one thousand troops and the flesh of the strong and the flesh of horses and of those sitting upon them and the flesh of all, both free men and slaves, the small and great."*
>
> [19]*And I saw the beast and the kings of the earth and their armies gathered to make war against the One sitting on the horse and against His army.* [20]*And the beast was captured and, with him, the false prophet who performed the signs before him, by which he deceived those who received the mark of the beast and who worshiped his image; these two were cast alive into the lake of fire burning with sulfur.* [21]*And the rest were killed with the sword of the One sitting upon the horse, the sword having proceeded from His mouth; and all the birds were filled with their flesh.*

In Revelation 4:1, John went, in a vision, through the gates of heaven to witness the exaltation of Christ upon the heavenly throne at the right hand of the Father. This time, however, heaven's gates are opened for Christ to come down to the earth to fight His final battle against the evil forces.

The Coming of Christ as Warrior King (19:11–16)

Christ is portrayed as a Roman general riding on a white horse (Rev. 19:11). He is referred to as "faithful and true" (cf. 3:14), pointing to His promise that He will deliver His people. Because He is faithful and true, He is about to wage the final war in righteousness. Wars are usually matters of military oppression and bloodshed. But Christ's war is meant to establish His everlasting justice. This war will end the oppression of God's people and usher in His everlasting kingdom.

Christ's eyes are pictured as a flame, denoting His ability to judge; nothing can remain hidden from His penetrating insight (Rev. 19:12; cf. 1:14). On His head are many royal crowns—tokens of His absolute royal power and authority. He has a title inscribed that nobody knows except Himself. John later reveals that Christ's title is the "King of kings and Lord of lords," and this title is inscribed on His robe and His thigh (19:16). This title is also mentioned in Revelation 17:14, where Christ is portrayed as the all-conquering Lamb, fighting the battle against the beast and its supporters. This indicates that Revelation 19 completes the scene introduced in Revelation 17.

In Revelation 5, Christ has been exalted and given authority to rule. Paul states that at His exaltation, Christ was bestowed with "the name which is above every name," so "every tongue will confess that Jesus Christ is Lord" (Phil. 2:9–11). However, not "every tongue" on earth has recognized His rightful lordship. His rule has been constantly challenged by Satan's rebellious claim to rule the earth (Luke 4:6). Now, Christ is coming with authority and power to abolish Satan's usurping rule and to assume His rightful rule as the only true King and Lord over the earth (cf. 1 Cor. 15:24).

Christ's robe is stained with blood (Rev. 19:13). This description evokes Isaiah's portrayal of God returning in a bloodstained robe from punishing Edom (Isa. 63:1–3). The fact that Christ's robe is stained with blood before the battle suggests that this is the blood of Christ's persecuted followers (see Rev. 17:6; 19:2). Christ is coming now to avenge their blood and to vindicate them (cf. Dan. 12:1).

Christ's identifying name in the final battle is the Word of God. In verse 15, a sharp sword proceeds from His mouth, which He uses to strike down the nations (see Rev. 19:21). A sword is a symbol of the Word of God (Eph. 6:17; Heb. 4:12). Here is the fulfillment of Isaiah's prophecy that the Messiah would "strike the earth with the rod of His mouth, and with the breath of His lips He will slay the wicked" (Isa. 11:4). Christ is about to tread "the winepress of the wine of the wrath of God, the Almighty" (Rev. 19:15).

It is significant that the weapon of the final battle symbolically comes out of Christ's mouth. It affirms that the battle of Armageddon is not a literal and military war, but a spiritual combat, meant to resolve the fundamental issue that started the Great Controversy. It is the battle of ideas concerning God's rightful rule over the universe. Satan is finally unmasked in front of the universe. This follows Paul's statement that Christ will defeat this apostate religious system "with the breath of His mouth and bring [it] to an end by the appearance of His coming" (2 Thess. 2:8).

However, Christ is not alone in the final battle. He is accompanied by "the armies who are in heaven" (Rev. 19:14). These armies ride on white horses and are clothed in "fine linen, white and clean" (19:14). This linen is the robe of the end-time saints, signifying their righteous deeds (19:8). This shows that God's people are referred to here. Revelation 17:14 clearly shows that the end-time saints will accompany

Christ in the final battle. They are also referred to as "the kings from the East" (cf. 16:12). While these saints are still on earth, waiting for translation (1 Thess. 4:14–16), they are already spiritually in the heavenly places, sharing in Christ's glory (cf. Eph. 2:6). This contrasts with those on the opposite side, who are referred to as "those who dwell on the earth" (cf. Rev. 6:10; 8:13; 11:10; 13:8, 14; 14:6). In Revelation 19, God's people join Christ in His triumphant victory over their enemies.

The Great Supper of God (19:17–21)

The time has come for the satanic confederacy to receive their deserved justice. John sees an angel calling, in a loud voice, the scavengers of the sky to gather together for "the great supper of God" to eat the flesh of the earth's armies (Rev. 19:17). This call to the birds of prey contrasts with the previous invitation to the Lamb's wedding supper (19:9). Those called to the Lamb's wedding supper are blessed, while the unrepentant are threatened with becoming the gruesome supper of these birds. The readers of Revelation are offered a choice: either accept the invitation to the Lamb's wedding supper or be among Christ's opponents, who will be eaten by scavengers.

This horrific scene reflects the scene from Ezekiel's vision in which God's judgment on the pagan nations of Gog is portrayed as a sacrificial feast, prepared for the birds of the air and the beasts of the field. These creatures are invited to participate in the great supper of God: to eat the flesh and drink the blood of mighty men and the earth's princes. They are welcomed to glut themselves at the Lord's table with horses, charioteers, mighty men, and all the men of war (Ezek. 39:17–21).

The scavengers' menu includes people of every sociopolitical level: the kings, the commanders of one thousand troops (Gr. *chiliarchoi*), the strong people, the horses with their horsemen, the free men, the slaves, the small, and the great (Rev. 19:18). All these people received the mark of the beast (13:16) and sided with Babylon in the final battle. These people are portrayed in the sixth seal scene as "the kings of the earth and the magistrates and the military commanders and the rich and the powerful and every slave and free person" trying to hide from God and the Lamb (6:15–17). The parallel between the two passages shows that the destruction of the wicked occurs in the context of the Second Coming.

John now sees the worldwide confederacy of political powers fighting Christ and His saints (Rev. 19:19). Revelation 17:14 says that the kings of the earth "will wage war against the Lamb, and the Lamb will overcome them." In the sixth plague scene, the satanic triumvirate sends their envoys to entice the world's governing powers to engage in the final war against God's end-time people (16:13–14). As the result, a worldwide religious and political confederacy is formed under the satanic trinity. They assemble for the great battle at Armageddon (16:16).

At that point, Christ—or "Michael, the great prince" (Dan. 12:1)—appears, completely overthrowing the worldwide confederacy. His coming in glory and power destroys the political confederacy. Revelation 6:15–17 shows the kings and mighty men running in panic, trying to hide from the Lamb's wrath. The apostle Paul explains that Christ will bring destruction to the end-time apostate religious system "with the breath of His mouth and bring [it] to an end by the appearance of His coming" (2 Thess. 2:8). Furthermore, two members of the satanic triumvirate—the sea beast and the earth beast—are captured and thrown into the lake of fire (Rev. 19:20). The lake of fire is not an everlasting burning hell but a description of the earth as it is destroyed by fire. Here, there will be an ultimate end to rebellion against God—the same as in Revelation 20:14.

The rest of the people are killed with the sword proceeding from Christ's mouth. As Paul states, they are destroyed by the glory of Christ's power (2 Thess. 1:8–10). The whole earth now resembles a battlefield, filled with the bodies of those killed. This awful scene concludes with the statement that "all the birds were filled with their flesh" (Rev. 19:21). The defeat of the worldwide confederacy of rebellious humanity, who gathered against God and His people in the final combat, will be total.

This concludes the description of the battle of Armageddon, which began in chapter 16. Babylon is overthrown when Satan's two allies are cast into the lake of fire. Those who supported Babylon are slain, and await the final judgment. The only being left on earth is Satan. His fate is described in Revelation 20.

The Millennium and the Final Judgment

 Revelation 20:1–15

Revelation 19 describes the conclusion of the battle of Armageddon, which culminates with the coming of Christ. The final battle's outcome is the destruction of the confederate evil forces and the deliverance of God's faithful people. Satan's two allies have been thrown into the lake of fire. All who supported Babylon have been killed by the glory of Christ's appearance and are awaiting the final judgment. Revelation 20 describes the situation during the millennium and the fate of Satan and his followers at the final judgment.

The Millennium (20:1–10)

The battle of Armageddon results in the desolation and depopulation of the earth. The destructive winds of the seven last plagues (Rev. 7:1) have caused much destruction, turning the earth into a barren desert. As Ellen White described it, the whole earth will look like "a desolate wilderness. The ruins of cities and villages destroyed by the earthquake, uprooted trees, ragged rocks thrown out by the sea or torn out of the earth itself, are scattered over its surface, while vast caverns mark the spot where the mountains have been rent from their foundations."[1] The coming of Christ brings the destruction of the wicked, whose bodies cover the whole earth. The state of the earth is much like the earth in its chaotic form before Creation (cf. Gen. 1:2). It also resembles Palestine during the Exile as portrayed by Jeremiah:

> I looked on the earth, and behold, it was formless and void; and to the heavens, and they had no light. . . . I looked, and behold, there was no man, and all the birds of the heavens had fled. I looked, and behold, the fruitful land was a wilderness, and all its cities were pulled down before the Lord, before His fierce anger. (Jer. 4:23–26)

In such a chaotic state, this planet becomes the place of Satan's imprisonment during the one thousand years, until he receives his final punishment in the lake of fire (Rev. 20:10):

> *¹And I saw an angel coming down from heaven, having in his hand the key of the abyss and a great chain in his hand. ²And he seized the dragon, the ancient serpent, the one who is the devil and Satan, and bound him for a thousand years, ³and he threw him into the abyss and locked it and sealed it over him, in order that he might not deceive the nations any longer until the thousand years were completed; after these things, it is necessary for him to be loosed for a little time.*
>
> *⁴And I saw the thrones, and they sat upon them, and judgment was given to them. And [I saw] the souls of those beheaded because of the testimony of Jesus and because of the word of God, and those who did not worship the beast nor his image and did not receive the mark upon their foreheads and upon their hands; and they came to life and reigned with Christ for a thousand years. ⁵(The rest of the dead did not come to life until the thousand years were completed.) This is the first resurrection. ⁶Blessed and holy is the one who has a part in the first resurrection; over these, the second death does not have authority, but they will be priests of God and of Christ, and they will reign with Him for the thousand years.*
>
> *⁷And when the thousand years are completed, Satan will be loosed from his prison, ⁸and he will go out to deceive the nations who are in the four corners of the earth, Gog and Magog, to gather them for the battle, whose number is as the sand of the sea. ⁹And they went up to the breadth of the earth and surrounded the camp of the saints, namely, the beloved city, and fire came down from heaven and devoured them. ¹⁰And the devil who deceived them was thrown into the lake of fire and sulfur, where both the beast and the false prophet were, and they will be tormented day and night forever and ever.*

The one thousand years, known as the millennium, is the period that begins with the Second Coming of Christ (see Rev. 19:11–21).

Revelation does not explain whether this is a literal or symbolic period of time. Although either is possible, the symbolism of the text points to the latter. However, the book points to the millennium as a real period of time concerning Satan with the fallen angels on one side and God's resurrected people on the other.

The Binding of Satan (20:1–3)

John observes an angel coming from heaven with the key to the abyss and a great chain in his hand. He seizes the dragon and binds him; then he throws the dragon into the abyss and securely imprisons him for a thousand years, so "he might not deceive the nations any longer until the thousand years were completed; after these things, it is necessary for him to be loosed for a little time" (Rev. 20:3).

This whole scene is expressed in figurative language. The dragon is identified as Satan, the ancient serpent of Genesis 3 and the great adversary of God and His people (cf. Rev. 12:9). The chain which binds Satan is also symbolic, for a spiritual being cannot be bound with chains. As shown earlier, the abyss is the place where Satan and his demonic forces are confined until they receive their rightful retribution (cf. Luke 8:31; 2 Pet. 2:4). The word for "abyss" is used in Genesis 1:2 in the Greek Old Testament—known as the Septuagint—to describe the earth as "formless and void" at the beginning of Creation. In Revelation 20, the abyss denotes the chaotic state of the earth, caused by the seven last plagues.

Satan is chained in Revelation 20, during the Second Coming. The desolate earth serves as his prison for one thousand years (Rev. 20:7). He is chained there with the fallen angels by a chain of circumstances. There are no humans left alive to tempt and harm (20:3). Those who died believing in Christ were resurrected and joined the living saints, and both groups have been taken to heaven (1 Thess. 4:16–17). Those who rejected God are dead (Rev. 19:21). All Satan and his demonic forces can do is contemplate the consequences of their rebellion against God. At the end of the millennium, Satan will be released from his imprisonment to once again perform his deceitful activities (20:3, 7–10).

The Saints in Heaven (20:4–6)

While Satan and his fallen angels are confined to the earth, the glorified saints sit on thrones and are authorized to judge. Some of them never tasted death but were transformed and translated to heaven (1 Thess. 4:17). The rest are those who were raised to life at the coming of Christ. Many of them died as martyrs because of their faithfulness to "the word of God and because of the testimony" of Jesus, as portrayed in the fifth seal scene (Rev. 6:9–11). Among those resurrected are God's end-time people, who chose not to side with Babylon and receive the mark of the beast. They went to the grave to "rest from their labors" (14:13). Now, they have come back to life, transformed, and will be taken to heaven for the one thousand years with the living saints (1 Thess. 4:15–17).

Revelation clearly specifies that raising the saints to life is the first resurrection, which takes place at the beginning of the millennium (Rev. 20:5). The rest of humanity will be resurrected at the conclusion of the millennium, which coincides with Satan's release from his solitary confinement (20:5–7). Those raised in the first resurrection are "blessed and holy," because they are not subject to "the second death" (20:6), which will be the fate of the wicked when they are thrown into the lake of fire (20:14–15; 21:8). Here is the fulfillment of the promise given to the faithful in Smyrna—that they "shall not be harmed by the second death" (2:11).

Although the text does not explicitly state where the resurrected redeemed are during the millennium, Revelation 7:9–17 and 19:1–10 show that they are in heaven. Earlier, Jesus used language that corresponds to Hebrew wedding customs to describe His return to the earth (see Rev. 19:7–9). After betrothing His bride, He returned to His Father's house in heaven to prepare a place for His people. After preparing this place, Christ will come back to take His people to this heavenly place (John 14:3). Peter also talks about the imperishable inheritance reserved for God's people in heaven (1 Pet. 1:4). All this shows that God's people will spend the millennium in the heavenly place prepared for them by Christ.

What will God's people do in heaven during the millennium? The text says that they will reign with Christ as priests and kings for one thousand years (Rev. 20:6). Here, Christ's promise to the overcomers in Laodicea is fulfilled: they will share His throne (3:21). God's wandering people, who often suffered persecution and humiliation on earth because of their faithfulness to the gospel, will be exalted to share Jesus's throne. As priests, they are in the immediate presence of God and have access to the records of God's governance over the universe.

During their millennial reign, the resurrected saints are authorized to exercise judgment (Rev. 20:4). This recalls Jesus's promise to His disciples that, at His coming, they will "sit upon twelve thrones, judging the twelve tribes of Israel" (Matt. 19:28). Paul pointed to the time when the saints will judge the world and even the angels (1 Cor. 6:2–3). The saints exercising judgment during the millennium has to do with the question Satan raised at the beginning of the Great Controversy, concerning the fairness of God's actions in the universe. Throughout history, Satan has introduced many doubts concerning God's character and His dealings with the beings He created.

During the millennium, God puts Himself on trial to be judged by the humans that He has saved. He allows the resurrected saints to access the records of history's events to find answers to all questions concerning the fairness of His decisions regarding those who were lost. During the process, God will "bring to light the things hidden in the darkness and disclose the motives of men's hearts" (1 Cor. 4:5). The redeemed saints are also able to find answers to questions dealing with God's leading in their own lives on earth.

At the conclusion of the millennium, all questions involving God's justice are forever settled. Satan's accusations are refuted. God's people are able to see beyond a shadow of doubt the greatness of God's love and care manifested, even in their own lives on earth. They are now ready to witness the administration of God's justice at the final judgment.

The Releasing of Satan (20:7–10)

At the conclusion of the millennium, Satan is released from his solitary confinement in the abyss. Releasing Satan is similar to releasing the demonic hordes from the abyss and allowing them to harm people at the time of the fifth trumpet (Rev. 9:1). Satan's release takes place simultaneously with the resurrection of the unsaved dead during the second resurrection (see 20:5). If Satan was chained by the absence of people on earth, his release is initiated by the resurrection of the wicked (20:7–8). His release, however, is only for a short time.

The resurrection of the wicked provides a new opportunity for Satan to operate as he did in the past. He sees his final opportunity to dethrone God and have dominion over the world. By his deceitful activities, he is able to gather the wicked from all time periods against God's people, who are encamped in the Holy City—the New Jerusalem (Rev. 20:8). Although the descent of the New Jerusalem is not mentioned until Revelation 21, it is evident that the city with the saints inside has descended prior to the time of Satan's attack. Under Satan's leadership, the wicked surround the Holy City, ready to attack and destroy God's people—similar to what they did during the battle of Armageddon. The attack does not take place, though, because God intervenes to protect His people within the city. Then fire comes from heaven, destroying Satan and his hordes.

In portraying this scene, John uses language that evokes the prophecies against Gog and Magog in Ezekiel—just as he used language that referred to Old Testament Babylon to portray the end-time apostate religious system in chapters 16–18. In Ezekiel 38–39, Gog and Magog are the enemies assembled against Israel in Palestine that will be utterly destroyed by God. John applies this Old Testament motif to describe Satan's final attack on the saints at the millennium's conclusion and to show God's miraculous intervention to protect His people (see Ezek. 38:22–23; 39:6).

The last attack on the Holy City demonstrates the hardness of the hearts within those who rejected God. Though God's miraculous intervention makes them realize the delusion of Satan's deception, they do not change. Their rebellious hearts are filled with the same hatred against God and His people that they previously demonstrated. This affirms, once again, that they have been rightly allotted for destruction.

The scene concludes with the total defeat of Satan and those who followed him. Fire, hurled from heaven, consumes them. Satan and the fallen angels meet their end in the lake of fire, thus sharing the fate of the two other triumvirate members (Rev. 20:10). The text states that they will be "tormented day and night forever and ever" (20:10; cf. 14:10–11). As shown earlier, the phrase "forever and ever" denotes a continuation of an action until it completes God's purpose. Satan's punishment is irreversible. All who have followed him must share his fate (while God's people are safe in the city under God's protection). This is described in detail in verses 11–15.

The Final Judgment (20:11-15)

Having briefly stated the fate of Satan and his army, John now gives a more detailed description of how the destruction of the wicked will take place:

> *¹¹And I saw a great white throne and One sitting upon it from whose face the earth and the heaven fled, and no place was found for them. ¹²And I saw the dead, the great and the small, standing before the throne; and books*

were opened, and another book was opened, which is the book of life; and the dead were judged by what has been written in the books, according to their works. ¹³And the sea gave up the dead who were in it, and Death and Hades gave up their dead who were in them, and each of them was judged according to his works. ¹⁴And Death and Hades were thrown into the lake of fire; this is the second death, the lake of fire. ¹⁵And if anyone was not found written in the book of life, he was thrown into the lake of fire.

As Satan and his army surround the Holy City and are about to carry out their attack, God suddenly appears seated on a throne. God's throne, which has been a source of hope and deliverance for God's people throughout the Great Controversy's history (cf. Heb. 4:16), now becomes a source of terror to the wicked. In the face of God's presence and in the greatness of the moment, the universe convulses in cataclysmic terror (Rev. 20:11).

The time has come for the dead to be judged (cf. Rev. 11:18). All the dead—regardless of how they died—are raised at the second resurrection and are brought to judgment: "The sea gave up the dead who were in it, and Death and Hades gave up their dead who were in them, and each of them was judged according to his works" (20:13). Every person who has ever lived on the earth but spurned God is brought to judgment before the throne of God. People from all time periods and every socioeconomic class are there. No one is exempt; all must give an account of the wrongs they committed.

The time has now come for God to "judge the world in righteousness" (Pss. 96:13; 98:9). The books of record are opened. Two kinds of books are mentioned here. The first books are the records of human deeds, showing whether a person has been loyal to God or to Satan. The second one is the book of life with the names of those who belong to God (Luke 10:20; Phil. 4:3; Rev. 3:5). The ones whose names are not in the book of life will end up in the lake of fire (20:15). They are now "judged by what has been written in the books, according to their works" (20:12; cf. Rom. 2:6).

As the unsaved stand before God's throne, it is as if a curtain is removed and their whole life unfolds before their eyes. They can see how much God tried to save them; yet, they knowingly and willingly spurned His mercy and refused His offer of salvation. Now they realize what they have lost as a consequence of the choices they made. Yet, they acknowledge God's justice. God's kingdom would not be a happy place for them. They have lived their lives in rebellion against God, so spending eternity in His presence would not be joyous for them. This is why their destruction in the lake of fire appears to be a manifestation of God's mercy toward them, rather than vengeful punishment by a wrathful deity.

Thus, all who spurned God's mercy meet their end in the lake of fire, which is "prepared for the devil and his angels" (Matt. 25:41). The lake of fire is not an everlasting burning hell, as many Christians believe. Rather, it is a metaphorical description of the whole earth burning with fire (Rev. 20:9). It is significant that John equates the lake of fire with the second death (20:14). This is in contrast to the first death, referred to in the Bible as a sleep. The lake of fire refers to complete destruction (Matt. 10:28)—not the beginning of eternal conscious torment. It is the place where all rebels against God meet their ultimate end. The fire burns long enough to completely consume everything, until nothing is left to burn. Its flames completely destroy everything, leaving "neither root nor branch" (Mal. 4:1): "Satan the root, his followers the branches."[2] They will all cease to exist.

The second death also means the end of death: "Death and Hades were thrown into the lake of fire" (Rev. 20:14). As Paul stated: "The last enemy that will be abolished is death" (1 Cor. 15:26). Eternal life for the redeemed can only begin when this great enemy is abolished. An eternity without sin and sinners is now ready to begin.

The Restored Earth

 Revelation 21:1–22:5

Revelation 21–22 brings us John's last vision on Patmos. The Great Controversy concludes with the triumph of God over the forces of evil. Satan and his hordes are destroyed in the lake of fire. Purged of all traces of sin and evil, this earth becomes the eternal home of the redeemed. The last two chapters of the book give a description of the new earth and its capital—the New Jerusalem.

The New Earth (21:1–8)

Revelation 21 opens with a general description of the new heaven and the new earth. Similar to elsewhere in the Bible, Revelation depicts the new earth in terms of what life there will not be like:

> ¹Then I saw a new heaven and a new earth; for the first heaven and the first earth passed away, and the sea is no longer there. ²And I saw the holy city, New Jerusalem, coming down out of heaven from God, made ready as a bride adorned for her husband. ³And I heard a loud voice from the throne, saying, "Behold, the tabernacle of God is among men, and He will dwell among them, and they shall be His peoples, and God Himself will be among them, ⁴and He will wipe away every tear from their eyes; and there no longer shall be death, neither sorrow nor crying nor pain, for the first things have passed away." ⁵And He who sits on the throne said, "Behold, I am making all things new." And He said, "Write, for these words are faithful and true." ⁶Then He said to me, "It is done. I am the Alpha and the Omega, the beginning and the end. I will

give to the one who thirsts from the spring of the water of life without cost. ⁷He who overcomes will inherit these things, and I will be his God and he will be My son. ⁸But for the cowardly and unbelieving and abominable and murderers and immoral persons and sorcerers and idolaters and all liars, their part will be in the lake that burns with fire and brimstone, which is the second death."

The description of the new world in Revelation 21–22 is given in the language of Genesis 1–3. "In the beginning God created the heavens and the earth" (Gen. 1:1). On the newly created earth, God made the Garden of Eden the home of humans. With the arrival of sin, however, this was lost. The earth became subject to corruption and decay (Rom. 8:19–22). Pain, tears, and death took the place of joy, happiness, and life.

But God promised that He would "create new heavens and a new earth; and the former things shall not be remembered or come to mind" (Isa. 65:17). In Revelation 21–22, this promise is fulfilled. With the new earth, God restores the lost Garden of Eden. All that was lost because of sin is now restored through Jesus Christ. In such a way, God's original plan for the human race is finally realized.

The Earth Restored (21:1)

With the eradication of sin, "a new heaven and a new earth" replaces the former heaven and earth (Rev. 21:1). In Jewish tradition, there were three heavens: the first one was the earth's atmosphere (the sky); the second, the starry universe; and the third, the dwelling place of God (cf. 2 Cor. 12:2). Revelation 21:1 refers to the earth's atmosphere or the sky. In the previous chapter, the old earth and the sky could not endure God's presence (Rev. 20:11). Thus, this planet will undergo a total transformation. The word "new" (Gr. *kainos*) denotes something new in form and quality rather than new in origin and time. The new earth is the renewed earth—purged by fire and restored to its original state (1 Pet. 3:10–13).

The first thing John observes on the new earth is that "the sea is no longer" (Rev. 21:1). This may mean that the oceans we know today will cease to exist. The phrase may also be understood metaphorically as the absence of evil. The sea is where the enemy of God and His people comes from (13:1). By removing the sea, evil, which caused fear and suffering, is also removed.

It appears, however, that this statement, "the sea is no longer there," reflects John's experience on Patmos. The fact that he refers to "*the* sea" shows that he has a particular sea in mind: the one surrounding Patmos during his tribulation. For him, the sea has become a symbol of evil, separation, and suffering. His own suffering on Patmos becomes the precursor to the experience of God's people throughout history. It is no wonder that, in his last vision, the first thing he observes is that "the sea is no longer" on the new earth. To John, the absence of the sea on the new earth means the absence of evil, which caused suffering and pain.

Life on the New Earth (21:2–8)

God's presence guarantees a life free of pain and death for His people on the restored earth. Sin separated humans from God. With the destruction of sin, God's presence among His people on earth has been restored. This presence is realized with the New Jerusalem "coming down out of heaven from God" (Rev. 21:2). The descent of the Holy City occurred at the end of the millennium (20:9). The fact that it came from heaven shows that the city is not a rebuilt Jerusalem in Palestine but a heavenly city designed and constructed by God (Heb. 11:10).

The New Jerusalem is referred to as God's tabernacle among His people. "He will dwell among them, and they shall be His peoples, and God Himself will be among them" (Rev. 21:3). There is no temple in the New Jerusalem; the actual presence of God makes the city the temple of the new earth (21:22). In Old Testament times, the temple symbolized God's presence among His people (Exod. 25:8; 29:45; Lev. 26:11–12). Because of Israel's unfaithfulness, God removed His presence from them (Matt. 23:37–38). Nonetheless, God promised that He would once again make His dwelling place with His people and be their God, and they would be His people (Ezek. 37:27). The New Jerusalem does not need a symbol of God's presence, because God's presence will be real in the city.

God's abiding presence defines the life of God's people on the new earth. Revelation describes life on the new earth in terms of what it will not be: no tears, death, sorrow, crying, and pain (Rev. 21:4; cf. 7:15–17). All these are the consequences of sin. Now, sin no longer exists, for "the first things have passed away" (21:4). Millennia earlier, Isaiah prophesied that "He will swallow up death for all time, and the Lord God will wipe tears away from all faces, and He will remove the reproach of His people from all the earth; for the LORD has spoken"

(Isa. 25:8). Revelation describes the fulfillment of this prophecy on the restored earth.

When Jesus dwelt on the earth, His presence banished all tears, pain, and sorrow. This was best expressed in the words of Mary and Martha at the death of their brother Lazarus: "Lord, if You had been here, my brother would not have died" (John 11:21). The sisters knew that death could not exist in the presence of Christ. In the same way, the abiding presence of God on the new earth will mean freedom from the pain and suffering we know today.

At this point, there is a proclamation from God's throne: "Behold, I am making all things new." This declaration is affirmed with the statement: "These words are faithful and true" (21:5). They are as faithful and true as God is faithful and true. This is also repeated in Revelation 22:6. Promises are as strong as the people giving them and their ability to do what they say they will do. The promise of a life free from sin and suffering comes from God, who is "the Alpha and the Omega, the first and the last, the beginning and the end." This claim begins and concludes the book (see 1:8; 22:13). As God, in the beginning, made this world out of nothing, so at the end of history, He will restore this world to its original state.

This section concludes with a warning. The overcomers are promised the status of being the children of God with all the rights of heirs (Rev. 21:7). They will inherit all the things promised to the overcomers in the messages to the seven churches in Revelation 2:3. But those who spurn God's mercy—the cowards, unfaithful, abominable, murderers, fornicators, idolaters, liars, and sorcerers—are excluded from the heavenly city (21:8; 21:27; 22:15). Their lot is the second death in the lake of fire prepared for Satan and his angels (Matt. 25:41).

The New Jerusalem (21:9–22:5)

Having described life in the restored earth, John now describes its capital—the New Jerusalem. He first describes the city's exterior (Rev. 21:9–21a) and then moves inside the city (21:21b–22:5):

> *⁹Then one of the seven angels who had the seven bowls full of the seven last plagues came and spoke with me, saying, "Come here, I will show you the bride, the wife of the Lamb." ¹⁰And he carried me away in the Spirit to a great and high mountain and showed me the holy city,*

Jerusalem, coming down out of heaven from God, ¹¹having the glory of God. Her brilliance was like a very costly stone, as a stone of crystal-clear jasper. ¹²It had a great and high wall, with twelve gates, and at the gates, twelve angels; and names were written on them, which are the names of the twelve tribes of the sons of Israel. ¹³There were three gates on the east and three gates on the north and three gates on the south and three gates on the west. ¹⁴And the wall of the city had twelve foundation stones, and on them were the twelve names of the twelve apostles of the Lamb.

¹⁵The one who spoke with me had a gold measuring rod to measure the city and its gates and its wall. ¹⁶The city is laid out as a square, and its length is as great as the width; and he measured the city with the rod, 12,000 stadia; its length and width and height are equal. ¹⁷And he measured its wall, 144 cubits, according to human measurements, which are also angelic measurements. ¹⁸The material of the wall was jasper; and the city was pure gold, like clear glass. ¹⁹The foundation stones of the city wall were adorned with every kind of precious stone. The first foundation stone was jasper; the second, sapphire; the third, chalcedony; the fourth, emerald; ²⁰the fifth, sardonyx; the sixth, sardius; the seventh, chrysolite; the eighth, beryl; the ninth, topaz; the tenth, chrysoprase; the eleventh, jacinth; the twelfth, amethyst. ²¹And the twelve gates were twelve pearls; each one of the gates was a single pearl. And the street of the city was pure gold, like transparent glass.

²²I saw no temple in it, for the Lord God, the Almighty, and the Lamb are its temple. ²³And the city has no need of the sun or of the moon to shine on it, for the glory of God has illumined it, and its lamp is the Lamb. ²⁴The nations will walk by its light, and the kings of the earth will bring their glory into it. ²⁵In the daytime (for there will be no night there), its gates will never be closed; ²⁶and they will bring the glory and the honor of the nations into it; ²⁷and nothing unclean, and no one who practices abomination and lying, shall ever come into it, but only those whose names are written in the Lamb's book of life.

22 ¹Then he showed me a river of the water of life, clear as crystal, coming from the throne of God and of the Lamb, ²in the middle of its street. On either side of the river was the tree of life, bearing twelve kinds of fruit, yielding its fruit every month; and the leaves of the tree were for the healing of the nations. ³There will no longer be any curse; and the throne of God and of the Lamb will be in it, and His bond-servants will serve Him; ⁴they will see His face, and His name will be on their foreheads. ⁵And there will no longer be any night; and they will not have need of the light of a lamp nor the light of the sun, because the Lord God will illumine them; and they will reign forever and ever.

John is now invited to observe the New Jerusalem. The angel refers to the city as "the bride, the wife of the Lamb" (Rev. 21:9); it is prepared as "a bride adorned for her husband" (21:2). In the Old Testament, the earthly Jerusalem is often spoken of as a bride lavishly adorned for God (Isa. 49:18; 62:5). In Revelation 19:7–8, the same metaphor is applied to God's people. The New Jerusalem and God's people are identical.

The New Jerusalem is a real place inhabited by real people. The city and life therein are beyond our comprehension, surpassing any human imagination. Paul reminds us: "Things which eye has not seen and ear has not heard, and which have not entered the heart of man, all that God has prepared for those who love Him" (1 Cor. 2:9). No imaginative language is adequate or sufficient to describe the heavenly reality. Therefore, it is portrayed in symbolic language. The city is pictured in terms of the fortified cities of the time, the Old Testament temple, the restored temple from Ezekiel 40–48, and the restored Garden of Eden (Gen. 2–3).

The Exterior of the City (21:10–21a)

The New Jerusalem is situated on "a great and high mountain" (Rev. 21:10). It has been suggested that this high mountain is, figuratively speaking, a mound made on the ruins of Babylon. Rebuilding a city on a mound of a previously destroyed city was a well-known practice in ancient times (see Josh. 11:13; Jer. 30:18). Thus, it is over the ruins of end-time Babylon, so to speak, that the New Jerusalem rises in all its glory.[1] This scene's purpose is to affirm God's ultimate triumph over the end-time apostate system.

John first observes the city from a distance. The city radiates the glory of God and appears to him as a jasper stone sparkling like crystal (Rev. 21:11). In the Old Testament temple, God's glory denoted His presence (Exod. 40:34–35; Ezek. 43:1–5). The New Jerusalem is surrounded by a high wall with twelve gates—three gates on each of the four sides—with angels by them (Rev. 21:12–13). This echoes the description of the temple in Ezekiel's vision (Ezek. 40:5; 48:30–35). The gates on each side allow entry from any direction. This points to the universal scope of the city. Jesus foretold that many will come from the east, west, north, and south and sit at the table in God's kingdom (Luke 13:29). This prediction is fulfilled in the New Jerusalem, where everybody has unlimited access to God's presence.

As John comes closer, he notices that the city walls are made of jasper and transparent gold (Rev. 21:18)—this accentuates the splendor of the city. This is reminiscent of the description of the temple in Jerusalem by Josephus. According to this Jewish historian, the temple was covered by plates of gold, "and at the first rising of the sun, reflected back a very fiery splendor, and made those who forced themselves to look upon it to turn their eyes away, just as they would have done at the sun's own rays."[2]

The gates of the New Jerusalem are made of huge pearls (Rev. 21:21). Upon them are inscribed the names of the twelve tribes of Israel, as in Ezekiel's vision (21:12; Ezek. 48:30–35). The New Jerusalem has twelve foundations, decorated with precious stones, with the names of the twelve apostles inscribed on them (Rev. 21:19–20). These precious stones parallel the precious stones that decorated the high priest's breastplate in the Old Testament, upon which were engraved the names of the twelve tribes of Israel (Exod. 28:17–20). In Revelation, the twelve tribes of Israel represent God's people of the Old Testament and the twelve apostles represent God's people of the New Testament. Combining the twelve tribes and the twelve apostles shows that the city is the place for all of God's people from both Old Testament and New Testament times.

The measurement of the New Jerusalem denotes a perfect cube; the city is 12,000 stadia (about 1,500 miles) in length, width, and height (Rev. 21:16). The cube generally consists of twelve edges. Each edge is 12,000 stadia long, which totals 144,000 stadia for the entire city. Revelation 7:4 shows that 144,000 is the number of the totality of God's people. The New Jerusalem is a colossal city, large enough to accommodate all of God's people—all who ever lived on the earth.

The significance of the New Jerusalem's cube shape is found in the fact that the Holy of Holies in the Old Testament temple was also a perfect cube (1 Kings 6:20). The city, thus, functions not only as the temple but also as the Holy of Holies. In the earthly temple, the Holy of Holies housed the Ark of the Covenant, which represented God's throne. The throne of God and of the Lamb is located in the New Jerusalem (Rev. 22:3). Jeremiah prophesied that, in the messianic age, people would not talk about the Ark of the Covenant, because Jerusalem would be called "the throne of the LORD" (Jer. 3:16–17). In the earthly temple, only the high priest was allowed to enter the Holy of Holies to meet God there. In the New Jerusalem, this privilege is granted to all the redeemed (Rev. 22:3–4). "They are before the throne of God and serve Him in worship day and night in His temple, and the One sitting on the throne will tabernacle over them" (7:15).

Inside the City (21:21b–27)

As John moves inside the city, he sees a street made of "pure gold, like transparent glass" (Rev. 21:21b). He notes that the city does not need the light of the sun or moon, because the glory of God provides light for its residents (21:23; 22:5). Thus, there is no night in the city (21:25). Here is the fulfillment of another of Isaiah's prophecies regarding the glorified Zion: "No longer will you have the sun for light by day, nor for brightness will the moon give you light; but you will have the LORD for an everlasting light, and your God for your glory. Your sun will no longer set, nor will your moon wane; for you will have the LORD for an everlasting light" (Isa. 60:19–20).

The nations will walk in the light of the city, and the kings will bring their glory into it (Rev. 21:24–26). This is another echo of Isaiah's prophecy: "Nations will come to your light, and kings to the brightness of your rising" (Isa. 60:3). The nations and the kings of the restored earth are the redeemed (see Rev. 1:6; 5:9; 7:9). The city gates will never be closed (21:25). "Your gates will be open continually," Isaiah foresaw. "They will not be closed day and night" (Isa. 60:11). The open gates make it possible for all people to come into the presence of God.

The only condition for entering the New Jerusalem is to have one's name registered in the Lamb's book of life (Rev. 21:27). The ones who are unclean and practice abominations and lies are excluded from the city (see 22:15). These are the ones who worshiped the beast (13:8) and drank from Babylon's cup, which was filled with abominations and unclean things (17:4). They have found their ultimate end in the lake of fire (20:15; 21:8).

Revelation continually reminds us to take our relationship with Jesus Christ seriously, because it concerns our eternal destiny. Today, we must make Christ the Lord of our lives and let nothing come between Him and us. We must accept His mercy and allow His blood to cleanse us of all sin for, as Isaiah prophesied, the residents of the restored Jerusalem "will be called holy—everyone who is recorded for life in Jerusalem" (Isa. 4:3). The purpose of Revelation is to make us focus on Christ as our only hope of reaching our future homeland.

On the Banks of the River (22:1–5)

In the conclusion of the Holy City vision, John is shown a river of life, flowing from the throne of God and the Lamb in the middle of the main street (Rev. 22:1). This is reminiscent of the river flowing from Eden, watering the garden and making it fruitful (Gen. 2:10). The Old Testament prophets often spoke of the river of living waters flowing from the restored temple in Jerusalem and giving life to all (Ezek. 47:1–12; Joel 3:18; Zech. 14:8). These prophecies are now fulfilled.

This river of life flowing in the New Jerusalem contrasts with the Euphrates waters, where end-time Babylon dwelt (Rev. 17:1). The Euphrates River flowed through ancient Babylon. At that river, God's people sat as captives, longing for Jerusalem (Ps. 137). Now, in Revelation, Babylon is no longer, and the captivity of God's people is over. It is at the side of the river of life that God's wandering people have found their eternal rest.

On the banks of the river is the tree of life (Rev. 22:2). The tree of life symbolizes eternal life (cf. Gen. 3:22). Because of the curse caused by sin, humans lost access to the tree of life in the Garden of Eden and became subject to death (3:22–24). Now, in the New Jerusalem, the curse is removed; the redeemed once again have access to the tree of life and share the gift of eternal life that Adam enjoyed prior to the entrance of sin (Rev. 22:3).

The tree of life yields fruit every month, and its leaves are for "the healing of the nations" (Rev. 22:2). Ezekiel saw in a vision the same tree: "By the river on its bank, on one side and on the other, will grow all kinds of trees for food. Their leaves will not wither and their fruit will not fail. They will bear every month because their water flows from the sanctuary, and their fruit will be for food and their leaves for healing" (Ezek. 47:12).

Many readers of Revelation assume that the leaves on the tree of life have some healing power to prevent and heal sickness and disease. However, remember two things. First, the book makes very clear that, with the eradication of sin and evil, there is no sickness or death any longer in the restored earth (Rev. 21:4). This excludes any need for physical healing.

Second, the text clearly specifies that the leaves of the tree are to heal the nations, not individuals. The New Jerusalem is inhabited by people of all nations, tribes, and languages (Rev. 7:9). Zechariah prophesied: "Many nations will join themselves to the LORD in that day and will become My people" (Zech. 2:11). "Many nations" constitute the people of God. All the barriers that separated nations are removed. The curative leaves on the tree of life heal all the wounds caused by the barriers that have divided people and have torn them apart for ages—national, racial, linguistic, social, and others. "Nation will not lift up sword against nation, and never again will they train for war. Each of them will sit under his vine and under his fig tree, with no one to make them afraid" (Mic. 4:3–4). On the banks of the river of life, each person invites "his neighbor to sit" (Zech. 3:10) under the tree of life. The redeemed on the restored earth are now one people, belonging to the one great family of God.

In the New Jerusalem, there is no longer any curse (Rev. 22:3). Because of the curse which sin brought upon the world, humans were banished from the Garden of Eden. With the eradication of sin, God's people are brought back to the restored Eden. Zechariah prophesied: "People will live in it, and there will no longer be a curse, for Jerusalem will dwell in security" (Zech. 14:11).

The greatest of all the privileges the redeemed will enjoy in the New Jerusalem is seeing God face to face (Rev. 22:4), as Adam did before sin. The perennial desire of humans throughout history has been to see God's face, something that even Moses was denied (Exod. 33:18–20). This is now fulfilled in the New Jerusalem. The redeemed now see God as He is (1 John 3:2). They serve Him and worship Him in His temple (see Rev. 7:15). His name is on their foreheads as the reward for refusing to have the mark of the beast on their foreheads (see 14:1; 15:2). The conclusion of the Great Controversy marks the beginning of their intimate fellowship with God. "And they will reign forever and ever" (22:5).

A Tale of Two Cities

The portrayal of the New Jerusalem in Revelation is intended to stimulate a desire for it. John describes this city of the Lamb in contrast to the harlot city, Babylon:

End-Time Babylon	The New Jerusalem
The city of Satan	The city of God
The great city	The holy city
An earthly city	A heavenly city
Rebellious	Faithful
The harlot city	The bride city of the Lamb
Decorated with gold and precious stones	Decorated with gold and precious stones
The habitation of demons	The dwelling place of God
The place of unclean things	No unclean things within it
The Euphrates flows through it	The river of life flows through it
Offers the cup of abominations	Offers the water of life
Nations and kings give their power and authority to it	Nations and kings bring their glory into it
Its inhabitants are not recorded in the book of life	Its inhabitants are recorded in the book of life
Destroyed forever	Exists forever
Light will never shine in it again	The Lamb is its light, and God illuminates it

The New Jerusalem is portrayed in Revelation as the fulfillment of human longings and dreams. God's people throughout history lived and died hoping for that city (Heb. 11:10, 16; 13:14). It is God's response to Babylon's offer of prosperity based on human strategy and effort. Babylon represents futile human dreams of and ambitions for power, fame, and money. However, the final word is with

God. Babylon comes to its end, and the New Jerusalem rises on top of its ruins.

Thus, Revelation gives us a contrasting tale of two cities. Readers must make their choice: either to choose Babylon and consequently suffer its fate or to choose the New Jerusalem and live life without end in boundless happiness. Christ urges us to choose to be there (Rev. 22:17).

The Conclusion
of the Book

 Revelation 22:6–21

The description of the restored earth, with its capital, the New Jerusalem, completes the prophecies of Revelation. In concluding the book, John wants to remind his readers of the things he declared in the introduction, to pronounce a final warning, and to give his closing remarks.

>⁶And he said to me: "These words are faithful and true, and the Lord God of the spirits of the prophets sent His angel to show His servants the things which must soon take place."
>
>⁷"And behold, I am coming soon. Blessed is the one who heeds the words of the prophecy of this book."
>
>⁸And I, John, am the one who has heard and seen these things. And when I heard and saw them, I fell down to worship at the feet of the angel who showed me these things. ⁹And he said to me: "See, do not do this; I am your fellow servant and of your brothers the prophets and of those who keep the words of this book; worship God." ¹⁰And he said to me: "Do not seal the words of the prophecy of this book, for the time is near. ¹¹Let the unrighteous still do unrighteousness, and let the filthy still be filthy, and let the righteous still do righteousness, and let the holy still be holy."
>
>¹²"Behold, I am coming soon, and My reward is with Me to give to each as his work is. ¹³I am the Alpha and the Omega, the first and the last, the beginning and the end.
>
>¹⁴"Blessed are those who wash their robes, that their authority may be over the tree of life and they may enter

the gates into the city. *¹⁵Outside are the dogs and the sorcerers and the fornicators and the murderers and the idolaters and everyone who loves and practices the lie.*

¹⁶"I, Jesus, have sent My angel to testify to you these things for the churches; I am the Sprout and the offspring of David, the bright Morning Star." ¹⁷And the Spirit and the bride say: "Come!" And let the one who hears say: "Come!" And let the one who thirsts come. Let the one who desires take the water of life freely.

¹⁸I, myself, testify to everyone who hears the words of the prophecy of this book: if anyone adds to them, God will add to him the plagues written in this book. ¹⁹And if anyone takes away from the words of the book of this prophecy, God will take away his part from the tree of life and from the holy city, which are written in this book.

²⁰The One who testifies to these things says, "Yes, I am coming soon." Amen. Come, Lord Jesus.

²¹The grace of the Lord Jesus be with all.

Authentication of the Book

The concluding section of Revelation begins with an affirmation that all John has heard and seen on Patmos is faithful and true. John was given the same affirmation earlier in Revelation 21:5. This is significant because Christ is the One who is faithful and true (Rev. 3:14; 19:11). He is "the Alpha and the Omega, the first and the last, the beginning and the end" (22:13; cf. 1:8). He is the A to Z of human history. He knows the end from the beginning. He is the One who gave John the prophecies of Revelation to show His people "the things which must soon take place" (22:6; cf. 1:1). The prophecies of Revelation are, thus, as reliable as Christ is reliable, and they will all surely come true.

Here is a strong reminder to the readers that Jesus Himself, not John, is the author of Revelation, because the book begins with the declaration that it is the revelation of Jesus Christ (Rev. 1:1). Revelation is both from and about Christ. John simply witnessed what Christ showed him in a vision and faithfully recorded what he saw and heard (1:2).

Revelation's conclusion also affirms that Jesus is the book's author. In Revelation 22:16, Jesus identifies Himself in the first person: "I, Jesus, have sent My angel to testify to you these things for the churches; I am the Sprout and the offspring of David, the bright Morning Star."

This statement appears to be Jesus's signature on the book. Here, He clearly states that the prophecies of Revelation have come from Him. He also states that the prophecies of Revelation are written for the churches—both of John's day and throughout history. In them, Christ unveils the church's future until the end of earth's history. He has not given us the prophecies of Revelation to satisfy our curiosity about the future but to assure His people of His presence with them until He comes back and takes them to their eternal home.

The Second Coming Affirmed

Three times in this concluding section, Jesus reminds His people that He is coming soon (Rev. 22:7, 12, 20). The return of Christ is the book's keynote (cf. 1:7). God's people must live in constant expectancy of Christ's imminent coming. In referring to His coming, Jesus does not use the future tense ("I will come") but the progressive futuristic present tense: "I am coming soon." Although the Second Coming is a future event, Jesus refers to it as if it is already taking place. Because of that, God's people must take seriously the prophecies of Revelation in order to be ready to meet Christ when He comes in power and glory: "Blessed is the one who heeds the words of the prophecy of this book" (22:7).

Once again, overwhelmed by what he has just seen and heard, John prostrates himself to worship the angel speaking to him (Rev. 22:8). However, as previously stated in Revelation 19:10, the angel warns him not to do that. Only God is to be worshiped; the angel is only a servant in service to John, his fellow prophets, and all who heed the words of the prophecy recorded in Revelation (22:9).

Subsequently, the angel instructs John not to seal the prophecies of Revelation (Rev. 22:10). This contrasts with the command given to the prophet Daniel to seal the end-time prophecies of his book (Dan. 12:4, 9). The reason for this prohibition was that those prophecies concerned events that were to take place in the distant future, and as such, they were not relevant to the people of Daniel's time. The prophecies of Revelation, on the other hand, were not to be kept sealed, "for the time is near" (Rev. 22:10). They have to be repeatedly read and studied by God's people as this world's history nears its end (cf. 1:3).

Next, a declaration is made in connection with the nearness of Christ's coming: "Let the unrighteous still do unrighteousness, and let the filthy still be filthy, and let the righteous still do righteousness, and let the holy still be holy" (Rev. 22:11). This parallels the unsealing of Daniel's end-time prophecies: those who will heed the prophecies and those who will reject them will be separated. Those who accept them "will be purged, purified and refined, but the wicked will act wickedly; and none of the wicked will understand, but those who have insight will understand" (Dan. 12:10). Revelation 22:11 shows that people can reject the prophetic message for some time; however, the time is coming when it will be too late to change. At a certain point in history, prior to Christ's coming, the door of opportunity to repent and turn to God will close, and grace will no longer be available. Christ will reward each according to his or her works (Rev. 22:12).

The book reminds us, once again, that the way to enter into eternal life is to have one's robes washed: "Blessed are those who wash their robes" (Rev. 22:14). This is the last of the seven beatitudes in Revelation. The clean and white robes stand for "the righteous deeds of the saints" (19:8). They are made white by the Lamb's blood (7:14). The righteous deeds of God's people are, thus, the result of Christ's outworking in their lives. It is because of what He has done for them and in them that they will stand in the presence of God and serve Him continually in His temple—the New Jerusalem (7:14).

As Daniel 12:10 shows, while understanding end-time prophecies will result in the purification of God's people, the wicked will persevere in their wicked ways. Revelation identifies them as dogs or unholy ones (Matt. 7:6), sorcerers, fornicators, murderers, idolaters, and all who love and practice a lie (Rev. 22:15). Such are excluded from the city; their end is in the lake of fire (21:8).

Final Appeal and Warning

In response to Jesus's declaration that He is coming soon, the Holy Spirit makes a call through the bride, the church: "Come!" Those who respond must call others to come to Christ: "Let the one who thirsts come. Let the one who desires take the water of life freely" (Rev. 22:17). This call echoes Jesus's appeal at the Feast of Booths: "If anyone is thirsty, let him come to Me and drink" (John 7:37). The water Christ talks about is a free gift: "I will give to the one who thirsts from the spring of the water of life without cost" (Rev. 21:6). This water of life will quench the thirst of every person who drinks it.

The water spoken of by Christ refers to the messages of Revelation. It is not enough just to read Revelation; we must "drink" its words and study its messages, treasuring them in our minds and hearts (see Rev. 1:3).[1] "Blessed is the one who heeds the words of the prophecy of this book" (22:7).

At this point, Jesus warns against adding to or removing from the words of the book's prophecy (Rev. 21:18–19). This warning echoes the admonition of Moses to Israel at the end of their wilderness journey: "You shall not add to the word which I am commanding you, nor take away from it, that you may keep the commandments of the LORD your God which I command you" (Deut. 4:2; cf. 12:32). Revelation is the Word of God given by Christ (Rev. 1:2). Tampering with the prophecies of Revelation carries far-reaching consequences. Those who add to the prophetic words of the book are threatened with the plagues described in the book. Those who subtract from it will be deprived of eternal life in the New Jerusalem.

Remember that this warning is not about tampering with the actual words of Revelation—as if some concept of verbal inspiration was at stake. Adding to the words of Revelation's prophecies has to do with distorting and misinterpreting those prophecies to suit one's own purposes. It also has to do with enforcing speculative ideas and views not warranted by the text. This particularly applies to the end-time prophecies of Revelation. Remember that we are dealing with unfulfilled prophecies, which we will only understand after they have been fulfilled (John 14:29). We must stay with what is clearly stated in the text and shun any speculations based on allegorical interpretations derived from headline news or current events.

On the other hand, one may take away from the words of Revelation by deliberately undermining their divine origin and their prophetic character, because it might look unpopular or not be widely accepted. A person who responds to Revelation in this way is just as guilty of tampering with the book's prophecies as the one who adds to it. Both will suffer eternal loss.

Once again and for the last time, Christ reminds readers that He will quickly return: "Yes, I am coming soon" (Rev. 22:20). On behalf of all God's people, John responds with a longing exclamation: "Amen. Come, Lord Jesus."

The book of Revelation closes with a benediction: "The grace of the Lord Jesus be with all" (Rev. 22:21). This phrase is much more than just a customary benediction. Its purpose is to assure God's people throughout history that their only hope is in Christ's grace. Christ is the answer to all human hopes and longings amidst the enigmas and uncertainties of life. The future may look frightening and gloomy, but God will always be with His people until the very time of the end (Matt. 28:20). He holds the future in His hands. His grace is promised to all who take the messages of Revelation seriously. His grace will equip His people to go through the tumultuous times of the final crisis. It is through Christ's grace that the book's promises will become a reality when Christ comes back and claims His faithful people as His bride and brings them to their eternal home.

Yes, come, Lord Jesus.

Endnotes

What Revelation Is All About

1. Ellen G. White, *The Acts of the Apostles* (Nampa, ID: Pacific Press, 2005), 585.

2. Robert H. Mounce, *The Book of Revelation: New International Commentary on the New Testament* (Grand Rapids, MI: Eerdmans, 1977), 68.

3. Bruce M. Metzger, *Breaking the Code: Understanding the Book of Revelation* (Nashville, TN: Abingdon, 1993), 23.

4. *The Septuagint with Apocrypha: Greek and English,* Trans. Lancelot C. L. Brenton (Peabody, MA: Hendrickson, 1986).

Vision of the Risen Christ

1. Pliny mentions Patmos as a place of banishment (*Natural History*, 4.12.23).

2. See Irenaeus, *Irenaeus Against Heresies*, 5.30.3; Eusebius Pamphilus, *Eusebius' Ecclesiastical History*, 3.18–20.

3. William M. Ramsay, *The Letters to the Seven Churches*, 2nd ed. (Peabody, MA: Hendrickson, 1994), 61.

4. Josephus, "The Jewish Antiquities, 3.7.2–4," *The Works of Josephus*, trans. William Whiston (Peabody, MA: Hendrickson Publishers, 1987), 88–89.

5. See Mishnah *Tamid* 3.9; also Alfred Edersheim, *The Temple: Its Ministry and Services*, 2nd ed. (Peabody, MA: Hendrickson Publishers, 1994), 125.

6. See David E. Aune, *Revelation 1–5: Word Biblical Commentary 52a* (Dallas, TX: Word Books, 1997), 104–15.

7. Jon Paulien, *The Bible Explorer* (Harrisburg, PA: TAG, 1996), Audio Series, 2.3.

8. Ellen G. White, *Selected Messages* (Washington, DC: Review and Herald, 1958), 2:396.

Messages to the Churches (Part 1)

1. cf. Philip Schaff, *History of the Christian Church*, 3rd ed. (Grand Rapids, MI: Eerdmans, 1910), 13–20.

2. Irenaeus, *Irenaeus Against Heresies*, 1.26.3; 3.11 (*The Ante-Nicene Fathers*, 1:352, 426–429); Hippolytus of Rome, *The Refutation of All Heresies*, 7.24 (*The Ante-Nicene Fathers*, 5:115).

3. See William Barclay, *The Daily Study Bible: The Revelation of John*, 2nd ed. (Philadelphia, PA: Westminster John Knox Press, 1976), 1:76–78.

4. Fritz Rienecker, *A Linguistic Key to the Greek New Testament* (Grand Rapids, MI: Zondervan, 1976), 815.

5. Robert H. Charles, *A Critical and Exegetical Commentary on the Revelation of St. John*, International Critical Commentary (London: T. & T. Clark, 1959), 1:60.

6. William Ramsay, *The Letters to the Seven Churches*, 2nd ed. (Peabody, MA: Hendrickson, 1994), 214.

Messages to the Churches (Part 2)

1. Ramsay, *The Letters to the Seven Churches*, 238.
2. Ibid., 269.
3. Mounce, *The Book of Revelation*, 109; Ramsay, *The Letters to the Seven Churches*, 267.
4. Tacitus, *Annals*, 14.27.

The Throne-Room Scene

1. See Plato, *Phaedo*, 110e (The Loeb Classical Library), 1:378–379.
2. J. Massyngberde Ford, *Revelation*, Anchor Bible, vol. 38 (New York: Doubleday, 1975), 71.
3. Richard M. Davidson, "Sanctuary Typology," in *Symposium on Revelation— Book 1*, Daniel and Revelation Committee Series 6 (Silver Spring, MD: Biblical Research Institute, 1992), 123.
4. Rev. 4:4, 10; 5:8, 11, 14; 7:11, 13; 11:16; 14:3; 19:4.
5. Rev. 4:10–11; 5:8–14; 7:11–12; 11:16–18; 19:4.
6. See Mishnah, *Yoma*, 1.5.
7. Henry B. Swete, *The Apocalypse of St. John* (Grand Rapids, MI: Eerdmans, 1951), 71.
8. Ellen G. White, *The Desire of Ages* (Nampa, ID: Pacific Press, 1989), 834.
9. As rightly observed by Jon Paulien, *The Gospel from Patmos* (Hagerstown, MD: Review and Herald, 2007), 104.
10. cf. 1 Kings 22:19; Isa. 6:1–3; Ezek. 1:22–28; 10:1–22; Dan. 7:9–10.
11. Paulien, *The Gospel from Patmos*, 104.

The Enthronement of Christ

1. George Eldon Ladd, *A Commentary on the Revelation of John* (Grand Rapids, MI: Eerdmans, 1972), 81.
2. Ellen G. White, "Letter 65, 1898," *Manuscript Releases* 9 (Silver Spring, MD: Ellen G. White Estate, 1990), 7.
3. Deuteronomy 17:18 specifies that the future king had to make for himself "a copy of *this law*" (emphasis added), which is a direct reference to Deuteronomy. The master copy, written by Moses, was stored in the sanctuary in the custody of Levites (Deut. 31:9, 24, 26), from which the newly crowned king had to make a copy for himself.
4. The test for the reign of the succeeding kings in Jerusalem was compliance with the covenant book, as David was also tested with it (cf. 1 Kings 11:6; 15:3, 11; 2 Kings 14:3; 16:2; 18:3; 22:2).
5. A fragment from Qumran has a reading similar to Isaiah 29:10–11 (4Q163 15–16).
6. *The Isaiah Targum*, 8:16–18, points to sealing the law because of disobedience and is associated with the threat of going into the Exile. Rabbis believed that sealing the law started during the time of King Ahaz and continued with the kings after him. See *The Babylonian Talmud Sanhedrin*, 103b; *The Midrash Rabbah Genesis, Lech Lecha*, 42.3; *The Midrash Rabbah Leviticus, Shemini*, 11.7; *The Midrash Rabbah Ruth, Proem*, 7; *The Midrash Rabbah Esther, Proem*, 2. See also Ranko Stefanovic, *The Background and Meaning of the Sealed Book of Revelation 5*, Andrews University Seminary Doctoral Dissertation Series 22 (Berrien Springs, MI: Andrews University Press, 1996), 278–280.

7. See Stefanovic, *The Background and Meaning*, 280–282.

8. The Jewish writings testify how the eagerly awaited Messiah was frequently conceived as the King in possession of the Torah. See Stefanovic, *The Background and Meaning*, 282–285.

9. Adela Yarbro Collins, *The Apocalypse*, New Testament Message 22 (Wilmington, DE: Michael Glazier, Inc., 1979), 39.

10. White, *The Desire of Ages*, 833–835.

11. The New Testament is replete with texts stating that at His ascension, Christ was seated "at the right side of God" and has been given authority, power, and universal dominion (Rom. 8:34; Eph. 1:20–22; Col. 3:1; Heb. 10:12; 12:2; 1 Pet. 3:21–22).

12. Ellen G. White, *The Acts of the Apostles* (Nampa, ID: Pacific Press, 1911), 38–39.

The Seven Seals

1. See the white hair of the exalted Christ (Rev. 1:14); the white stone of the overcomers in Pergamum (2:17); the white robes of the overcomers (3:4–5, 18), the twenty-four elders (4:4), the martyrs underneath the altar (6:11), and the Great Multitude (7:9, 13); the white cloud upon which the Son of Man sits (4:14); the white horse ridden by Christ (19:11); the white dress of heaven's armies (19:14); the white throne upon which God sits at the final judgment (20:11).

2. See Judg. 7:22; Isa. 19:2; Zech. 14:13.

3. See Deut. 7:13; 11:14; 28:51; 2 Chron. 32:28; Hosea 2:8; Joel 2:19.

4. cf. Jer. 14:12–13; 15:2–3; 21:6–9; 24:10; 29:17–18; Ezek. 5:12–17; 6:11–12; 12:16; 14:12–23; 33:27–29.

5. See Judg. 2:14; 3:8; 4:2; 6:1; 10:7; 13:1; Neh. 9:27, 30; Ps. 106:41; Jer. 20:4–5; 22:25; 27:6; 32:3, 28; 34:2; Ezek. 39:23; Dan. 1:2.

6. Regarding the earthquake, see Isa. 13:13; Jer. 4:34; Ezek. 38:19–20; Joel 2:10; Amos 8:8; Hag. 2:6. Regarding the darkening of the sun and moon, the falling of the stars, and the convulsion of the sky, see Isa. 13:10; 34:4; 50:3; Joel 2:31; 3:15.

7. Jon Paulien, "The Seven Seals," *Symposium on Revelation—Book 1*, Daniel and Revelation Committee Series 6 (Silver Spring, MD: Biblical Research Institute, 1992), 237.

8. Richard Bauckham, *The Climax of Prophecy* (London: T. & T. Clark, 1993), 71–83; cf. 4 Ezra 7:30–34.

The Sealed Saints

1. Ecclus. 39:28 (*The Oxford Annotated Apocrypha*, 180).

2. See Dan. 5:4–6 in *The Testaments of the Twelve Patriarchs*. See Charles, *A Critical and Exegetical Commentary on the Revelation of St. John*, 1:208–209.

3. Ellen G. White, *Selected Messages* (Washington, DC: Review and Herald, 1958), 1:174.

4. Ellen G. White, *Review and Herald*, March 9, 1905 (quoted in *The Seventh-day Adventist Bible Commentary*, 2nd ed. [Washington, DC: Review and Herald, 1980], 7:970).

The Seven Trumpets (Part 1)

1. For instance, Revelation 8:3–5 is sandwiched between verses 2 and 6; 12:7–12 between verses 6 and 13; and 15:2–8 between 15:l and 16:l.

2. The Greek text shows that the angel stood *upon* the altar rather than *at* the altar, as suggested by other translations. See Ranko Stefanovic, "The Angel at the Altar (Revelation 8:3–5): A Case Study on Intercalations in Revelation," *Andrews University Seminary Studies* (Berrien Springs, MI: Andrews University Press, 2006), 44.1, 79–94.

3. This altar must be a sizeable structure, resembling the one in the Jerusalem temple; the priest had to climb several stairs to the top to officiate over the sacrifices. According to the *Mishnah*, the size of the altar at its base was 32 by 32 by 1 cubits, while the altar proper was 30 by 30 by 5 cubits. It was narrower at the top, measuring 24 by 24 cubits. An area measuring one cubit around the top was where the priest stood as he offered the sacrifice (*Mishnah Middoth*, 3.1).

4. See *Mishnah Tamid*, 4.1–5.6. See Emil Schürer, *The History of the Jewish People in the Age of Jesus Christ*, 2nd ed. (London: T. & T. Clark, 1979), 299–308.

5. Regarding the symbol of the tree, see Pss. 1:3; 52:8; 92:12–14; Isa. 61:3; Jer. 11:15–17; 17:7–8; Ezek. 20:46–48; Matt. 3:10; 7:17–19; 21:18–19; Luke 13:6–9; 23:28–31. Regarding the green grass, see Ps. 72:16; Isa. 40:6–8; 44:2–4.

6. cf. Pss. 48:1; 78:68; Isa. 2:2–3; 13:4; 31:4; 41:15; 65:25; Jer. 51:24–25; Ezek. 35:2–3; Obad. 8–9.

7. See 4 Ezra 3; 2 Bar. 10:1–3; 11:1; 67:7; Sib. Oracles 5:137–154, 160–161.

The Seven Trumpets (Part 2)

1. This idea was also held by the Jewish people in John's day (see 1 Enoch 18:12–16; 54:5; 88:1–3).

2. Hans K. LaRondelle, *How to Understand the End-Time Prophecies of the Bible* (Bradenton, FL: First Impressions, 1997), 189.

The Mighty Angel with the Scroll

1. Quoted in *The Seventh-day Adventist Bible Commentary*, 7:971.

The Two Witnesses

1. Kenneth A. Strand, "An Overlooked Old Testament Background to Revelation 11:1," *Andrews University Seminary Studies* 22 (1984): 322–325.

2. Ford, *Revelation*, 177.

3. This twofold interpretation is also in Ellen White's writings. While she interpreted the two witnesses as representing the Old and New Testament scriptures (*The Great Controversy* [Nampa, ID: Pacific Press, 2005], 267), she also talks about the church prophesying in sackcloth during troublous times (*Testimonies for the Church* [Nampa, ID: Pacific Press, 1948], 4:594–595).

4. cf. Gen. 18:32; Isa. 6:13; Amos 6:9. See Jacques B. Doukhan, *Secrets of Daniel* (Hagerstown, MD: Review and Herald, 2000), 23 n. 7.

5. G. K. Beale, *The Book of Revelation*, The New International Greek Testament Commentary (Grand Rapids, MI: Eerdmans, 1999), 603.

6. According to White, in Revelation 4–5 and 8, John the Revelator observes what was happening in the first apartment of heaven's sanctuary, while in

Revelation 11:19, he looked into the Holy of Holies, which describes the beginning of the pre-Advent judgment that started in 1844 (see *The Great Controversy*, 415–416, 433–434; *Patriarchs and Prophets* (reprint; Nampa, ID: Pacific Press, 2005), 415–416; *The Spirit of Prophecy*, 4:273).

Satan: A Defeated Enemy

1. See Isa. 57:7–8; Jer. 3:6–10; Ezek. 16:8–42; 23; Hosea 1–3.

2. Leon Morris, *The Book of Revelation*, Tyndale New Testament Commentaries, 2nd ed. (Grand Rapids, MI: Eerdmans, 1987), 152.

3. David E. Aune, *Revelation 6–16*, Word Biblical Commentary 52b (Waco, TX: Thomas Nelson, 1998), 684–685.

4. Quoted in *The Seventh-day Adventist Bible Commentary*, 7:973–974.

5. Ellen G. White, *The Desire of Ages* (Nampa, ID: Pacific Press Publishing, 1989), 493.

The Beast from the Sea

1. See Rev. 12:9; 13:14; 18:23; 19:20; 20:3, 8, 10.

2. Angel Manuel Rodriguez, *Future Glory: The 8 Greatest End-Time Prophecies in the Bible* (Hagerstown, MD: Review and Herald, 2002), 104.

3. Pope Leo XIII, "Encyclical Letter: The Reunion of Christendom, June 20, 1894," *Seventh-day Adventist Bible Students' Source Book*, 684.

The Beast from the Earth

1. Beatrice S. Neall, "Sealed Saints and the Tribulation," in *Symposium on Revelation—Book 1*, Daniel and Revelation Committee Series 6 (Silver Spring, MD: Biblical Research Institute, 1992), 257.

2. William G. Johnsson, "The Saints' End-Time Victory over the Forces of Evil," in *Symposium on Revelation—Book 2*, Daniel and Revelation Committee Series 7 (Silver Spring, MD: Biblical Research Institute, 1992), 30.

3. Richard Rice, *Reign of God*, 2nd ed. (Berrien Springs, MI: Andrews University Press, 1997), 403.

4. Ellen G. White, *Testimonies for the Church* (Nampa, ID: Pacific Press, 2005), 6:17.

5. See *The Seventh-day Adventist Encyclopedia* (Washington, DC: Review and Herald, 1996), 11:221–225.

6. See James White, *A Word to the "Little Flock"* (Washington, DC: Review and Herald, 1944), 19.

God's Final Message to the World

1. See White, *The Great Controversy*, 649–650.

2. See 1QM 7.3–6.

3. See *The Greek New Testament*, 4th ed., ed. Kurt Aland, et al. (New York: United Bible Societies, 1993), 863.

4. cf. Ps. 60:3; Jer. 25:15–29; 49:12; Ezek. 23:32–34; Obad. 16.

The Seven Last Plagues

1. See White, *The Great Controversy*, 629.

The Battle of Armageddon

1. Herodotus, *The History of Herodotus*, 1.191. Herodotus's description of Babylon's capture by Cyrus has been confirmed in modern times by the Cyrus Cylinder, which describes the capture of Babylon by the Persians without any battle. See James B. Pritchard, *Ancient Near Eastern Texts Relating to the Old Testament*, 3rd ed. (Princeton, NJ: Princeton University Press, 1969), 315.

2. White, *The Great Controversy*, 624.

3. See *Mishnah Middoth*, 2.1; cf. F. F. Bruce, "The Revelation to John," *A New Testament Commentary* (Grand Rapids, MI: Zondervan, 1969), 657.

The Woman and the Beast

1. David Marshall, *Apocalypse!: Has the Countdown Begun?* (Alma Park, England: Autumn House, 2000), 147.

2. Johnsson, "The Saints' End-Time Victory over the Forces of Evil," 17.

Judgment on Babylon

1. Beale, *The Book of Revelation*, 901.

The Two Suppers

1. See Ranko Stefanovic, "The Gift of Prophecy and the Church: The Biblical Perspective," *Ellen White and Current Issues Symposium* 7 (2012): 39–69.

The Millennium and the Final Judgment

1. White, *The Great Controversy*, 657.

2. Ibid., 673.

The Restored Earth

1. Roberto Badenas, "New Jerusalem—The Holy City," *Symposium on Revelation—Book 2*, Daniel and Revelation Committee Series 7 (Silver Spring, MD: Biblical Research Institute, 1992), 255.

2. Josephus, *The Wars of the Jews*, 5.5.6 (Whiston, 707–708).

The Conclusion of the Book

1. Jacques B. Doukhan, *Secrets of Revelation* (Hagerstown, MD: Review and Herald, 2002), 204.

Scripture Index

Ezekiel